BASIL MONTAGU PICKERING'S NEW PUBLICATIONS.

Privy Council Tracts.

No. 3.—A HANDY BOOK OF PRIVY COUNCIL LAW.
  I. Ecclesiastical Cases.
  II. Patent Cases.
    Dedicated to the Right Honourable BARON HATHERLEY.
  Royal 8vo., pp. 75, 1s. 6d.

" This is No. III. of a series of which the first two are already well known, and duly appreciated wherever they are known. Able as the others are, this far surpasses them in weight, wit, and crushing argument. They deserve a leading article to themselves, and if we content ourselves with a brief notice it is only in the hope that we shall be able to say enough to induce our readers to procure the tracts themselves. They must interest every clergyman in his official character, and touch every Englishman in his love of liberty and justice. These are strong words. We are content to abide the decision of each of our readers as he riscs from their perusal. The writer of this tract not only charges the Committee of the Privy Council with blundering, partiality, and unlawyerlike argument—this has been done not ineffectually by others—but of ignorance of facts which they admit should have guided their decision, and of inconsistency in the application of their own principles and precedents. These charges are amply proved, *e.g.* p. 60. In another place (p. 43), a more glaring misstatement is pointed out, and involves, we deeply regret to be compelled to say it, the Archbishop of Canterbury; the paragraph has the significant marginal description—A FORGED DECRETAL! All the Privy Council cases from Gorham downwards are ably analyzed and contrasted. . . . . AFTER THIS EXPOSURE WE MUCH OVERRATE THE PATIENCE OF OUR COUNTRYMEN IF THE COMMITTEE IS TOLERATED AS A COURT AT ALL."
—*The Church Review.*

" A pamphlet of seventy-five closely printed pages, designed to illustrate the working of the Final Court of Appeal in ecclesiastical matters. A sketch of Contradictory Decisions in Patent Cases is

A

also appended. It is not necessary to agree with all the deductions of the author from the various decisions affecting the Church of England to see that this is A VALUABLE HANDBOOK."—*The Overland Mail.*

No. 2.—THE CASE OF "THE SEVEN BISHOPS"—THE CASE OF "THE 4,700." Dedicated to the LORD BISHOP OF LONDON. 1*s.*

"The wonderful parallel between the two cases must strike every reader."—*The Church Times.*

No. 1.—DR. STEPHENS ON THE ORNAMENTS RUBRIC. Dedicated to His Grace the ARCHBISHOP OF YORK. 1*s.*

". . . . This most useful pamphlet . . . . The pamphlet should be bought."—*The Literary Churchman.*

"A scathing reply to the judgment from the writings of Dr. Stephens himself."

SAD TONES FOR SICK TIMES. By Vox et Præterea Nihil. 1870. Crown 8vo., 3*s.*

This little volume is full of clever satire ; it requires from the reader a reasonable amount of knowledge of what is going on around him, especially in ecclesiastical matters, for there is much more wit in every one of the thirteen pieces contained in the volume than appears on the surface. It contains an admirable satire On the Irish Church, On the Lord Bishop and the Lord Mayor, On Convocation, On the Two Infallibles Protestant and Papal, On Oxford, On the Friends of Prosperity, On the Pope of Canterbury and the Privy Council, A New Version of Sam Butler's " He does not Pray but Prosecute," On the Lectionary Revisionaries, and On the Ritual Commissioners, this last is perhaps the best of the whole, it is certainly the most severe and the most pregnant with by-play and double entendre.

POETRY FOR CHILDREN. By CHARLES and MARY LAMB. Fcap. 8vo., with woodcut initials, head and tailpieces, cloth, 3*s.* 6*d.*

Also on sale copies of nearly all of the publications of my late father, WILLIAM PICKERING. *All orders, if not sent direct, should distinctly specify " Pickering's edition," as imitations are otherwise frequently substituted.*

RARE OLD BOOKS

NOW ON SALE BY

BASIL MONTAGU PICKERING.

CAXTON'S GOLDEN LEGEND. The Legende named in Latin Legenda Aurea, that is to say in Englyshe the golden legende: for lyke as passeth golde in valewe al other metallys soo thys legende excedeth all other bokes. *Fynyshed at Westmestre by me Wyllyam Caxton,* 1493. 4to. *220 guineas.*

Of this, the crown of Caxton's labours, only ten copies are known, and only one of these perfect. The present is very fine, tall, and sound; it is perfected by sixteen leaves by Harris, and bound by Riviere in the very best manner in French olive morocco, tooled to a Tudor pattern. Caxton was not only the printer, but he was also the translator of this volume. Mr. Blades describes this book as "without folios or catchwords, many woodcuts and woodcut initials," but this is inaccurate, for it has folios throughout; but he is quite correct in saying that there are *many* woodcuts, and they are very curious; this copy has the woodcut and the Life of S. Thomas A'Becket unmutilated, and is altogether a MOST DESIRABLE VOLUME.

HOLINSHED'S CHRONICLES OF ENGLAND, SCOTLANDE, AND IRELANDE, 1577. 2 very thick vols. folio, 𝔅lack 𝔏etter, NUMEROUS CURIOUS WOOD ENGRAVINGS, FINE COPY, *red morocco extra, panel sides, gilt backs and gilt leaves, by Riviere.* 42*l.*

THE FIRST EDITION OF THIS VALUABLE CHRONICLE, AND THE ONLY ONE HAVING WOODCUTS. It is commonly termed the SHAKE-SPEARE EDITION, because it was the one consulted by him in the compilation of his historical plays: indeed, he has incorporated long passages from it into some of them. In the second edition the language was much altered, and the numerous woodcuts omitted. It is extremely difficult to meet with such a good copy as the one here offered.

This copy has between pp. 1592-93, a leaf printed on one side, containing "The names of the Knights made at Leith after the brenning of Edinburgh, by the Earle of Hertforde," and between pp. 1868-69, a large folding woodcut representing the Siege of

Edinburgh, containing also "The names of such Gentlemen and Captaines as had charge of the siege and wynning of Edenburgh Castell, anno 1573," both of which are usually deficient. Also the FOUR rare leaves of Errata.

MORE (SIR THOMAS) WORKES, written by him in Englysh Tonge. 1557. Folio, black letter, *above* 1,500 *pages,* 3 *leaves supplied in most wonderful facsimile by Mr. Harris, morocco extra, panel sides, gilt edges,* 17*l.* 17*s.*

The above copy of this great old English writer's works is quite complete, having the eight leaves at the commencement, containing the poems "Mayster Thomas More wrote in his youth for his pastime," viz., " A merry jest how a sergeant would learne to play the frere." Another of the poems is a pageant, representing the various stages of man's life, which Shakespeare no doubt must have seen, and on which he founded his celebrated *touching description* of the seven ages of man's life, and " A ruful lamentacyon on the Deathe of Queene Elizabeth, mother to King Henry VIII. 1503," and several other poems. It has also the *unpaged* leaf between 1138-9. There are also seven leaves containing the " Twelve Rules of John Picus, Earle of Mirandula," translated into English Verse by Sir Thomas More.

Sir John Simeon's copy fetched 26*l.* 10*s.*

HAKLUYT (Richard), Principal Navigations, Voyages, Traffiques, and Discoveries of the English Nation, made by Sea or Overland, to the remote and farthest Quarters of the Earth, at any time within the compass of these 1600 years. 1599-1600. 3 vols. folio, black letter, *French red morocco extra, panel sides, and gilt leaves by Riviere,* 19*l.* 19*s.*

Best folio edition, containing the suppressed "Voyage to Cadiz," to be found but in very few copies.

Oldys, in admiration of the heroic deeds of our ancestors described in the above work, enthusiastically says : " This elaborate and excellent collection redounds as much to the glory of the English nation as any book that ever was published in it."

A SET OF RITSON'S POETICAL AND ANTIQUARIAN PIECES. 38 vols. *Uncut, half morocco,* 40 *guineas.*

FIRST EDITIONS OF TENNYSON, SHELLEY, KEATS, COLERIDGE, BYRON, COWPER, AND OTHER POETS. See Catalogues.

BASIL MONTAGU PICKERING

has been honoured by instructions from Her Majesty's Stationery
Office to publish on their behalf

BY AUTHORITY OF THE LORDS COMMISSIONERS OF HER MAJESTY'S
TREASURY AT THE RECOMMENDATION OF THE
ROYAL COMMISSION ON RITUAL.

THE BOOK OF COMMON PRAYER of 1636, with all the MS. alterations made by Convocation in 1661 (the draft of the present version showing at a glance in what particulars it differs from the preceding edition). From this long-lost document the copy appended to the Act of Uniformity was transcribed, from which transcription "the Sealed Book" of 1662 was printed. The book is reproduced by Major-General Sir Henry James' Photo-zincographic Process, and is an exact counterpart of the original folio volume; a limited number only were printed (at 2*l.* 2*s.*), and very few copies remain for sale. The volume possesses the highest value and interest to all those who would form a correct judgment as to the mind of the English Church in matters pertaining to doctrine and ritual.

THE DOOMSDAY BOOK OF ENGLAND, including "The Great Doomsday Book" and "The Little Doomsday Book;" accurate facsimiles of each by Sir Henry James' Photo-zincographic Process. The 2 vols. like the originals, and bound in half-morocco, 20*l.*

THE DOOMSDAY BOOKS in separate counties may be had at the following prices (exact facsimiles by Sir Henry James' Photo-zincographic Process).

In Great Doomsday Book.

	£.	s.	d.		£.	s.	d.
Bedfordshire	0	8	0	Cornwall	0	0	0
Berkshire	0	8	0	Derbyshire	0	8	8
Buckingham	0	8	0	Devonshire	0	8	0
Cambridge	0	10	0	Dorsetshire	0	0	0
Cheshire & Lancashire	0	8	0	Gloucestershire	0	8	0

Basil Montagu Pickering,

Published for " Her Majesty's Stationery Office."

	£.	s.	d.		£.	s.	d.
Hampshire . . .	0	10	0	Oxfordshire . . .	0	8	0
Herefordshire . .	0	8	0	Rutlandshire (*see*			
Hertfordshire . .	0	10	0	Leicestershire)			
Huntingdon . . .	0	8	0	Shropshire . . .	0	8	0
Kent	0	8	0	Somersetshire . .	0	10	0
Lancashire (*see* Chesh-				Staffordshire . . .	0	8	0
ire and Lancash.)				Surrey	0	8	0
Leicester and Rutland	0	8	0	Sussex	0	10	0
Lincolnshire . . .	1	1	0	Warwickshire . .	0	8	0
Middlesex . . .	0	8	0	Wiltshire . . .	0	10	0
Nottinghamshire .	0	10	0	Worcestershire .	0	8	0
Northamptonshire .	0	8	0	Yorkshire . . .	1	1	0

In Little Doomsday Book

	£.	s.	d.
Norfolk	1	3	0
Suffolk	1	2	0
Essex	0	16	0

Cost of the entire set, 17*l*. 3*s*.

THE NATIONAL MSS. OF ENGLAND.

Photo-zincographic facsimiles of the National MSS. of England.

Part I.	16*s*.
Part II.	1*s*.
Part III.	16*s*.
Part IV.	16*s*.

THE NATIONAL MSS. OF SCOTLAND.

National MSS. of Scotland, Part I.	21*s*.
Ditto Part II.	21*s*.

PUBLISHED FOR " THE TRUSTEES OF THE BRITISH MUSEUM."

BOOKS AND MANUSCRIPTS.

A CATALOGUE OF THE HEBREW BOOKS IN THE BRITISH MUSEUM. 8*vo*., 1*l*. 5*s*.

PHOTOGRAPHIC FACSIMILES OF THE EPISTLES OF CLEMENT OF ROME. 3*l*. 3*s*.

Published for the British Museum.

COMBE (T.), HAWKINS (E.), COCKERELL (C. R.) AND BIRCH (S.), DESCRIPTION OF ANCIENT MARBLES;
11 parts, 4to. 24l. 5s. 6d.
Ditto   ditto, *large paper*, 35l. 17s. 6d.

COMBE (T.) DESCRIPTION OF ANCIENT TERRA-COTTAS, 4to., 1l. 11s. 6d.
Ditto   ditto, *large paper*, 2l. 12s. 6d.

DAVIS (NATHAN) INSCRIPTIONS IN THE PHŒNICIAN CHARACTER FROM CARTHAGE, *folio*, 1l. 5s.

EGYPTIAN MONUMENTS FROM THE COLLECTION OF THE EARL OF BELMORE, *folio*, 15s.

CATALOGUE OF THE GEOGRAPHICAL COLLECTION IN THE LIBRARY OF GEORGE III., 2 vols. 8vo., 1l. 4s.

HAWKINS (ED.) CATALOGUE OF ANGLO-GALLIC COINS, 4to., 1l. 4s.

FRAGMENTS FROM THE ILIAD OF HOMER, from a Syrian Palimpsest, edited by W. Cureton. 4to., 2l. 2s.
Ditto   ditto, *large paper*, 3l. 3s.

INSCRIPTIONS IN THE HIERATIC AND DEMOTIC CHARACTER, *folio*, 1l. 7s. 6d.

INSCRIPTIONS IN THE HIMYARITIC CHARACTER FROM SOUTHERN ARABIA, *folio*, 1l. 4s.

NUMMI VETERES IN MUSEO R. P. KNIGHT, ab ipso descripti. 4to., 1l. 15s.

LAYARD (A. H.) INSCRIPTIONS IN THE CUNEIFORM CHARACTER FROM ASSYRIAN MONUMENTS, *folio*, 1l. 1s.

CUNEIFORM INSCRIPTIONS OF WESTERN ASIA, prepared for publication by Major-Gen. Sir H. C. Rawlinson and G. Norris. 3 vols., folio, 3l.

ELLIS (H.) A CATALOGUE OF THE MSS. FORMERLY F. HARGRAVE'S. 4to., 12s.

CATALOGUS CODICUM MANUSCRIPTORUM ORIENTALIUM. Pars I., Codices Syricos et Carshunicos amplectens. Pars II., Codicus Arabicorum partem amplectens. Pars III., Codices Æthiopicos amplectens, 4 parts in 3. *Folio*, 2l. 10s.

FACSIMILE OF THE CODEX ALEXANDRINUS. 3 vols., *folio*, 18*l*.

A CATALOGUE OF THE ARUNDEL MSS. *Folio*, 1*l*. 8*s*.
  Ditto   ditto, with *coloured plates*, 4*l*. 14*s*. 6*d*.

A CATALOGUE OF THE BURNEY MSS. *Folio*, 18*s*.
  Ditto   ditto, with *coloured plates*, 3*l*. 3*s*.

INDEX TO THE ARUNDEL AND BURNEY MSS. *Folio*, 15*s*.

CATALOGUE OF ADDITIONS TO MSS. IN THE BRITISH MUSEUM FROM 1836—1853. 4 vols., 8*vo*., 2*l*. 17*s*.

CATALOGUE OF SYRIAC MSS., Part I. 15*s*.

PAPYRI IN THE HIEROGLYPHIC AND HIERATIC CHARACTERS FROM THE COLLECTION OF THE EARL OF BELMORE. *Folio*, 6*s*.

SELECT PAPYRI IN THE HIERACTIC CHARACTER, 2 Parts in 5. *Folio*, 5*l*. 17*s*.

GREEK PAPYRI IN THE BRITISH MUSEUM, Part I. 4*to*., 10*s*.
  Ditto   ditto, *large paper*, 15*s*.

MAPS, CHARTS, AND PLANS.

A CATALOGUE OF THE MS. MAPS, CHARTS, AND PLANS. 2 vols., 8*vo*., 1*l*.

MUSIC.

A CATALOGUE OF THE MS. MUSIC IN THE BRITISH MUSEUM. 8*vo*., 5*s*.

PRINTS.

A CATALOGUE OF SATIRICAL PRINTS, Vol. I. 1*l*. 5*s*.

VASES.

A CATALOGUE OF THE GREEK AND ETRUSCAN VASES IN THE BRITISH MUSEUM. 2 vols., 8*vo*., 10*s*.
  Ditto   ditto, *fine paper*, 15*s*.

Also published for the Trustees of the British Museum, numerous works on Natural History. A detailed catalogue may be had on application to BASIL MONTAGU PICKERING.

BASIL MONTAGU PICKERING, 196, PICCADILLY, LONDON, W.

HISTORICAL SKETCHES.

HISTORICAL SKETCHES

RISE AND PROGRESS OF UNIVERSITIES
NORTHMEN AND NORMANS IN ENGLAND AND IRELAND
MEDIEVAL OXFORD
CONVOCATION OF CANTERBURY

BY

JOHN HENRY NEWMAN

OF THE ORATORY

SOMETIME FELLOW OF ORIEL COLLEGE

LONDON
BASIL MONTAGU PICKERING
196 PICCADILLY
1872

I.

RISE AND PROGRESS OF UNIVERSITIES.

TO

JAMES R. HOPE SCOTT, ESQ., Q.C.,

ETC., ETC.

A NAME EVER TO BE HAD IN HONOUR,

WHEN UNIVERSITIES ARE MENTIONED,

FOR THE ZEAL OF HIS EARLY RESEARCHES,

AND THE MUNIFICENCE OF HIS LATER DEEDS,

THIS VOLUME IS INSCRIBED,

A TARDY AND UNWORTHY MEMORIAL,

ON THE PART OF ITS AUTHOR,

OF THE LOVE AND ADMIRATION

OF MANY EVENTFUL YEARS.

DUBLIN, *Oct.* 28, 1856.

ADVERTISEMENT.

THE following illustrations of the idea of a University originally appeared in 1854, in the columns of the Dublin "Catholic University Gazette."

In 1856 they were published in one volume, under the title of "Office and Work of Universities."

Though the Author then put his name in the title-page, he thought it best to retain both the profession of *incognito* and the conversational tone in which he originally wrote; for the obvious reason, that, to have dropped either would have been to recast his work. For such a task he could not promise himself leisure; and, had he effected it, he might after all only have made himself more exact and solid at the price of becoming less readable, at least in the judgment of a day, which keenly appreciates the proverb, that "a great book is a great evil." In saying this, however, he has no intention of implying that he has spared thought or pains in his composition, or of apologising for its matter.

P.S. In the present edition (1872) he has exchanged its original title for one which he considers more appropriate to its contents.

ADVERTISEMENT

This little work, though issued at one shilling, was originally approved in 1854 in the judgment of the Dublin "Catholic University Gazette."

In 1856 it was included in one volume under the title "Office and Work of Universities."

Though the Author then put his name on the title-page, he thought it best to reserve both the positions of Catholic and the educational ones, in which he might make use of it, for the time being, had he then, to have deferred either would have been to postpone his work. For such a task an ephemeral publication cannot indulge; and had he thought it he might after all only have made his share scarcer, and spirit as they had of it, be coming less readable, at least to the judgment of a day; which mostly approves the world that "a great book is a great evil." The saying this, however, he has no intention of implying that he has spared thought or pains in his composition, or of apologising for its matter.

P.S. In the present edition (1859) he has exchanged its original title for one which he considers more appropriate to its contents.

UNIVERSITIES.

UNIVERSITIES.

CHAPTER I.

INTRODUCTORY.

I HAVE it in purpose to commit to paper, time after time, various thoughts of my own, seasonable, as I conceive, when a Catholic University is under formation, and apposite in a publication, which is to be the record and organ of its proceedings. An anonymous person, indeed, like myself, can claim no authority for anything he advances; nor have I any intention of introducing or sheltering myself under the sanction of the Institution which I wish to serve. My remarks will stand amid weightier matters like the non-official portion of certain government journals in foreign parts; and I trust they will have their use, though they are but individual in their origin, and immethodical in their execution. When I say anything to the purpose, the gain is the University's; when I am mistaken or unsuccessful, the failure is my own.

The Prelates of the Irish Church are at present engaged in an anxious and momentous task, which has the inconvenience of being strange to us, if it be not novel. A University is not founded every day; and seldom indeed has it been founded under the peculiar circumstances which will now attend its establishment in

Catholic Ireland. Generally speaking, it has grown up out of schools, or colleges, or seminaries, or monastic bodies, which had already lasted for centuries; and, different as it is from them all, has been little else than their natural result and completion. While then it has been expanding into its peculiar and perfect form, it has at the same time been by anticipation educating subjects for its service, and has been creating and carrying along with it the national sympathy. Here, however, as the world is not slow to object, this great institution is to take its place among us without antecedent or precedent, whether to recommend or explain it. It receives, we are told, neither illustration nor augury from the history of the past, and requires to be brought into existence as well as into shape. It has to force its way abruptly into an existing state of society which has never duly felt its absence; and it finds its most formidable obstacles, not in anything inherent in the undertaking itself, but in the circumambient atmosphere of misapprehension and prejudice into which it is received. Necessary as it really is, it has to be carried into effect in the presence of a reluctant or perplexed public opinion, and that, without any counterbalancing assistance whatever, as has commonly been the case with Universities, from royal favour or civil sanction.

This is what many a man will urge, who is favourable to the project itself, viewed apart from the difficulties of the time; nor can the force of such representations be denied. On the other hand, such difficulties must be taken for what they are really worth; they exist, not so much in adverse facts, as in the opinion of the world about the facts. That opinion is the adverse fact. It would be absurd to deny, that grave and good men, zealous for religion, and experienced in the state of the country, have had serious misgivings on the subject, and have thought the vision of a Catholic University too noble, too desirable, to be possible. Still, making every admission on this score which can be required of me, I think it is true, after all, that our main adversary is to be found, not in the unfavourable judgments of particular persons, though such there are, but in the vague and diffusive influence of what is called Public Opinion.

I am not so irrational as to despise Public Opinion; I have no thought of making light of a tribunal established in the conditions and necessities of human nature. It has its place in the very constitution of society; it ever has existed, it ever will exist, whether in the commonwealth of nations, or in the humble and secluded village. But wholesome as it is as a principle, it has, in common with all things human, great imperfections, and makes many mistakes. Too often it is nothing else than what the whole world opines, and no one in particular. Your neighbour assures you that every one is of one way of thinking; that there is but one opinion on the subject; and while he claims not to be answerable for it, he does not hesitate to propound and spread it. In such cases, every one is appealing to every one else; and the constituent members of a community one by one think it their duty to defer and succumb to the voice of that same community as a whole.

It would be extravagant to maintain that this is the adequate account of the sentiments which have for some time prevailed among us as to the establishment of our University; but, so far as it holds good, this follows, viz.: that the despondency, with which the project is regarded by so many persons, is the offspring, not of their judgment, but mainly (I say it, as will be seen directly, without any disrespect) of their imagination. Public Opinion

especially acts upon the imagination ; it does not convince, but it impresses ; it has the force of authority,
rather than of reason ; and concurrence in it is, not an
intelligent decision, but a submission or belief.　This
circumstance at once suggests to us how we are to proceed in the case under consideration.　Arguments are
the fit weapons with which to assail an erroneous judgment, but assertions and actions must be brought to
bear upon a false imagination.　The mind in that case
has been misled by representations ; it must be set right
by representations.　What it asks of us is, not reasoning,
but discussion.　In works on Logic, we meet with a sophistical argument, the object of which is to prove that
motion is impossible ; and it is not uncommon, before
scientifically handling it, to submit it to a practical refutation ;—Solvitur ambulando.　Such is the sort of reply
which I think it may be useful just now to make to
public opinion, which is so indisposed to allow that a
Catholic University of the English tongue can be set in
motion.　I will neither directly prove that it is possible,
nor answer the allegations in behalf of its impossibility ;
I shall attempt a humbler, but perhaps a not less effica-
cious service, in employing myself to the best of my
ability, and according to the patience of the reader, in
setting forth what a University is.　I will leave the controversy to others ; I will confine myself to description
and statement, concerning the nature, the character, the
work, the peculiarities of a University, the aims with
which it is established, the wants it may supply, the
methods it adopts, what it involves and requires, what
are its relations to other institutions, and what has been
its history.　I am sanguine that my labour will not be
thrown away, though it aims at nothing very learned,
nothing very systematic ; though it should wander from

one subject to another, as each happens to arise, and gives no promise whatever of terminating in the production of a treatise.

And in attempting as much as this, while I hope I shall gain instruction from criticisms of whatever sort, I do not mean to be put out by them, whether they come from those who know more, or those who know less than myself ;—from those who take exacter, broader, more erudite, more sagacious, more philosophical views than my own ; or those who have yet to attain such measure of truth and of judgment as I may myself claim. I must not be disturbed at the animadversions of those who have a right to feel superior to me, nor at the complaints of others who think I do not enter into or satisfy their difficulties. If I am charged with being shallow on the one part, or off-hand on the other, if I myself feel that fastidiousness at my own attempts, which grows upon an author as he multiplies his compositions, I shall console myself with the reflection, that life is not long enough to do more than our best, whatever that may be ; that they who are ever taking aim, make no hits ; that they who never venture, never gain ; that to be ever safe, is to be ever feeble ; and that to do some substantial good, is the compensation for much incidental imperfection.

With thoughts like these, which, such as they are, have been the companions and the food of my life hitherto, I address myself to my undertaking.

CHAPTER II.

WHAT IS A UNIVERSITY?

IF I were asked to describe as briefly and popularly as I could, what a University was, I should draw my answer from its ancient designation of a *Studium Generale*, or " School of Universal Learning." This description implies the assemblage of strangers from all parts in one spot ;—*from all parts ;* else, how will you find professors and students for every department of knowledge ? and *in one spot;* else, how can there be any school at all ? Accordingly, in its simple and rudimental form, it is a school of knowledge of every kind, consisting of teachers and learners from every quarter. Many things are requisite to complete and satisfy the idea embodied in this description ; but such as this a University seems to be in its essence, a place for the communication and circulation of thought, by means of personal intercourse, through a wide extent of country.

There is nothing far-fetched or unreasonable in the idea thus presented to us ; and if this be a University, then a University does but contemplate a necessity of our nature, and is but one specimen in a particular medium, out of many which might be adduced in others, of a provision for that necessity. Mutual education, in a large sense of the word, is one of the great and incessant occupations of human society, carried on partly with set purpose, and partly not. One generation forms another ; and the existing generation is ever acting and reacting upon itself in the persons of its individual members. Now, in this process, books, I need scarcely say, that is, the *litera scripta*, are one special instrument. It is true ; and emphatically so in this age. Considering the prodigious powers of the press, and how they are developed at this time in the never-intermitting issue of periodicals, tracts, pamphlets, works in series, and light literature, we must allow there never was a time which promised fairer for dispensing with every other means of information and instruction. What can we want more, you will say, for the intellectual education of the whole man, and for every man, than so exuberant and diversified and persistent a promulgation of all kinds of knowledge ? Why, you will ask, need we go up to knowledge, when knowledge comes down to us ? The Sibyl wrote her prophecies upon the leaves of the forest, and wasted them ; but here such careless profusion might be prudently indulged, for it can be afforded without loss, in consequence of the almost fabulous fecundity of the instrument which these latter ages have invented. We have sermons in stones, and books in the running brooks ; works larger and more comprehensive than those which have gained for ancients an immortality, issue forth every morning, and are projected onwards to the ends of the earth at the rate of hundreds of miles a day. Our seats are strewed, our pavements are powdered, with swarms of little tracts ; and the very bricks of our city walls preach wisdom, by informing us by their placards where we can at once cheaply purchase it.

I allow all this, and much more ; such certainly is our popular education, and its effects are remarkable. Nevertheless, after all, even in this age, whenever men are really serious about getting what, in the language of

trade, is called "a good article," when they aim at something precise, something refined, something really lumi-
nous, something really large, something choice, they go
to another market; they avail themselves, in some shape
or other, of the rival method, the ancient method, of oral
instruction, of present communication between man and
man, of teachers instead of learning, of the personal
influence of a master, and the humble initiation of a
disciple, and, in consequence, of great centres of pilgrimage and throng, which such a method of education
necessarily involves. This, I think, will be found to hold
good in all those departments or aspects of society, which
possess an interest sufficient to bind men together, or to
constitute what is called "a world." It holds in the
political world, and in the high world, and in the religious world; and it holds also in the literary and
scientific world.

If the actions of men may be taken as any test of
their convictions, then we have reason for saying this,
viz. :—that the province and the inestimable benefit of
the *litera scripta* is that of being a record of truth, and
an authority of appeal, and an instrument of teaching in
the hands of a teacher ; but that, if we wish to become
exact and fully furnished in any branch of knowledge
which is diversified and complicated, we must consult
the living man and listen to his living voice. I am not
bound to investigate the cause of this, and anything I
may say will, I am conscious, be short of its full analysis ;—perhaps we may suggest, that no books can get
through the number of minute questions which it is
possible to ask on any extended subject, or can hit upon
the very difficulties which are severally felt by each
reader in succession. Or again, that no book can con-
vey the special spirit and delicate peculiarities of its

subject with that rapidity and certainty which attend on the sympathy of mind with mind, through the eyes, the look, the accent, and the manner, in casual expressions thrown off at the moment, and the unstudied turns of familiar conversation. But I am already dwelling too long on what is but an incidental portion of my main subject. Whatever be the cause, the fact is undeniable. The general principles of any study you may learn by books at home ; but the detail, the colour, the tone, the air, the life which makes it live in us, you must catch all these from those in whom it lives already. You must imitate the student in French or German, who is not content with his grammar, but goes to Paris or Dresden : you must take example from the young artist, who aspires to visit the great Masters in Florence and in Rome. Till we have discovered some intellectual daguerreotype, which takes off the course of thought, and the form, lineaments, and features of truth, as completely and minutely, as the optical instrument reproduces the sensible object, we must come to the teachers of wisdom to learn wisdom, we must repair to the fountain, and drink there. Portions of it may go from thence to the ends of the earth by means of books ; but the fulness is in one place alone. It is in such assemblages and congregations of intellect that books themselves, the masterpieces of human genius, are written, or at least originated.

The principle on which I have been insisting is so obvious, and instances in point are so ready, that I should think it tiresome to proceed with the subject, except that one or two illustrations may serve to explain my own language about it, which may not have done justice to the doctrine which it has been intended to enforce.

For instance, the polished manners and high-bred bearing which are so difficult of attainment, and so

strictly personal when attained,—which are so much
admired in society, from society are acquired. All that
goes to constitute a gentleman,—the carriage, gait,
address, gestures, voice; the ease, the self-possession,
the courtesy, the power of conversing, the talent of not
offending; the lofty principle, the delicacy of thought,
the happiness of expression, the taste and propriety, the
generosity and forbearance, the candour and consideration, the openness of hand ;—these qualities, some of
them come by nature, some of them may be found
in any rank, some of them are a direct precept of
Christianity ; but the full assemblage of them, bound
up in the unity of an individual character, do we expect
they can be learned from books? are they not necessarily
acquired, where they are to be found, in high society ?
The very nature of the case leads us to say so; you
cannot fence without an antagonist, nor challenge all
comers in disputation before you have supported a thesis ; and in like manner, it stands to reason, you cannot
learn to converse till you have the world to converse
with; you cannot unlearn your natural bashfulness, or
awkwardness, or stiffness, or other besetting deformity,
till you serve your time in some school of manners.
Well, and is it not so in matter of fact ? The metropolis,
the court, the great houses of the land, are the centres
to which at stated times the country comes up, as to
shrines of refinement and good taste ; and then in due
time the country goes back again home, enriched with a
portion of the social accomplishments, which those very
visits serve to call out and heighten in the gracious dis-
pensers of them. We are unable to conceive how the
" gentlemanlike " can otherwise be maintained ; and
maintained in this way it is.

And now a second instance : and here too I am going

to speak without personal experience of the subject I am introducing. I admit I have not been in Parliament, any more than I have figured in the *beau monde ;* yet I cannot but think that statesmanship, as well as high breeding, is learned, not by books, but in certain centres of education. If it be not presumption to say so, Parliament puts a clever man *au courant* with politics and affairs of state in a way surprising to himself. A member of the Legislature, if tolerably observant, begins to see things with new eyes, even though his views undergo no change. Words have a meaning now, and ideas a reality, such as they had not before. He hears a vast deal in public speeches and private conversation, which is never put into print. The bearings of measures and events, the action of parties, and the persons of friends and enemies, are brought out to the man who is in the midst of them with a distinctness, which the most diligent perusal of newspapers will fail to impart to them. It is access to the fountain-heads of political wisdom and experience, it is daily intercourse, of one kind or another, with the multitude who go up to them, it is familiarity with business, it is access to the contributions of fact and opinion thrown together by many witnesses from many quarters, which does this for him. However, I need not account for a fact, to which it is sufficient to appeal ; that the Houses of Parliament and the atmosphere around them are a sort of University of politics.

As regards the world of science, we find a remarkable instance of the principle which I am illustrating, in the periodical meetings for its advance, which have arisen in the course of the last twenty years, such as the British Association. Such gatherings would to many persons appear at first sight simply preposterous.

Above all subjects of study, Science is conveyed, is propagated, by books, or by private teaching; experiments and investigations are conducted in silence; discoveries are made in solitude. What have philosophers to do with festive celebrities, and panegyrical solemnities with mathematical and physical truth? Yet on a closer attention to the subject, it is found that not even scientific thought can dispense with the suggestions, the instruction, the stimulus, the sympathy, the intercourse with mankind on a large scale, which such meetings secure. A fine time of year is chosen, when days are long, skies are bright, the earth smiles, and all nature rejoices; a city or town is taken by turns, of ancient name or modern opulence, where buildings are spacious and hospitality hearty. The novelty of place and circumstance, the excitement of strange, or the refreshment of well-known faces, the majesty of rank or of genius, the amiable charities of men pleased both with themselves and with each other; the elevated spirits, the circulation of thought, the curiosity; the morning sections, the outdoor exercise, the well-furnished, well-earned board, the not ungraceful hilarity, the evening circle; the brilliant lecture, the discussions or collisions or guesses of great men one with another, the narratives of scientific processes, of hopes, disappointments, conflicts, and successes, the splendid eulogistic orations; these and the like constituents of the annual celebration, are considered to do something real and substantial for the advance of knowledge which can be done in no other way. Of course they can but be occasional; they answer to the annual Act, or Commencement, or Commemoration of a University, not to its ordinary condition; but they are of a University nature; and I can well believe in their utility. They issue in the promotion of a certain living and, as it were, bodily communication of knowledge from one to another, of a general interchange of ideas, and a comparison and adjustment of science with science, of an enlargement of mind, intellectual and social, of an ardent love of the particular study, which may be chosen by each individual, and a noble devotion to its interests.

Such meetings, I repeat, are but periodical, and only partially represent the idea of a University. The bustle and whirl which are their usual concomitants, are in ill keeping with the order and gravity of earnest intellectual education. We desiderate means of instruction which involve no interruption of our ordinary habits ; nor need we seek it long, for the natural course of things brings it about, while we debate over it. In every great country, the metropolis itself becomes a sort of necessary University, whether we will or no. As the chief city is the seat of the court, of high society, of politics, and of law, so as a matter of course is it the seat of letters also ; and at this time, for a long term of years, London and Paris are in fact and in operation Universities, though in Paris its famous University is no more, and in London a University scarcely exists except as a board of administration. The newspapers, magazines, reviews, journals, and periodicals of all kinds, the publishing trade, the libraries, museums, and academies there found, the learned and scientific societies, necessarily invest it with the functions of a University ; and that atmosphere of intellect, which in a former age hung over Oxford or Bologna or Salamanca, has, with the change of times, moved away to the centre of civil government. Thither come up youths from all parts of the country, the students of law, medicine, and the fine arts, and the *employés* and *attachés* of literature. There they live, as chance determines; and they are satisfied with their temporary home, for they find in it all that was promised to them there. They have not come in vain, as far as their own object in coming is concerned. They have not learned any particular religion, but they have learned their own particular profession well. They have, moreover, become acquainted with the habits, manners, and opinions of their place of sojourn, and done their part in maintaining the tradition of them. We cannot then be without virtual Universities ; a metropolis is such : the simple question is, whether the education sought and given should be based on principle, formed upon rule, directed to the highest ends, or left to the random succession of masters and schools, one after another, with a melancholy waste of thought and an extreme hazard of truth.

Religious teaching itself affords us an illustration of our subject to a certain point. It does not indeed seat itself merely in centres of the world ; this is impossible from the nature of the case. It is intended for the many not the few ; its subject matter is truth necessary for us, not truth recondite and rare ; but it concurs in the principle of a University so far as this, that its great instrument, or rather organ, has ever been that which nature prescribes in all education, the personal presence of a teacher, or, in theological language, Oral Tradition. It is the living voice, the breathing form, the expressive countenance, which preaches, which catechises. Truth, a subtle, invisible, manifold spirit, is poured into the mind of the scholar by his eyes and ears, through his affections, imagination, and reason ; it is poured into his mind and is sealed up there in perpetuity, by propounding and repeating it, by questioning and requestioning, by correcting and explaining, by progressing and then recurring to first principles, by all those ways which are implied in the word "catechising." In the first ages, it was a work of long time; months, sometimes years, were devoted to the arduous task of disabusing the mind of the incipient Christian of its pagan errors, and of moulding it upon the Christian faith. The Scriptures indeed were at hand for the study of those who could avail themselves of them; but St. Irenæus does not hesitate to speak of whole races, who had been converted to Christianity, without being able to read them. To be unable to read or write was in those times no evidence of want of learning: the hermits of the deserts were, in this sense of the word, illiterate; yet the great St. Anthony, though he knew not letters, was a match in disputation for the learned philosophers who came to try him. Didymus again, the great Alexandrian theologian, was blind. The ancient discipline, called the *Disciplina Arcani*, involved the same principle. The more sacred doctrines of Revelation were not committed to books but passed on by successive tradition. The teaching on the Blessed Trinity and the Eucharist appears to have been so handed down for some hundred years; and when at length reduced to writing, it has filled many folios, yet has not been exhausted.

But I have said more than enough in illustration; I end as I began;—a University is a place of concourse, whither students come from every quarter for every kind of knowledge. You cannot have the best of every kind everywhere; you must go to some great city or emporium for it. There you have all the choicest productions of nature and art all together, which you find each in its own separate place elsewhere. All the riches of the land, and of the earth, are carried up thither; there are the best markets, and there the best workmen. It is the centre of trade, the supreme court of fashion, the umpire of rival talents, and the standard of things rare and precious. It is the place for seeing galleries of first-rate pictures, and for hearing wonderful voices and performers of transcendent skill. It is the place for great preachers, great orators, great nobles, great statesmen. In the nature of things, greatness and unity go together; excellence implies a centre. And such, for the third or fourth time, is a University; I hope I do not weary out the reader by repeating it. It is the place to which a thousand schools make contributions; in which the intellect may safely range and speculate, sure to find its equal in some antagonist activity, and its judge in the tribunal of truth. It is a place where inquiry is pushed forward, and discoveries verified and perfected, and rashness rendered innocuous, and error exposed, by the collision of mind with mind, and knowledge with knowledge. It is the place where the professor becomes eloquent, and is a missionary and a preacher, displaying his science in its most complete and most winning form, pouring it forth with the zeal of enthusiasm, and lighting up his own love of it in the breasts of his hearers. It is the place where the catechist makes good his ground as he goes, treading in the truth day by day into the ready memory, and wedging and tightening it into the expanding reason. It is a place which wins the admiration of the young by its celebrity, kindles the affections of the middle-aged by its beauty, and rivets the fidelity of the old by its associations. It is a seat of wisdom, a light of the world, a minister of the faith, an Alma Mater of the rising generation. It is this and a great deal more, and demands a somewhat better head and hand than mine to describe it well.

Such is a University in its idea and in its purpose; 6

such in good measure has it before now been in fact. Shall it ever be again? We are going forward in the strength of the Cross, under the patronage of the Blessed Virgin, in the name of St. Patrick, to attempt it.

CHAPTER III.

SITE OF A UNIVERSITY.

IF we would know what a University is, considered in its elementary idea, we must betake ourselves to the first and most celebrated home of European literature and source of European civilization, to the bright and beautiful Athens,—Athens, whose schools drew to her bosom, and then sent back again to the business of life, the youth of the Western World for a long thousand years. Seated on the verge of the continent, the city seemed hardly suited for the duties of a central metropolis of knowledge ; yet, what it lost in convenience of approach, it gained in its neighbourhood to the traditions of the mysterious East, and in the loveliness of the region in which it lay. Hither, then, as to a sort of ideal land, where all archetypes of the great and the fair were found in substantial being, and all departments of truth explored, and all diversities of intellectual power exhibited, where taste and philosophy were majestically enthroned as in a royal court, where there was no sovereignty but that of mind, and no nobility but that of genius, where professors were rulers, and princes did homage, hither flocked continually from the very corners of the *orbis terrarum*, the many-tongued generation, just. rising, or just risen into manhood, in order to gain wisdom.

Pisistratus had in an early age discovered and nursed the infant genius of his people, and Cimon, after the

Persian war, had given it a home. That war had established the naval supremacy of Athens ; she had become
an imperial state ; and the Ionians, bound to her by
the double chain of kindred and of subjection, were
importing into her both their merchandize and their
civilization. The arts and philosophy of the Asiatic
coast were easily carried across the sea, and there was
Cimon, as I have said, with his ample fortune, ready to
receive them with due honours. Not content with
patronizing their professors, he built the first of those
noble porticos, of which we hear so much in Athens, and
he formed the groves, which in process of time became
the celebrated Academy. Planting is one of the most
graceful, as in Athens it was one of the most beneficent,
of employments. Cimon took in hand the wild wood,
pruned and dressed it, and laid it out with handsome
walks and welcome fountains. Nor, while hospitable
to the authors of the city's civilization, was he ungrateful
to the instruments of her prosperity. His trees extended
their cool, umbrageous branches over the merchants,
who assembled in the Agora, for many generations.

Those merchants certainly had deserved that act of
bounty ; for all the while their ships had been carrying
forth the intellectual fame of Athens to the western
world. Then commenced what may be called her University existence. Pericles, who succeeded Cimon both
in the government and in the patronage of art, is said
by Plutarch to have entertained the idea of making
Athens the capital of federated Greece : in this he
failed, but his encouragement of such men as Phidias
and Anaxagoras led the way to her acquiring a far more
lasting sovereignty over a far wider empire. Little
understanding the sources of her own greatness, Athens
would go to war : peace is the interest of a seat of com-

merce and the arts ; but to war she went ; yet to her, whether peace or war, it mattered not. The political power of Athens waned and disappeared ; kingdoms rose and fell ; centuries rolled away,—they did but bring fresh triumphs to the city of the poet and the sage. There at length the swarthy Moor and Spaniard were seen to meet the blue-eyed Gaul ; and the Cappadocian, late subject of Mithridates, gazed without alarm at the haughty conquering Roman. Revolution after revolution passed over the face of Europe, as well as of Greece, but still she was there,—Athens, the city of mind,—as radiant, as splendid, as delicate, as young, as ever she had been.

Many a more fruitful coast or isle is washed by the blue Ægean, many a spot is there more beautiful or sublime to see, many a territory more ample ; but there was one charm in Attica, which in the same perfection was nowhere else. The deep pastures of Arcadia, the plain of Argos, the Thessalian vale, these had not the gift ; Bœotia, which lay to its immediate north, was notorious for its very want of it. The heavy atmosphere of that Bœotia might be good for vegetation, but it was associated in popular belief with the dulness of the Bœotian intellect : on the contrary, the special purity, elasticity, clearness, and salubrity of the air of Attica, fit concomitant and emblem of its genius, did that for it which earth did not ;—it brought out every bright hue and tender shade of the landscape over which it was spread, and would have illuminated the face even of a more bare and rugged country.

A confined triangle, perhaps fifty miles its greatest length, and thirty its greatest breadth ; two elevated rocky barriers, meeting at an angle ; three prominent mountains, commanding the plain,—Parnes, Pentelicus, and Hymettus ; an unsatisfactory soil ; some streams, not always full ;—such is about the report which the agent of a London company would have made of Attica. He would report that the climate was mild ; the hills were limestone ; there was plenty of good marble ; more pasture land than at first survey might have been expected, sufficient certainly for sheep and goats ; fisheries productive ; silver mines once, but long since worked out ; figs fair ; oil first-rate ; olives in profusion. But what he would not think of noting down, was, that that olive tree was so choice in nature and so noble in shape, that it excited a religious veneration ; and that it took so kindly to the light soil, as to expand into woods upon the open plain, and to climb up and fringe the hills. He would not think of writing word to his employers, how that clear air, of which I have spoken, brought out, yet blended and subdued, the colours on the marble, till they had a softness and harmony, for all their richness, which in a picture looks exaggerated, yet is after all within the truth. He would not tell, how that same delicate and brilliant atmosphere freshened up the pale olive, till the olive forgot its monotony, and its cheek glowed like the arbutus or beech of the Umbrian hills. He would say nothing of the thyme and thousand fragrant herbs which carpeted Hymettus ; he would hear nothing of the hum of its bees ; nor take much account of the rare flavour of its honey, since Gozo and Minorca were sufficient for the English demand. He would look over the Ægean from the height he had ascended ; he would follow with his eye the chain of islands, which, starting from the Sunian headland, seemed to offer the fabled divinities of Attica, when they would visit their Ionian cousins, a sort of viaduct thereto across the sea : but that fancy would not occur to him, nor any admiration of the dark violet billows with their white edges down below ; nor of those graceful, fan-like jets of silver upon the rocks, which slowly rise aloft like water spirits from the deep, then shiver, and break, and spread, and shroud themselves, and disappear, in a soft mist of foam ; nor of the gentle, incessant heaving and panting of the whole liquid plain ; nor of the long waves, keeping steady time, like a line of soldiery, as they resound upon the hollow shore,—he would not deign to notice that restless living element at all, except to bless his stars that he was not upon it. Nor the distinct detail, nor the refined colouring, nor the graceful outline and roseate golden hue of the jutting crags, nor the bold shadows cast from Otus or Laurium by the declining sun ;—our agent of a mercantile firm would not value these matters even at a low figure. Rather we must turn for the sympathy we seek to yon pilgrim student, come from a semi-barbarous land to that small corner of the earth, as to a shrine, where he might take his fill of gazing on those emblems and coruscations of invisible unoriginate perfection. It was the stranger from a remote province, from Britain or from Mauritania, who in a scene so different from that of his chilly, woody swamps, or of his fiery choking sands, learned at once what a real University must be, by coming to understand the sort of country, which was its suitable home.

Nor was this all that a University required, and found in Athens. No one, even there, could live on poetry. If the students at that famous place had nothing better than bright hues and soothing sounds, they would not have been able or disposed to turn their residence there to much account. Of course they must have the means

of living, nay, in a certain sense, of enjoyment, if
Athens was to be an Alma Mater at the time, or to
remain afterwards a pleasant thought in their memory.
And so they had : be it recollected Athens was a port,
and a mart of trade, perhaps the first in Greece ; and
this was very much to the point, when a number of
strangers were ever flocking to it, whose combat was to
be with intellectual, not physical difficulties, and who
claimed to have their bodily wants supplied, that they
might be at leisure to set about furnishing their minds.
Now, barren as was the soil of Attica, and bare the face
of the country, yet it had only too many resources for
an elegant, nay luxurious abode there. So abundant
were the imports of the place, that it was a common
saying, that the productions, which were found singly
elsewhere, were brought all together in Athens. Corn
and wine, the staple of subsistence in such a climate,
came from the isles of the Ægean ; fine wool and car-
peting from Asia Minor ; slaves, as now, from the
Euxine, and timber too ; and iron and brass from the
coasts of the Mediterranean. The Athenian did not
condescend to manufactures himself, but encouraged
them in others ; and a population of foreigners caught
at the lucrative occupation both for home consumption
and for exportation. Their cloth, and other textures for
dress and furniture, and their hardware—for instance,
armour—were in great request. Labour was cheap ;
stone and marble in plenty ; and the taste and skill,
which at first were devoted to public buildings, as temples and porticos, were in course of time applied to the
mansions of public men. If nature did much for
Athens, it is undeniable that art did much more.

Here some one will interrupt me with the remark :
" By the bye, where are we, and whither are we going ?—

what has all this to do with a University? at least what
has it to do with education? It is instructive doubtless;
but still how much has it to do with your subject?"
Now I beg to assure the reader that I am most con-
scientiously employed upon my subject; and I should
have thought every one would have seen this: however,
since the objection is made, I may be allowed to pause
awhile, and show distinctly the drift of what I have been
saying, before I go farther. *What* has this to do with
my subject! why, the question of the *site* is the very
first that comes into consideration, when a *Studium
Generale* is contemplated; for that site should be a
liberal and noble one; who will deny it? All authorities agree in this, and very little reflection will be sufficient to make it clear. I recollect a conversation I once
had on this very subject with a very eminent man. I
was a youth of eighteen, and was leaving my University
for the Long Vacation, when I found myself in company
in a public conveyance with a middle-aged person, whose
face was strange to me. However, it was the great academical luminary of the day, whom afterwards I knew
very well. Luckily for me, I did not suspect it; and
luckily too, it was a fancy of his, as his friends knew, to
make himself on easy terms especially with stage-coach
companions. So, what with my flippancy and his condescension, I managed to hear many things which were
novel to me at the time; and one point which he was
strong upon, and was evidently fond of urging, was the
material pomp and circumstance which should environ a
great seat of learning. He considered it was worth the
consideration of the government, whether Oxford should
not stand in a domain of its own. An ample range, say
four miles in diameter, should be turned into wood and
meadow, and the University should be approached on

all sides by a magnificent park, with fine trees in groups and groves and avenues, and with glimpses and views of the fair city, as the traveller drew near it. There is nothing surely absurd in the idea, though it would cost a round sum to realise it. What has a better claim to the purest and fairest possessions of nature, than the seat of wisdom? So thought my coach companion; and he did but express the tradition of ages and the instinct of mankind.

For instance, take the great University of Paris. That famous school engrossed as its territory the whole south bank of the Seine, and occupied one half, and that the pleasanter half, of the city. King Louis had the island pretty well as his own,—it was scarcely more than a fortification; and the north of the river was given over to the nobles and citizens to do what they could with its marshes; but the eligible south, rising from the stream, which swept around its base, to the fair summit of St. Genevieve, with its broad meadows, its vineyards and its gardens, and with the sacred elevation of Montmartre confronting it, all this was the inheritance of the University. There was that pleasant Pratum, stretching along the river's bank, in which the students for centuries took their recreation, which Alcuin seems to mention in his farewell verses to Paris, and which has given a name to the great Abbey of St. Germain-des-Prés. For long years it was devoted to the purposes of innocent and healthy enjoyment; but evil times came on the University; disorder arose within its precincts, and the fair meadow became the scene of party brawls; heresy stalked through Europe, and Germany and England no longer sending their contingent of students, a heavy debt was the consequence to the academical body. To let their land was the only resource left to them:

buildings rose upon it, and spread along the green sod, and the country at length became town. Great was the grief and indignation of the doctors and masters, when this catastrophe occurred. " A wretched sight," said the Proctor of the German nation, "a wretched sight, to witness the sale of that ancient manor, whither the Muses were wont to wander for retirement and pleasure. Whither shall the youthful student now betake himself, what relief will he find for his eyes, wearied with intense reading, now that the pleasant stream is taken from him ?" Two centuries and more have passed since this complaint was uttered ; and time has shown that the outward calamity, which it recorded, was but the emblem of the great moral revolution, which was to follow ; till the institution itself has followed its green meadows, into the region of things which once were and now are not.

And in like manner, when they were first contemplating a University in Belgium, some centuries ago, " Many," says Lipsius, " suggested Mechlin, as an abode salubrious and clean, but Louvain was preferred, as for other reasons, so because no city seemed, from the disposition of place and people, more suitable for learned leisure. Who will not approve the decision ? Can a site be healthier or more pleasant ? The atmosphere pure and cheerful ; the spaces open and delightful ; meadows, fields, vines, groves, nay, I may say, a *rus in urbe*. Ascend and walk round the walls ; what do you look down upon ? Does not the wonderful and delightful variety smooth the brow and soothe the mind ? You have corn, and apples, and grapes ; sheep and oxen ; and birds chirping or singing. Now carry your feet or your eyes beyond the walls ; there are streamlets, the river meandering along ; country-houses, convents, the superb fortress ; copses or woods fill up the scene, and spots

for simple enjoyment." And then he breaks out into
poetry :

> Salvete Athenæ nostræ, Athenæ Belgicæ,
> Te Gallus, te Germanus, et te Sarmata
> Invisit, et Britannus, et te duplicis
> Hispaniæ alumnus, etc.

Extravagant, then, and wayward as might be the
thought of my learned coach companion, when, in the
nineteenth century, he imagined, Norman-wise, to turn
a score of villages into a park or pleasaunce, still, the
waywardness of his fancy is excused by the justness of
his principle ; for certainly, such as he would have made
it, a University ought to be. Old Antony-à-Wood, dis-
coursing on the demands of a University, had expressed
the same sentiment long before him ; as Horace in
ancient times, with reference to Athens itself, when he
spoke of seeking truth "in the *groves* of Academe."
And to Athens, as will be seen, Wood himself appeals,
when he would discourse of Oxford. Among "those
things which are required to make a University," he
puts down,—

"First, a good and pleasant site, where there is a
wholesome and temperate constitution of the air ; composed with waters, springs or wells, woods and pleasant
fields ; which being obtained, those commodities are
enough to invite students to stay and abide there. As
the Athenians in ancient times were happy for their
conveniences, so also were the Britons, when by a remnant of the Grecians that came amongst them, they or
their successors selected such a place in Britain to plant
a school or schools therein, which for its pleasant situation was afterwards called Bellositum or Bellosite, now
Oxford, privileged with all those conveniences before
mentioned."

By others the local advantages of that University have been more philosophically analyzed ;—for instance, with a reference to its position in the middle of southern England ; its situation on several islands in a broad plain, through which many streams flowed ; the surrounding marshes, which, in times when it was needed, protected the city from invaders ; its own strength as a military position ; its easy communication with London, nay with the sea, by means of the Thames ; while the London fortifications hindered pirates from ascending the stream, which all the time was so ready and convenient for a descent.

Alas ! for centuries past that city has lost its prime honour and boast, as a servant and soldier of the Truth. Once named the second school of the Church, second only to Paris, the foster-mother of St. Edmund, St. Richard, St. Thomas Cantilupe, the theatre of great intellects, of Scotus the subtle Doctor, of Hales the irrefragible, of Occam the special, of Bacon the admirable, of Middleton the solid, and of Bradwardine the profound, Oxford has now lapsed to that level of mere human loveliness, which in its highest perfection we admire in Athens. Nor would it have a place, now or hereafter, in these pages, nor would it occur to me to speak its name, except that, even in its sorrowful deprivation, it still retains so much of that outward lustre, which, like the brightness on the prophet's face, ought to be a ray from an illumination within, as to afford me an illustration of the point on which I am engaged, viz., what should be the material dwelling-place and appearance, the local circumstances, and the secular concomitants of a great University. Pictures are drawn in tales of romance, of spirits seemingly too beautiful in their fall to be really fallen, and the holy Pope at Rome,

Gregory, in fact, and not in fiction, looked upon the blue eyes and golden hair of the fierce Saxon youth in the slave market, and pronounced them Angels, not Angles ; and the spell which this once loyal daughter of the Church still exercises upon the foreign visitor, even now when her true glory is departed, suggests to us how far more majestic and more touching, how brimfull of indescribable influence would be the presence of a University, which was planted within, not without Jerusalem, —an influence, potent as her truth is strong, wide as her sway is world-wide, and growing, not lessening, by the extent ,of space over which its attraction would be exerted.

Let the reader then listen to the words of the last learned German, who has treated of Oxford, and judge for himself if they do not bear me out, in what I have said of the fascination which the very face and smile of a University possess over those who come within its range.

"There is scarce a spot in the world," says Huber, "that bears an historical stamp so deep and varied as Oxford ; where so many noble memorials of moral and material power, coöperating to an honourable end, meet the eye all at once. He who can be proof against the strong emotions which the whole aspect and genius of the place tend to inspire, must be dull, thoughtless, uneducated, or of very perverted views. Others will bear us witness, that, even side by side with the Eternal Rome, the Alma Mater of Oxford may be fitly named, as producing a deep, a lasting, and peculiar impression.

" In one of the most fertile districts of the Queen of the Seas, whom nature has so richly blessed, whom for centuries past no footstep of foreign armies has desecrated, lies a broad green vale, where the Cherwell and

the Isis mingle their full, clear waters. Here and there
primeval elms and oaks overshadow them ; while in
their various windings they encircle gardens, meadows,
and fields, villages, cottages, farm-houses, and country-
seats, in motley mixture. In the midst rises a mass of
mighty buildings, the general character of which varies
between convent, palace, and castle. Some few Gothic
church-towers and Romaic domes, it is true, break
through the horizontal lines; yet the general impression
at a distance and at first sight, is essentially different
from that of any of the towns of the middle ages. The
outlines are far from being so sharp, so angular, so irregular, so fantastical ; a certain softness, a peculiar repose, reigns in those broader, terrace-like rising masses.
Only in the creations of Claude Lorraine or Poussin
could we expect to find a spot to compare with the
prevailing character of this picture, especially when lit
up by a favourable light. The principal masses consist
of Colleges, the University buildings, and the city
churches ; and by the side of these the city itself is lost
on distant view. But on entering the streets, we find
around us all the signs of an active and prosperous
trade. Rich and elegant shops in profusion afford a
sight to be found nowhere but in England ; but with all
this glitter and show, they sink into a modest, and, as it
were, a menial attitude, by the side of the grandly severe
memorials of the higher intellectual life, memorials which
have been growing out of that life from almost the beginning of Christianity itself. Those rich and elegant shops
are, as it were, the domestic offices of these palaces of
learning, which ever rivet the eye of the observer, while
all besides seems perforce to be subservient to them.
Each of the larger and more ancient Colleges looks like
a separate whole—an entire town, whose walls and monu-

ments proclaim the vigorous growth of many centuries ; and the town itself has happily escaped the lot of modern beautifying, and in this respect harmonizes with the Colleges." *

There are those who, having felt the influence of this ancient School, and being smit with its splendour and its sweetness, ask wistfully, if never again it is to be Catholic, or whether at least some footing for Catholicity may not be found there. All honour and merit to the charitable and zealous hearts who so inquire ! Nor can we dare to tell what in time to come may be the inscrutable purposes of that grace, which is ever more comprehensive than human hope and aspiration. But for me, from the day I left its walls, I never, for good or bad, have had anticipation of its future ; and never for a moment have I had a wish to see again a place, which I have never ceased to love, and where I lived for nearly thirty years. Nay, looking at the general state of things at this day, I desiderate for a School of the Church, if an additional School is to be granted to us, a more central position than Oxford has to show. Since the age of Alfred and of the first Henry, the world has grown, from the west and south of Europe, into four or five continents ; and I look for a city less inland than that old sanctuary, and a country closer upon the highway of the seas. I look towards a land both old and young ; old in its Christianity, young in the promise of its future ; a nation, which received grace before the Saxon came to Britain, and which has never quenched it ; a Church, which comprehends in its history the rise and fall of Canterbury and York, which Augustine and Paulinus found, and Pole and

* Huber on English Universities. F. W. Newman's translation.

Fisher left behind them.   I contemplate a people which
has had a long night, and will have an inevitable day.
I am turning my eyes towards a hundred years to come,
and I dimly see the island I am gazing on, become the
road of passage and union between two hemispheres,
and the centre of the world.   I see its inhabitants rival
Belgium in populousness, France in vigour, and Spain
in enthusiasm ; and I see England taught by advancing
years to exercise in its behalf that good sense which is
her characteristic towards every one else.   The capital
of that prosperous and hopeful land is situate in a
beautiful bay and near a romantic region ; and in it I
see a flourishing University, which for a while had to
struggle with fortune, but which, when its first founders
and servants were dead and gone, had successes far
exceeding their anxieties.   Thither, as to a sacred soil,
the home of their fathers, and the fountain-head of their
Christianity, students are flocking from East, West, and
South, from America and Australia and India, from
Egypt and Asia Minor, with the ease and rapidity of a
locomotion not yet discovered, and last, though not
least, from England,—all speaking one tongue, all
owning one faith, all eager for one large true wisdom ;
and thence, when their stay is over, going back again to
carry over all the earth " peace to men of good will."

CHAPTER IV.

UNIVERSITY LIFE.

ATHENS.

HOWEVER apposite may have been the digression into which I was led when I had got about half through the foregoing Chapter, it has had the inconvenience of what may be called running me off the rails ; and now that I wish to proceed from the point at which it took place, I shall find some trouble, if I may continue the metaphor, in getting up the steam again, or if I may change it, in getting into the swing of my subject.

It has been my desire, were I able, to bring before the reader what Athens may have been, viewed as what we have since called a University ; and to do this, not with any purpose of writing a panegyric on a heathen city, or of denying its many deformities, or of concealing what was morally base in what was intellectually great, but just the contrary, of representing things as they really were ; so far, that is, as to enable him to see what a University is, in the very constitution of society and in its own idea, what is its nature and object, and what it needs of aid and support external to itself to complete that nature and to secure that object.

So now let us fancy our Scythian, or Armenian, or African, or Italian, or Gallic student, after tossing on the Saronic waves, which would be his more ordinary course to Athens, at last casting anchor at Piræus. He is

3

of any condition or rank of life you please, and may
be made to order, from a prince to a peasant. Perhaps he is some Cleanthes, who has been a boxer in
the public games. How did it ever cross his brain to
betake himself to Athens in search of wisdom? or, if
he came thither by accident, how did the love of it
ever touch his heart? But so it was, to Athens he
came with three drachms in his girdle, and he got his
livelihood by drawing water, carrying loads, and the
like servile occupations. He attached himself, of all
philosophers, to Zeno the Stoic,—to Zeno, the most
high-minded, the most haughty of speculators; and
out of his daily earnings the poor scholar brought his
master the daily sum of an obolus, in payment for attending his lectures. Such progress did he make, that
on Zeno's death he actually was his successor in his
school; and, if my memory does not play me false,
he is the author of a hymn to the Supreme Being,
which is one of the noblest effusions of the kind in
classical poetry. Yet, even when he was the head of a
school, he continued in his illiberal toil as if he had
been a monk; and, it is said, that once, when the wind
took his pallium, and blew it aside, he was discovered
to have no other garment at all;—something like the
German student who came up to Heidelberg with nothing upon him but a great coat and a pair of pistols.

Or it is another disciple of the Porch,—Stoic by nature, earlier than by profession,—who is entering the city;
but in what different fashion he comes! It is no other
than Marcus, Emperor of Rome and philosopher. Professors long since were summoned from Athens for his
service, when he was a youth, and now he comes, after
his victories in the battle field, to make his acknowledg-
ments at the end of life, to the city of wisdom, and to

submit himself to an initiation into the Eleusinian mysteries.

Or it is a young man of great promise as an orator, were it not for his weakness of chest, which renders it necessary that he should acquire the art of speaking without over-exertion, and should adopt a delivery sufficient for the display of his rhetorical talents on the one hand, yet merciful to his physical resources on the other. He is called Cicero; he will stop but a short time, and will pass over to Asia Minor and its cities, before he returns to continue a career which will render his name immortal; and he will like his short sojourn at Athens so well, that he will take good care to send his son thither at an earlier age than he visited it himself.

But see where comes from Alexandria (for we need not be very solicitous about anachronisms), a young man from twenty to twenty-two, who has narrowly escaped drowning on his voyage, and is to remain at Athens as many as eight or ten years, yet in the course of that time will not learn a line of Latin, thinking it enough to become accomplished in Greek composition, and in that he will succeed. He is a grave person, and difficult to make out; some say he is a Christian, something or other in the Christian line his father is for certain. His name is Gregory, he is by country a Cappadocian, and will in time become preëminently a theologian, and one of the principal Doctors of the Greek Church.

Or it is one Horace, a youth of low stature and black hair, whose father has given him an education at Rome above his rank in life, and now is sending him to finish it at Athens; he is said to have a turn for poetry: a hero he is not, and it were well if he knew it; but he is caught by the enthusiasm of the hour, and goes off campaigning with Brutus and Cassius, and will leave his shield behind him on the field of Philippi.

Or it is a mere boy of fifteen : his name Eunapius ; though the voyage was not long, sea sickness, or confinement, or bad living on board the vessel, threw him into a fever, and, when the passengers landed in the evening at Piræus, he could not stand. His countrymen who accompanied him, took him up among them and carried him to the house of the great teacher of the day, Proæresius, who was a friend of the captain's, and whose fame it was which drew the enthusiastic youth to Athens. His companions understand the sort of place they are in, and, with the licence of academic students, they break into the philosopher's house, though he appears to have retired for the night, and proceed to make themselves free of it, with an absence of ceremony, which is only not impudence, because Proæresius takes it so easily. Strange introduction for our stranger to a seat of learning, but not out of keeping with Athens ; for what could you expect of a place where there was a mob of youths and not even the pretence of control ; where the poorer lived any how, and got on as they could, and the teachers themselves had no protection from the humours and caprices of the students who filled their lecture-halls ? However, as to this Eunapius, Proæresius took a fancy to the boy, and told him curious stories about Athenian life. He himself had come up to the University with one Hephæstion, and they were even worse off than Cleanthes the Stoic ; for they had only one cloak between them, and nothing whatever besides, except some old bedding ; so when Proæresius went abroad, Hephæstion lay in bed, and practised himself in oratory ; and then Hephæstion put on the cloak, and Proæresius crept under the coverlet. At another time there was so fierce a feud between what would be called "town and gown" in an English University, that the Professors did not dare lecture in public, for fear of ill treatment.

But a freshman like Eunapius soon got experience for himself of the ways and manners prevalent in Athens. Such a one as he had hardly entered the city, when he was caught hold of by a party of the academic youth, who proceeded to practise on his awkwardness and his ignorance. At first sight one wonders at their childishness; but the like conduct obtained in the medieval Universities; and not many months have passed away since the journals have told us of sober Englishmen, given to matter-of-fact calculations, and to the anxieties of money-making, pelting each other with snow-balls on their own sacred territory, and defying the magistracy, when they would interfere with their privilege of becoming boys. So I suppose we must attribute it to something or other in human nature. Meanwhile, there stands the new-comer, surrounded by a circle of his new associates, who forthwith proceed to frighten, and to banter, and to make a fool of him, to the extent of their wit. Some address him with mock politeness, others with fierceness; and so they conduct him in solemn procession across the Agora to the Baths; and as they approach, they dance about him like madmen. But this was to be the end of his trial, for the Bath was a sort of initiation; he thereupon received the pallium, or University gown, and was suffered by his tormentors to depart in peace. One alone is recorded as having been exempted from this persecution; it was a youth graver and loftier than even St. Gregory himself: but it was not from his force of character, but at the instance of Gregory, that he escaped. Gregory was his bosom-friend, and was ready in Athens to shelter him when he came. It was another

Saint and another Doctor; the great Basil, then, (it would appear,) as Gregory, but a catechumen of the Church.

But to return to our freshman. His troubles are not at an end, though he has got his gown upon him. Where is he to lodge? whom is he to attend? He finds himself seized, before he well knows where he is, by another party of men, or three or four parties at once, like foreign porters at a landing, who seize on the baggage of the perplexed stranger, and thrust half a dozen cards into his unwilling hands. Our youth is plied by the hangers-on of professor this, or sophist that, each of whom wishes the fame or the profit of having a housefull. We will say that he escapes from their hands,—but then he will have to choose for himself where he will put up; and, to tell the truth, with all the praise I have already given, and the praise I shall have to give, to the city of mind, nevertheless, between ourselves, the brick and wood which formed it, the actual tenements, where flesh and blood had to lodge (always excepting the mansions of great men of the place), do not seem to have been much better than those of Greek or Turkish towns, which are at this moment a topic of interest and ridicule in the public prints. A lively picture has lately been set before us of Gallipoli. Take, says the writer,* a multitude of the dilapidated outhouses found in farm-yards in England, of the rickety old wooden tenements, the cracked, shut-terless structures of planks and tiles, the sheds and stalls, which our bye lanes, or fish-markets, or river-sides can supply; tumble them down on the declivity of a bare bald hill; let the spaces between house and house, thus accidentally determined, be understood to form streets,

* Mr. Russell's Letters in the *Times* newspaper (1854).

winding of course for no reason, and with no meaning, up and down the town ; the roadway always narrow, the breadth never uniform, the separate houses bulging or retiring below, as circumstances may have determined, and leaning forward till they meet overhead ;— and you have a good idea of Gallipoli. I question whether this picture would not nearly correspond to the special seat of the Muses in ancient times. Learned writers assure us distinctly that the houses of Athens were for the most part small and mean ; that the streets were crooked and narrow ; that the upper stories projected over the roadway ; and that staircases, balustrades, and doors that opened outwards, obstructed it ; —a remarkable coincidence of description. I do not doubt at all, though history is silent, that that roadway was jolting to carriages, and all but impassable ; and that it was traversed by drains, as freely as any Turkish town now. Athens seems in these respects to have been below the average cities of its time. " A stranger," says an ancient, "might doubt, on the sudden view, if really he saw Athens."

I grant all this, and much more, if you will ; but, recollect, Athens was the home of the intellectual and beautiful ; not of low mechanical contrivances, and material organization. Why stop within your lodgings, counting the rents in your wall or the holes in your tiling, when nature and art call you away ? You must put up with such a chamber, and a table, and a stool, and a sleeping board, any where else in the three continents ; one place does not differ from another indoors ; your magalia in Africa, or your grottos in Syria are not perfection. I suppose you did not come to Athens to swarm up a ladder, or to grope about a closet : you came to see and to hear, what hear and see you could not elsewhere. What food for the intellect is it possible to procure indoors, that you stay there looking about you? do you think to read there? where are your books? do you expect to purchase books at Athens— you are much out in your calculations. True it is, we at this day, who live in the nineteenth century, have the books of Greece as a perpetual memorial; and copies there have been, since the time that they were written; but you need not go to Athens to procure them, nor would you find them in Athens. Strange to say, strange to the nineteenth century, that in the age of Plato and Thucydides, there was not, it is said, a bookshop in the whole place: nor was the book trade in existence till the very time of Augustus. Libraries, I suspect, were the bright invention of Attalus or the Ptolemies;* I doubt whether Athens had a library till the reign of Hadrian. It was what the student gazed on, what he heard, what he caught by the magic of sympathy, not what he read, which was the education furnished by Athens.

He leaves his narrow lodging early in the morning; and not till night, if even then, will he return. It is but a crib or kennel,—in which he sleeps when the weather is inclement or the ground damp; in no respect a home. And he goes out of doors, not to read the day's news- paper, or to buy the gay shilling volume, but to imbibe the invisible atmosphere of genius, and to learn by heart the oral traditions of taste. Out he goes; and, leaving the tumble-down town behind him, he mounts the Acropolis to the right, or he turns to the Areopagus on

---

* I do not go into controversy on the subject, for which the reader must have recourse to Lipsius, Morhof, Boeckh, Bekker, etc.; and this of course applies to whatever historical matter I introduce, or shall introduce.

the left. He goes to the Parthenon to study the sculptures of Phidias; to the temple of the Dioscuri to see the paintings of Polygnotus. We indeed take our Sophocles or Æschylus out of our coat-pocket; but, if our sojourner at Athens would understand how a tragic poet can write, he must betake himself to the theatre on the south, and see and hear the drama literally in action. Or let him go westward to the Agora, and there he will hear Lysias or Andocides pleading, or Demosthenes haranguing. He goes farther west still, along the shade of those noble planes, which Cimon has planted there; and he looks around him at the statues and porticos and vestibules, each by itself a work of genius and skill, enough to be the making of another city. He passes through the city gate, and then he is at the famous Ceramicus; here are the tombs of the mighty dead; and here, we will suppose, is Pericles himself, the most elevated, the most thrilling of orators, converting a funeral oration over the slain into a philosophical panegyric of the living.

Onwards he proceeds still; and now he has come to that still more celebrated Academe, which has bestowed its own name on Universities down to this day; and there he sees a sight which will be graven on his memory till he dies. Many are the beauties of the place, the groves, and the statues, and the temple, and the stream of the Cephissus flowing by; many are the lessons which will be taught him day after day by teacher or by companion; but his eye is just now arrested by one object; it is the very presence of Plato. He does not hear a word that he says; he does not care to hear; he asks neither for discourse nor disputation; what he sees is a whole, complete in itself, not to be increased by addition, and greater than anything else. It will be a point in the history of his life ; a stay for his memory to rest on, a burning thought in his heart, a bond of union with men of like mind, ever afterwards. Such is the spell which the living man exerts on his fellows, for good or for evil. How nature impels us to lean upon others, making virtue, or genius, or name, the qualification for our doing so ! A Spaniard is said to have travelled to Italy, simply to see Livy ; he had his fill of gazing, and then went back again home. Had our young stranger got nothing by his voyage but the sight of the breathing and moving Plato, had he entered no lecture-room to hear, no gymnasium to converse, he had got some measure of education, and something to tell of to his grandchildren.

But Plato is not the only sage, nor the sight of him the only lesson to be learned in this wonderful suburb. It is the region and the realm of philosophy. Colleges were the inventions of many centuries later ; and they imply a sort of cloistered life, or at least a life of rule, scarcely natural to an Athenian. It was the boast of the philosophic statesman of Athens, that his countrymen achieved by the mere force of nature and the love of the noble and the great, what other people aimed at by laborious discipline ; and all who came among them were submitted to the same method of education. We have traced our student on his wanderings from the Acropolis to the Sacred Way ; and now he is in the region of the schools. No awful arch, no window of many-coloured lights marks the seats of learning there or elsewhere; philosophy lives out of doors. No close atmosphere oppresses the brain or inflames the eyelid; no long session stiffens the limbs. Epicurus is reclining in his garden ; Zeno looks like a divinity in his porch ; the restless Aristotle, on the other side of the city, as if in antagonism to Plato, is walking his pupils off their legs in his Lyceum by the Ilyssus. Our student has determined on entering himself as a disciple of Theophrastus, a teacher of marvellous popularity, who has brought together two thousand pupils from all parts of the world. He himself is of Lesbos; for masters, as well as students, come hither from all regions of the earth,—as befits a University. How could Athens have collected hearers in such numbers, unless she had selected teachers of such power? it was the range of territory, which the notion of a University implies, which furnished both the quantity of the one, and the quality of the other. Anaxagoras was from Ionia, Carneades from Africa, Zeno from Cyprus, Protagoras from Thrace, and Gorgias from Sicily. Andromachus was a Syrian, Proæresius an Armenian, Hilarius a Bithynian, Philiscus a Thessalian, Hadrian a Syrian. Rome is celebrated for her liberality in civil matters; Athens was as liberal in intellectual. There was no narrow jealousy, directed against a Professor, because he was not an Athenian; genius and talent were the qualifications; and to bring them to Athens, was to do homage to it as a University. There was a brotherhood and a citizenship of mind.

Mind came first, and was the foundation of the academical polity; but it soon brought along with it, and gathered round itself, the gifts of fortune and the prizes of life. As time went on, wisdom was not always sentenced to the bare cloak of Cleanthes; but, beginning in rags, it ended in fine linen. The Professors became honourable and rich; and the students ranged themselves under their names, and were proud of calling themselves their countrymen. The University was divided into four great nations, as the medieval antiquarian would style them; and in the middle of the fourth century, Proæresius was the leader or proctor of the Attic, Hephæstion of the Oriental, Epiphanius of the Arabic, and Diophantus of the Pontic. Thus the Professors were both patrons of clients, and hosts and *proxeni* of strangers and visitors, as well as masters of the schools : and the Cappadocian, Syrian, or Sicilian youth who came to one or other of them, would be encouraged to study by his protection, and to aspire by his example.

Even Plato, when the schools of Athens were not a hundred years old, was in circumstances to enjoy the *otium cum dignitate.* He had a villa out at Heraclea ; and he left his patrimony to his school, in whose hands it remained, not only safe, but fructifying, a marvellous phenomenon in tumultuous Greece, for the long space of eight hundred years. Epicurus too had the property of the Gardens where he lectured ; and these too became the property of his sect. But in Roman times the chairs of grammar, rhetoric, politics, and the four philosophies, were handsomely endowed by the State ; some of the Professors were themselves statesmen or high function-aries, and brought to their favourite study senatorial rank or Asiatic opulence.

Patrons such as these can compensate to the freshman, in whom we have interested ourselves, for the poorness of his lodging and the turbulence of his companions. In every thing there is a better side and a worse ; in every place a disreputable set and a respectable, and the one is hardly known at all to the other. Men come away from the same University at this day, with contradic-tory impressions and contradictory statements, accord-ing to the society they have found there ; if you believe the one, nothing goes on there as it should be : if you believe the other, nothing goes on as it should *not.* Virtue,

however, and decency are at least in the minority every
where, and under some sort of a cloud or disadvantage ;
and this being the case, it is so much gain whenever an
Herodes Atticus is found, to throw the influence of
wealth and station on the side even of a decorous philosophy. A consular man, and the heir of an ample
fortune, this Herod was content to devote his life to
a professorship, and his fortune to the patronage of
literature. He gave the sophist Polemo about eight
thousand pounds, as the sum is calculated, for three
declamations. He built at Athens a stadium six hundred feet long, entirely of white marble, and capable of
admitting the whole population. His theatre, erected
to the memory of his wife, was made of cedar wood
curiously carved. He had two villas, one at Marathon,
the place of his birth, about ten miles from Athens, the
other at Cephissia, at the distance of six ; and thither
he drew to him the *élite*, and at times the whole body of
the students. Long arcades, groves of trees, clear pools
for the bath, delighted and recruited the summer visitor.
Never was so brilliant a lecture-room as his evening
banqueting-hall ; highly connected students from Rome
mixed with the sharp-witted provincial of Greece or
Asia Minor ; and the flippant sciolist, and the nonde-
script visitor, half philosopher, half tramp, met with a
reception, courteous always, but suitable to his deserts.
Herod was noted for his repartees ; and we have instances on record of his setting down, according to the
emergency, both the one and the other.

A higher line, though a rarer one, was that allotted
to the youthful Basil. He was one of those men who
seem by a sort of fascination to draw others around them
even without wishing it. One might have deemed that
his gravity and his reserve would have kept them at a

distance ; but, almost in spite of himself, he was the centre of a knot of youths, who, pagans as most of them were, used Athens honestly for the purpose for which they professed to seek it ; and, disappointed and displeased with the place himself, he seems nevertheless to have been the means of their profiting by its advantages. One of these was Sophronius, who afterwards held a high office in the State : Eusebius was another, at that time the bosom-friend of Sophronius, and afterwards a Bishop. Celsus too is named, who afterwards was raised to the government of Cilicia by the Emperor Julian. Julian himself, in the sequel of unhappy memory, was then at Athens, and known at least to St. Gregory. Another Julian is also mentioned, who was afterwards commissioner of the land tax. Here we have a glimpse of the better kind of society among the students of Athens ; and it is to the credit of the parties composing it, that such young men as Gregory and Basil, men as intimately connected with Christianity, as they were well known in the world, should hold so high a place in their esteem and love. When the two saints were departing, their companions came around them with the hope of changing their purpose. Basil persevered ; but Gregory relented, and turned back to Athens for a season.

CHAPTER V.

FREE TRADE IN KNOWLEDGE.

THE SOPHISTS.

WHEN the Catholic University is mentioned, we hear people saying on all sides of us,—" Impossible! how can you give degrees? what will your degrees be worth? where are your endowments? where are your edifices? where will you find students? what will government have to say to you? who wants you? who will acknowledge you? what do you expect? what is left for you?"

Now, I hope I may say without offence, that this surprise on the part of so many excellent men, is itself not a little surprising. When I look around at what the Catholic Church now is in this country of Ireland, and am told what it was twenty or thirty years ago; when I see the hundreds of good works, which in that interval have been done, and now stand as monuments of the zeal and charity of the living and the dead; when I find that in those years new religious orders have been introduced, and that the country is now covered with convents; when I gaze upon the sacred edifices, spacious and fair, which during that time have been built out of the pence of the poor; when I reckon up the multitude of schools now at work, and the sacrifices which gave them birth; when I reflect upon the great political exertions and successes which have made the same period memorable in all history to come; when I contrast what was then almost a nation of bondsmen, with the intelligence, and freedom of thought, and hope for the future, which is its present characteristic; when I meditate on the wonderful sight of a people springing again fresh and vigorous from the sepulchre of famine and pestilence; and when I consider that those bonds of death which they have burst, are but the specimen and image of the adamantine obstacles, political, social, and municipal, which have all along stood in the way of their triumphs, and how they have been carried on to victory by the simple energy of a courageous faith; it sets me marvelling to find some of those very men, who have been heroically achieving impossibilities all their lives long, now beginning to scruple about adding one little sneaking impossibility to the list, and I feel it to be a great escape for the Church that they did not insert the word "impossible" into their dictionaries and encyclopedias at a somewhat earlier date.

However, this by the way: as to the objection itself, which has led to this not unnatural reflection, perhaps the reader may have observed, if he has taken the trouble to follow me, that in what I have said above I have already been covertly aiming at it; and now I propose to handle it avowedly, at least as far as my limits will allow in one Chapter.

He will recollect, perhaps, that in former Chapters I have already been maintaining, that a University consists, and has ever consisted, in demand and supply, in wants which it alone can satisfy and which it does satisfy, in the communication of knowledge, and the relation and bond which exists between the teacher and the taught. Its constituting, animating principle is this moral attraction of one class of persons to another; which is prior in its nature, nay commonly in its history, to any other tie

whatever ; so that, where this is wanting, a University is
alive only in name, and has lost its true essence, whatever be the advantages, whether of position or of afflu-
ence, with which the civil power or private benefactors
contrive to encircle it. I am far indeed from undervaluing those external advantages ; a certain share of them
is necessary to its well-being : but on the whole, as it is
with the individual, so will it be with the body:—it is
talents and attainments which command success. Consideration, dignity, wealth, and power, are all very
proper things in the territory of literature ; but they
ought to know their place ; they come second, not first ;
they must not presume, or make too much of themselves,
or they had better be away. First intellect, then secular
advantages, as its instruments and as its rewards ; I say
no more than this, but I say no less.

Nor am I denying, as I shall directly show, that,
under any circumstances, professors will ordinarily lecture, and students ordinarily attend them, with a view, in
some shape or other, to secular advantage. Certainly ;
few persons pursue knowledge simply for its own sake.
But though remuneration of some sort, both to the
teachers and to the taught, may be inseparable from
the fact of a University, still it may be separable from
its idea. Much less am I forgetting (to view the subject
on another side), that intellect is helpless, because
ungovernable and self-destructive, unless it be regulated by a moral rule and by revealed truth. Nor am
I saying anything in disparagement of the principle,
that establishments of literature and science should be
in subordination to ecclesiastical authority.

I would not make light of any of these considerations ;
some I shall even assume at once, as necessary for my
purpose ; of some I shall say more hereafter ; here,

however, I am merely suggesting to the reader's better judgment what constitutes a University, what is just enough to constitute it, or what a University consists in, viewed in its essence. What this is, seems to me most simply explained and ascertained, as I noticed in a former Chapter, by the instance of metropolitan centres. It would appear as if the very same kinds of need, social and moral, which give rise to a metropolis, give rise also to a University; nay, that every metropolis *is* a University, as far as the rudiments of a University are concerned. Youths come up thither from all parts, in order to better themselves generally;—not as if they necessarily looked for degrees in their own several pursuits, and degrees recognized by the law; not as if there were to be any competition for fellowships in chemistry, for instance, or engineering,— but they come to gain that instruction which will turn most to their account in after life, and to form good and serviceable connexions, and that, as regards the fine arts, literature, and science, as well as in trade and the professions. I do not see why it should be more difficult for Ireland to trade, if I may use the term, upon the field of knowledge, than for the inhabitants of San Francisco or of Melbourne to make a fortune by their gold fields, or for the North of England by its coal. If gold is power, wealth, influence; and if coal is power, wealth, influence; so is knowledge.

> "When house and lands are gone and spent,
>   Then learning is most excellent";

and, as some men go to the Antipodes for the gold, so others may come to us here for the knowledge. And it is as reasonable to expect students, though we have no charter from the State, provided we hold out the in-

ducement of good teachers, as to expect a crowd of
Britishers, Yankees, Spaniards, and Chinamen at the
diggings, though there are no degrees for the successful
use of the pickaxe, sieve, and shovel.

And history, I think, corroborates this view of the
matter. In all times there have been Universities ; and
in all times they have flourished by means of this profession of teaching and this desire of learning. They
have needed nothing else but this for their existence.
There has been a demand, and there has been a supply ;
and there has been the supply necessarily before the demand, though not before the need. This is how the
University, in every age, has made progress. Teachers
have set up their tent, and opened their school, and
students and disciples have flocked around them, in
spite of the want of every advantage, or even of the
presence of every conceivable discouragement. Years,
nay, centuries perhaps, passed along of discomfort and
disorder : and these, though they showed plainly enough
that, for the well-being and perfection of a University,
something more than the desire for knowledge is required, yet they showed also how irrepressible was that
desire, how reviviscent, how indestructible, how adequate to the duties of a vital principle, in the midst of
enemies within and without, amid plague, famine, desti-
tution, war, dissension, and tyranny, evils physical and
social, which would have been fatal to any other but a
really natural principle naturally developed.

Do not let the reader suppose, however, that I am
anticipating for Dublin at this day such dreary periods
or such ruinous commotions, as befel the schools of the
medieval period. Such miseries were the accidents of
the times ; and this is why we hear so much then of protectors of learning—the Charlemagnes and Alfreds,—as

the compensation of those miseries. It may be asked, whether royal protectors do not tell against the inherent vitality, on which I have been insisting, of Universities ; but in truth, powerful sovereigns, such as they, did but clear and keep the ground, on which Universities were to build. Learning in the middle ages had great foes and great friends ; we too, were we setting up a school of learning in a rude period of society, should have to expect perils on the one hand, and to court protectors on the other ; as it is, however, we can afford to treat with comparative unconcern the prospect both of the one and of the other. We may hope, and we may be content, to be just let alone ; or, if we must be anxious about the future, we may reasonably use the words of the proverb, " Save me from my friends." Charlemagne was indeed a patron of learning, but he was its protector far more ; it is our happiness, for which we cannot be too thankful to the Author of all good, that we need no protector ; for it is our privilege just now, whatever comes of the morrow, to live in the midst of a civilization, the like of which the world never saw before. The descent of enemies on our coasts, the forays of indigenous marauders, the sudden rise of town mobs, the unbridled cruelty of rulers, the resistless sweep of pestilence, the utter insecurity of life and property, and the recklessness which is its consequence, all that deforms the annals of the medieval Universities, is to us for the present but a matter of history. The statesman, the lawyer, the soldier, the policeman, the reformer, the economist, have most of them seriously wronged and afflicted us Catholics in other ways, national, social, and religious ; but, on the side on which I have here to view them, they are acting in our behalf as a blessing from heaven. They are giving us that tranquillity for which the Church so variously and so anxiously prays ; that real freedom, which enables us to consult her interests, to edify her holy house, to adorn her sanctuary, to perfect her discipline, to inculcate her doctrines, and to enlighten and form her children, " with all confidence," as Scripture speaks, " without prohibition." We are able to set up a *Studium Generale*, without its concomitant dangers and inconveniences ; and the history of the past, while it adumbrates for us the pattern of a University, and supplies us with a specimen of its good fruits, conveys to us no presage of the recurrence of those melancholy conflicts, in which the cultivated intellect was in those times engaged, sometimes with brute force, and sometimes, alas ! with Revealed Religion.

Charlemagne then was necessary, but not so much for the University, as against its enemies ; he was confessedly a patron of letters, effectual as well as munificent, but he could not any how have dispensed with his celebrated professors, and they, as the history of literature, both before and after him, shows, could probably have dispensed with him. Whether we turn to the ancient world or to the modern, in either case we have evidence in behalf of this position : we have the spectacle of the thirst of knowledge acting for and by itself, and making its own way.

Here I shall confine myself to ancient history : both in Athens and in Rome, we find it pushing forward, in independence of the civil power. The professors of literature seated themselves in Athens without the favour of the government ; and they opened their mission in Rome in spite of its state traditions. It was the rising generation, it was the mind of youth unfettered by the conventional ideas of the ruling politics, which in either instance became their followers. The ex-

citement they created in Athens is described by Plato
in one of his Dialogues, and has often been quoted.
Protagoras came to the bright city with the profession
of teaching "the political art"; and the young flocked
around him.   They flocked to him, be it observed, not
because he promised them entertainment or novelty,
such as the theatre might promise, and a people pro-
verbially fickle and curious might exact; nor, on the
other hand, had he any definite recompense to hold
out,—a degree, for instance, or a snug fellowship, or
an India writership, or a place in the civil service.   He
offered them just the sort of inducement, which carries
off a man now to a conveyancer, or a medical prac-
titioner, or an engineer,—he engaged to prepare them
for the line of life which they had chosen as their own,
and to prepare them better than Hippias or Prodicus,
who were at Athens with him.   Whether he was really
able to do this, is another thing altogether; or rather
it makes the argument stronger, if he were unable; for,
if the very promise of knowledge was so potent a spell,
what would have been its real possession?

But now let us hear the state of the case from the
mouth of Hippocrates himself,—the youth, who in his
eagerness woke Socrates, himself a young man at the
time, while it was yet dark, to tell him that Protagoras
was come to Athens.   "When we had supped, and were
going to bed,"* he says, "then my brother told me that
Protagoras was arrived, and my first thought was to
come and see you immediately; but afterwards it
appeared to me too late at night.   As soon, however,
as sleep had refreshed me, up I got, and came here."
"And I," continued Socrates, giving an account of the
conversation, "knowing his earnestness and excitability,

* Carey's translation is followed almost verbatim.

said : 'What is that to you? does Protagoras do you any harm?' He laughed and said : 'That he does, Socrates ; because he alone is wise, and does not make *me* so.' 'Nay,' said I, 'do you give him money enough, and he will make you wise too.' 'O Jupiter and ye gods,' he made answer, 'that it depended upon that, for I would spare nothing of my own, or of my friends' property either ; and I have now come to you for this very purpose, to get you to speak to him in my behalf. For, besides that I am too young, I have never yet seen Protagoras, or heard him speak ; for I was but a boy when he came before. However, all praise him, Socrates, and say that he has the greatest skill in speaking. But why do we not go to him, that we may find him at home?'"

They went on talking till the light ; and then they set out for the house of Callias, where Protagoras, with others of his own calling, was lodged. There they found him pacing up and down the portico, with his host and others, among whom, on one side of him, was a son of Pericles (his father being at this time in power), while another son of Pericles, with another party, was on the other. A party followed, chiefly of foreigners, whom Protagoras had " bewitched, like Orpheus, by his voice." On the opposite side of the portico sat Hippias, with a bench of youths before him, who were asking him questions in physics and astronomy. Prodicus was still in bed, with some listeners on sofas round him. The house is described as quite full of guests. Such is the sketch given us of this school of Athens, as there represented. I do not enter on the question, as I have already said, whether the doctrine of these Sophists, as they are called, was true or false ; more than very partially true it could not be, whether in morals or in physics, from the circumstances of the age ; it is sufficient that it powerfully interested the hearers. We see what it was that filled the Athenian lecture-halls and porticos ; not the fashion of the day, not the patronage of the great, not pecuniary prizes, but the reputation of talent and the desire of knowledge,—ambition, if you will, personal attachment, but not an influence, political or other, external to the School. "Such Sophists," says Mr. Grote, referring to the passage in Plato, "had *nothing to recommend them* except superior *knowledge* and *intellectual fame*, combined with an imposing *personality*, making itself felt in the lectures and conversation."

So much for Athens, where Protagoras had at least this advantage, that Pericles was his private friend, if he was not publicly his patron ; but now when we turn to Rome, in what is almost a parallel page in her history, we shall find that literature, or at least philosophy, had to encounter there the direct opposition of the ruling party in the state, and of the hereditary and popular sentiment. The story goes, that when the Greek treatises which Numa had had buried with him, were accidentally brought to light, the Romans had burned them, from the dread of such knowledge coming into fashion. At a later date decrees passed the Senate for the expulsion from the city, first of philosophers, then of rhetoricians, who were gaining the attention of the rising generation. A second decree was passed some time afterwards to the same effect, assigning, in its vindication, the danger, which existed, of young men losing, by means of these new studies, their taste for the military profession.

Such was the nascent conflict between the old rule and policy of Rome, and the awakening intellect, at the time of that celebrated embassy of the three philoso-

phers, Diogenes the Stoic, Carneades the Academic,
and Critolaus the Peripatetic, sent to Rome from Athens
on a political affair. Whether they were as skilful in
diplomacy as they were zealous in their own particular
line, need not here be determined ; any how, they
lengthened out their stay at Rome, and employed themselves in giving lectures. "Those among the youth,"
says Plutarch, "who had a taste for literature went to
them, and became their constant and enthusiastic
hearers. Especially, the graceful eloquence of Carneades, which had a reputation equal to its talent,
secured large and favourable audiences, and was noised
about the city. It was reported that a Greek, with a
perfectly astounding power both of interesting and of
commanding the feelings, was kindling in the youth a
most ardent emotion, which possessed them, to the
neglect of their ordinary indulgences and amusements,
with a sort of rage for philosophy." Upon this, Cato
took up the matter upon the traditionary ground ; he
represented that the civil and military interests of Rome
were sure to suffer, if such tastes became popular ; and
he exerted himself with such effect, that the three philosophers were sent off with the least possible delay, "to
return home to their own schools, and in future to confine their lessons to Greek boys, leaving the youth of
Rome, as heretofore, to listen to the magistrates and
the laws." The pressure of the government was successful at the moment ; but ultimately the cause of
education prevailed. Schools were gradually founded ;
first of grammar, in the large sense of the word, then of
rhetoric, then of mathematics, then of philosophy, and
then of medicine, though the order of their introduction,
one with another, is not altogether clear. At length
the Emperors secured the interests of letters by an estab-

lishment, which has lasted to this day in the Roman
University, now called *Sapienza*.

Here are two striking instances in very different
countries, to prove that it is the thirst for knowledge,
and not the patronage of the great, which carries on the
cause of literature and science to its ultimate victory;
and all that can be said against them is, that I have
gone back a great way to find them. But a general
truth is made up of particular instances, which cannot
be brought forward all at once, nor crowded into half a
dozen pages of a work like this. I shall continue the
subject some future time; meanwhile I will but observe
that, while these ancient instances teach us that a University is *founded* on principles *sui generis* and proper to
itself, so do they coincidently suggest that it may
boldly *appeal* to those principles before they are yet
brought into exercise, and may, or rather must, take the
initiative in its own success. It must be set up before it
can be sought; and it must offer a supply, in order to
create a demand. Protagoras and Carneades needed
nothing more than to advertise themselves in order to
gain disciples; if we have a confidence that we have
that to offer to Irishmen, to Catholics, which is good and
great, and which at present they have not, our success
may be tedious and slow in coming, but ultimately
come it must.

Therefore, I say, let us set up our University; let us
only set it up, and it will teach the world its value by
the fact of its existence. What ventures are made, what
risks incurred by private persons in matters of trade!
What speculations are entered on in the departments of
building or engineering! What boldness in innovation
or improvement has been manifested by statesmen during the last twenty years! Mercantile undertakings

indeed may be ill-advised, and political measures may be censurable in themselves, or fatal in their results. I am not considering them here in their motive or their object, in their expedience or their justice, but in the manner in which they have been carried out. What largeness then of view, what intrepidity, vigour, and resolution are implied in the Reform Bill, in the Emancipation of the Blacks, in the finance changes, in the Useful Knowledge movement, in the organization of the Free Kirk, in the introduction of the penny postage, and in the railroads! This is an age, if not of great men, at least of great works; are Catholics alone to refuse to act on faith? England has faith in her skill, in her determination, in her resources in war, in the genius of her people; is Ireland alone to fail in confidence in her children and her God? *Fortes fortuna adjuvat;* so says the proverb. If the chance concurrence of half a dozen of sophists, or the embassy of three philosophers, could do so much of old to excite the enthusiasm of the young, and to awaken the intellect into activity, is it very presumptuous, or very imprudent, in us at this time, to enter upon an undertaking, which comes to us with the authority of St. Peter, the blessing of St. Patrick, the coöperation of the faithful, the prayers of the poor, and all the ordinary materials of success, resources, intellect, pure intention, and self devotion, to bring it into effect? Shall it be said in future times, that the work needed nought but good and gallant hearts, and found them not?

CHAPTER VI.

DISCIPLINE AND INFLUENCE.

I HAVE had some debate with myself, whether what are called myths and parables, and similar compositions of a representative nature, are in keeping with this work; yet, considering that the early Christians recognized the *Logi* of the classical writers as not inconsistent with the gravity of their own literature, not to mention the precedent afforded by the sacred text, I think I may proceed, without apology to myself or others, to impart to the reader in confidence, while it is fresh on my mind, a conversation which I have just had with an intimate English friend, on the general subject to which these columns are devoted. I do not say that it was of a very important nature; still to those who choose to reflect, it may suggest more than it expresses. It took place only a day or two ago, on occasion of my paying him a flying visit.

My friend lives in a spot as convenient as it is delightful. The neighbouring hamlet is the first station out of London of a railroad; while not above a quarter of a mile from his boundary wall flows the magnificent river, which moves towards the metropolis through a richness of grove and meadow of its own creation. After a liberal education, he entered a lucrative business; and, making a competency in a few years, exchanged

New Broad Street for the "fallentis semita vitæ." Soon after his marriage, which followed this retirement, his wife died, and left him solitary. Instead of returning to the world, or seeking to supply her place, he gave himself to his garden and his books ; and with these companions he has passed the last twenty years. He has lived in a largish house, the "monarch of all he surveyed;" the sorrows of the past, his creed, and the humble chapel not a stone's throw from his carriage-gate, have saved him from the selfishness of such a sovereignty, and the oppressiveness of such a solitude ; yet not, if I may speak candidly, from some of the inconveniences of a bachelor life. He has his own fixed views, from which it is difficult to move him, and some people say that he discourses rather than converses, though, somehow, when I am with him, from long familiarity, I manage to get through as many words as he.

I do not know that such peculiarities can in any case be called moral defects ; certainly not, when contrasted with the great mischiefs which a life so enjoyable as his might have done to him, and has not. He has indeed been in possession of the very perfection of earthly happiness, at least as I view things ;—mind, I say of "earthly;" and I do not say that earthly happiness is desirable. On the contrary, man is born for labour, not for self ; what right has any one to retire from the world and profit no one ? He who takes his ease in this world, will have none in the world to come. All this rings in my friend's ears quite as distinctly as I may fancy it does in mine, and has a corresponding effect upon his conduct ; who would not exchange consciences with him ? but still the fact remains, that a life such as his is in itself dangerous, and that, in proportion to its attractiveness. If indeed there were no country beyond the grave, it would be our wisdom to make of our present dwelling-place as much as ever we could ; and this would be done by the very life which my friend has chosen, not by any absurd excesses, not by tumult, dissipation, excitement, but by the "moderate and rational use," as Protestant sermons say, "of the gifts of Providence."

Easy circumstances, books, friends, literary connexions, the fine arts, presents from abroad, foreign correspondents, handsome appointments, elegant simplicity, gravel walks, lawns, flower beds, trees and shrubberies, summer houses, strawberry beds, a greenhouse, a wall for peaches, "hoc erat in votis";—nothing out of the way, no hot-houses, graperies, pineries,—"Persicos odi, puer, apparatus,"—no mansions, no parks, no deer, no preserves ; these things are not worth the cost, they involve the bother of dependents, they interfere with enjoyment. One or two faithful servants, who last on as the trees do, and cannot change their place :—the ancients had slaves, a sort of dumb waiter, and the real article ; alas ! they are impossible now. We must have no one with claims upon us, or with rights ; no incumbrances ; no wife and children ; they would hurt our dignity. We must have acquaintance within reach, yet not in the way ; ready, not troublesome or intrusive. We must have something of name, or of rank, or of ancestry, or of past official life, to raise us from the dead level of mankind, to afford food for the imagination of our neighbours, to bring us from time to time strange visitors, and to invest our home with mystery. In consequence we shall be loyal subjects, good conservatives, fond of old times, averse to change, suspicious of novelty, because we know perfectly when we are well off, and that in our case "progredi *est* regredi." To a life such as this, a man is more attached, the longer he lives ;

and he would be more and more happy in it too, were it not for the *memento* within him, that books and gardens do not make a man immortal ; that, though they do not leave him, he at least must leave them, all but "the hateful cypresses," and must go where the only book is the book of doom, and the only garden the Paradise of the just.

All this has nothing to do with our University, but nevertheless they are some of the reflections which came into my mind, as I left the station I have spoken of, and turned my face towards my friend's abode. As I went along, on the lovely afternoon of last Monday, which had dried up the traces of a wet morning, and as I fed upon the soothing scents and sounds which filled the air, I began to reflect how the most energetic and war-like race among the descendants of Adam, had made, by contrast, this Epicurean life, the " otium cum dignitate," the very type of human happiness. A life in the country in the midst of one's own people, was the dream of Roman poets from Virgil to Juvenal, and the reward of Roman statesmen from Cincinnatus to Pliny. I called to mind the Corycian old man, so beautifully sketched in the fourth Georgic, and then my own fantastic protesta-tion in years long dead and gone, that, if I were free to choose my own line of life, it should be that of a gardener in some great family, a life without care, without excite-ment, in which the gifts of the Creator screened off man's evil doings, and the romance of the past coloured and illuminated the matter-of-fact present.

"Otium divos," I suppose the reader will say. Smiling myself at the recollection of my own absurdity, I passed along the silent avenues of solemn elms, which, belong-ing to a nobleman's domain, led the way towards the humbler dwelling for which I was bound ; and then I recurred to the Romans, wandering in thought, as in a time of relaxation one is wont; and I contrasted, or rather investigated, the respective aspects, one with another, under which a country life, so dear to that conquering people nationally, presented itself severally to Cicero, to Virgil, to Horace, and to Juvenal, and I asked myself under which of them all was my friend's home to be regarded. Then suddenly the scene changed, and I was viewing it in my own way; for I had known him since I was a schoolboy, in his father's time; and I recollected with a sigh how I had once passed a week there of my summer holidays, and what I then thought of persons and things I met there, of its various inmates, father, mother, brothers, and sisters, all of them, except himself and me, now numbered with the departed. Thus Cicero and Horace glided off from my field of view, like the circles of a magic lantern; and my ears, no longer open to the preludes of the nightingales around me, which were preparing for their nightly concert, heard nothing but

The voices of the dead, and songs of other years.

Thus, deep in sad thoughts, I reached the well-known garden gate, and unconsciously opened it, and was upon the lower lawn, advancing towards the house, before I apprehended shrubberies and beds, which were sensibly before me, otherwise than through my memory. Then suddenly the vivid past gave way, and the actual present flowed in upon me, and I saw my friend pacing up and down on the side furthest from me, with his hands behind him, and a newspaper or some such publication in their grasp.

It is an old-fashioned place; the house may be of the date of George the Second; a square hall in the middle, and in the centre of it a pillar, and rooms all around. The servants' rooms and offices run off on the right; a rookery covers the left flank, and the drawing-room opens upon the lawn. There a large plane tree, with its massive branches, whilome sustained a swing, when there were children on that lawn, blithely to undergo an exercise of head, at the very thought of which the grown man sickens. Three formal terraces gradually conduct down to one of the majestic avenues, of which I have already spoken; the second and third, intersected by grass walks, constitute the kitchen-garden. As a boy, I used to stare at the magnificent cauliflowers and large apricots which it furnished for the table; and how difficult it was to leave off, when once one got among the gooseberry bushes in the idle morning!

I had now got close upon my friend; and, in return for the schoolboy reminiscences and tranquil influences of the place, was ungrateful enough to begin attacking him for his epicurean life. "Here you are, you old pagan," I said, "as usual, fit for nothing so much as to be one of the interlocutors in a dialogue of Cicero's."

"*You* are a pretty fellow," he made answer, "to accuse me of paganism, who have yourself been so busily engaged just now in writing up Athens;" and then I saw that it was several numbers of the *Gazette*, which he had in his hand, and which perhaps had given energy to his step.

After giving utterance to some general expressions of his satisfaction at the publication, and the great interest he took in the undertaking to which it was devoted, he suddenly stopped, turned round upon me, looked hard in my face, and taking hold of a button of my coat, said abruptly : "But what on earth possessed you, my good friend, to have anything to do with this Irish University? what was it to you? how did it fall in your way?"

5

I could not help laughing out; "O I see," I cried, "you consider me a person who cannot keep quiet, and must ever be in one scrape or another."

" Yes, but seriously, tell me," he urged, "what *had* you to do with it? what was Ireland to you? you had your own line and your own work; was not that enough?"

" Well, my dear Richard," I retorted, "better do too much than too little."

" A *tu quoque* is quite unworthy of you," he replied; " answer me, charissime, what had you to do with an Irish undertaking? do you think they have not clever men enough there to work it, but you must meddle?"

" Well," I said, " I do not think it *is* an Irish undertaking, that is, in such a sense that it is not a Catholic undertaking, and one which intimately and directly interests other countries besides Ireland."

" Say England," he interposed.

" Well, I say and mean England: I think it most intimately concerns England; unless it was an affair of England, as well as of Ireland, I should have sympathized in so grand a conception, I should have done what I could to aid it, but I should have had no call, as you well say, I should have considered it presumption in me, to take an active part in its execution."

He looked at me with a laughing expression in his eye, and was for a moment silent; then he began again:

" You must think yourself a great genius," he said, "to fancy that place is not a condition of capacity. You are an Englishman; your mind, your habits are English; you have hitherto been acting only upon Englishmen, with Englishmen; do you really anticipate that you will be able to walk into a new world, and to do any good service there, because you have done it here? *Ne sutor ultra crepidam.* I would as soon believe that you could shoot your soul into a new body, according to the Eastern tale, and make it your own."

I made him a bow; "I thank you heartily," I said, "for the seasonable encouragement you give me in a difficult undertaking; you are determined, Richard, that I shall not get too much refreshment from your shrubberies."

"I beg your pardon," he made answer, "do not mistake me; I am only trying to draw you out; I am curious to know how you came to make this engagement; you know we have not had any talk together for some time."

"It may be as you say," I answered; "that is, I may be found quite unequal to what I have attempted; but, I assure you, not for want of zealous and able assistance, of sympathizing friends,—not because it is in Ireland, instead of England, that I have to work."

"They tell me," he replied, "that they don't mean to let you have any Englishmen about you if they can help it."

"You seem to know a great deal more about it here than I do in Ireland," I answered: "I have not heard this; but still, I suppose, in former times, when men were called from one country to another for a similar purpose, as Peter from Ireland to Naples, and John of Melrose to Paris, they did in fact go alone."

"Modest man!" he cried, "to compare yourself to the sages and doctors of the Middle Age! But still the fact is not so: far from going alone, the very number they could and did spare from home is the most remarkable evidence of the education of the Irish in those times. Moore, I recollect, emphatically states, that it was abroad that the Irish sought, and abroad that they found, the rewards of their genius. If any people ought to suffer foreigners to come to them, it is they who have, with so much glory to themselves, so often gone to foreigners. In the passage I have in my eye, Moore calls it 'the peculiar fortune of Ireland, that both in talent and in fame her sons have prospered more signally abroad than at home ; that not so much those who confined their labours to their native land, as those who carried their talents and zeal to other lands, won for their country the high title of the Island of the Holy and the Learned.' But, not to insist on the principle of reciprocity, jealousy of foreigners among them is little in keeping with that ancient hospitality of theirs, of which history speaks as distinctly."

" Really," I made answer, " begging your pardon, you do not quite know what you are talking about. You never were in Ireland, I believe ; am I likely to know less than you ? If there be a nation, which in matters of intellect does not want 'protection,' to use the political word, it is the Irish. A stupid people would have a right to claim it, when they would set up a University ; but, if I were you, I would think twice before I paid so bad a compliment to one of the most gifted nations of Europe, as to suppose that it could not keep its ground, that it would not take the lead, in the intellectual arena, though competition was perfectly open. If their 'grex philosophorum' spread in the medieval time over Europe, in spite of the perils of sea and land, will they not be sure to fill the majority of chairs in their own University in an age like this, from the sheer claims of talent, though those chairs were open to the world ? No ; a monopoly would make the cleverest people idle ; it would sink the character of their undertaking, and Ireland herself would be the first to exclaim against the places of a great school of learning becoming mere pieces of patronage and occasions for jobbing, like the sees of the Irish Establishment."

My friend did not reply, but looked grave; at length he said that he was not stating what ought to be, but what would be; Irishmen boasted, and justly, that in ancient times they went to Melrose, to Malmesbury, to Glastonbury, to East Anglia, to Oxford; that they established themselves in Paris, Ratisbon, Padua, Pavia, Naples, and other continental schools; but there was in fact no reciprocity now; Paris had not been simply for Frenchmen, nor Oxford simply for Englishmen, but Ireland must be solely for the Irish.

"Really, in truth," I made answer, "to speak most seriously, I think you are prejudiced and unjust, and I should be very sorry indeed to have to believe that you expressed an English sentiment. I am sure you do not. However, you speak of what you simply do not know. In Ireland, as in every country, there is of course a wholesome jealousy towards persons placed in important posts, such as my own, lest they should exercise their power unfairly; there is a fear of jobs, not a jealousy of English; and I don't suppose you think I am likely to turn out a jobber. This is all I can grant you at the utmost, and perhaps I grant too much. But I do most solemnly assure you, that, as far as I have had the means of bearing witness, there is an earnest wish in the promoters and advocates of this great undertaking to get the best men for its execution, wherever they are to be found, in England, or in France, or in Belgium, or in Germany, or in Italy, or in the United States; though there is an anticipation too, which is far from unreasonable, that for most of the Professorships of the University the best men *will* be found in Ireland. Of course in particular cases, there ever will be a difference of opinion who is the best man ; but this does not interfere at all, as is evident, with the honest desire on all sides, to make the Institution a real honour to Ireland and a defence of Ireland's faith."

My companion again kept silence, and so we walked on ; then he suddenly said : "Come let us have some tea, since you tell me," (I had told him by letter,) "that you cannot take a bed ; the last train is not over-late."

As we walked towards the house, "The truth is," he continued, speaking slowly, "I had another solution of my own difficulty myself. I cannot help thinking that your *Gazette* makes more of *persons* than is just, and does not lay stress enough upon order, system, and rule, in conducting a University. This is what I have said to myself. 'After all, suppose there *be* an exclusive system, it does not much matter ; a great institution, if well organized, moves of itself, independently of the accident of its particular functionaries.' . . . Well now, is it not so ?" he added briskly ; "you have been laying too much stress upon *persons ?* "

I hesitated how best I should begin to answer him, and he went on :—"Look at the Church herself ; how little she depends on individuals ; in proportion as she can develop her system, she dispenses with them. In times of great confusion, in countries under conversion, great men are given to her, great Popes, great Evangelists ; but there is no call for Hildebrands or Ghislieris in the nineteenth century, or for Winfrids or Xaviers in modern Europe. It is so with states ; despotisms require great monarchs, Turkish or Russian ; constitutions manage to jog on without them ; this is the meaning of the famous saying, 'Quantulâ sapientiâ regitur mundus !' What a great idea again, to use Guizot's expression, is the Society of Jesus! what a creation of genius is its organization ; but so well adapted is the institution to its object, that for that very reason it can afford to crush individualities, however gifted ; so much so, that, in spite of the rare talents of its members, it has even become an objection to it in the mouth of its enemies, that it has not produced a thinker like Scotus or Malebranche. Now, I consider your papers make too much of persons, and put system out of sight ; and this is the sort of consolation which occurs to me, in answer to the misgivings which come upon me, about the exclusiveness with which the University seems to me to be threatened."

"You know," I answered, "these papers have not got half through their subject yet. I assure you I do not at all forget, that something more than able Professors are necessary to make a University."

"Still," said he, " I should like to be certain you were sufficiently alive to the evils which spring from over-valuing them. You have talked to us a great deal about Platos, Hephæstions, Herods, and the rest of them, sophists one and all, and very little about a constitution. All that you have said has gone one way. You have professed a high and mighty independence of state patronage, and a conviction that the demand and supply of knowledge is all in all ; that the supply must be provided before the demand in order to create it ; and that great minds are the instruments of that supply. You have founded your ideal University on individuals. Then, I say, on this hypothesis, be sure you have for your purpose the largest selection possible ; do not proclaim that you mean to have the tip-top men of the age, and then refuse to look out beyond one country for them, as if any country, though it be Ireland, had a monopoly of talent. Observe, I say this on your hypothesis; but I confess I am disposed to question its soundness, and it is in that way I get over my own misgiving about you. I say that, may be, your University *need not* have the best men; it may fall back on a jogtrot system, a routine, and perhaps it ought to do so."

" Forbid it!" said I; "you cannot suppose that what you have said is new to me, or that I do not give it due weight. Indeed I could almost write a dissertation on the subject which you have started, that is, on the functions and mutual relations, in the conduct of human affairs, of Influence and Law. I should begin by saying that these are the two moving powers which carry on the world, and that in the supernatural order they are absolutely united in the Source of all perfection. I should observe that the Supreme Being is both,—a living, individual Agent, as sovereign as if an Eternal Law were not; and a Rule of right and wrong, and an Order fixed and irreversible, as if He had no will, or supremacy, or characteristics of personality. Then I should say that here below the two principles are separated, that each has its own function, that each is necessary for the other, and that they ought to act together; yet that it too often happens that they become rivals of one another, that this or that acts of itself, and will encroach upon the province, or usurp the rights of the other; and that then every thing goes wrong. Thus I should start, and would you not concur with me? Would it not be sufficient to give you hope that I am not taking a onesided view of the subject of University education?"

He answered, as one so partial to me was sure to answer; that he had no sort of suspicion that I was acting without deliberation, or without viewing the matter as a whole; but still he could not help saying

that he thought he saw a bias in me which he had not
expected, and he would be truly glad to find himself
mistaken. " Do you know," he said, " I am surprised to
find that you, of all men in the world, should be taking
the intellectual line, and should be advocating the professorial system. Surely it was once far otherwise ; I
thought our line used to be, that knowledge without
principle was simply mischievous, and that Professors
did but represent and promote that mischievous knowledge. This used to be our language : and, beyond all
doubt, a great deal may be said in justification of it. What
is heresy in ecclesiastical history but the action of personal influence against law and precedent ? and what
were such heterodox teachers as the Arian leaders in
primitive times, or Abelard in the middle ages, but the
eloquent and attractive masters of philosophical schools ?
And what again were Arius and Abelard but the fore-
runners of modern German professors, a set of clever
charlatans, or subtle sophists, who aim at originality,
show, and popularity, at the expense of truth ? Such
men are the *nucleus* of a system, if system it may be
called, of which disorder is the outward manifestation,
and scepticism the secret life. This you used to think ;
but now you tell us that demand and supply are all in
all, and that supply must precede demand ;—and that
this is a University in a nutshell."

I laughed, and said he was unfair to me, and rather
had not understood me at all. " We are neither of us
theologians or metaphysicians," said I ; " yet I suppose
we know the difference between a direct cause and a *sine
quâ non*, and between the essence of a thing and its
integrity. Things are not content to be in fact just
what we contemplate them in the abstract, and nothing
more ; they require something more than themselves,

sometimes as necessary conditions of their being, sometimes for their well-being. Breath is not part of man; it
comes to him from without; it is merely the surrounding air, inhaled, and then exhaled; yet no one can live
without breathing. Place an animal under an exhausted
receiver, and it dies: yet the air does not enter into its
definition. When then I say, that a Great School or
University consists in the communication of knowledge,
in lecturers and hearers, that is, in the Professorial
system, you must not run away with the notion that
I consider personal influence enough for its well-being.
It is indeed its essence, but something more is necessary
than barely to get on from day to day; for its sure and
comfortable existence we must look to law, rule, order;
to religion, from which law proceeds; to the collegiate
system, in which it is embodied; and to endowments,
by which it is protected and perpetuated. This is the
part of the subject which my papers have not yet
touched upon; nor could they well treat of what comes
second, till they had done justice to what comes first."

I thought that here he seemed disposed to interrupt
me, so I interposed: "Now, please, let me bring out
what I want to say, while I am full of it. I say then,
that the personal influence of the teacher is able in some
sort to dispense with an academical system, but that the
system cannot in any sort dispense with personal influence. With influence there is life, without it there
is none; if influence is deprived of its due position, it
will not by those means be got rid of, it will only break
out irregularly, dangerously. An academical system
without the personal influence of teachers upon pupils,
is an arctic winter; it will create an ice-bound, petrified,
cast-iron University, and nothing else. You will not
call this any new notion of mine; and you will not

suspect, after what happened to me a long twenty-five years ago, that I can ever be induced to think otherwise. No! I have known a time in a great School of Letters, when things went on for the most part by mere routine, and form took the place of earnestness. I have experienced a state of things, in which teachers were cut off from the taught as by an insurmountable barrier; when neither party entered into the thoughts of the other; when each lived by and in itself; when the tutor was supposed to fulfil his duty, if he trotted on like a squirrel in his cage, if at a certain hour he was in a certain room, or in hall, or in chapel, as it might be; and the pupil did his duty too, if he was careful to meet his tutor in that same room, or hall, or chapel, at the same certain hour; and when neither the one nor the other dreamed of seeing each other out of lecture, out of chapel, out of academical gown. I have known places where a stiff manner, a pompous voice, coldness and condescension, were the teacher's attributes, and where he neither knew, nor wished to know, and avowed he did not wish to know, the private irregularities of the youths committed to his charge.

" This was the reign of Law without Influence, System without Personality. And then again, I have seen in this dreary state of things, as you yourself well know, while the many went their way and rejoiced in their liberty, how that such as were better disposed and aimed at higher things, looked to the right and to the left, as sheep without a shepherd, to find those who would exert that influence upon them which its legitimate owners made light of; and how, wherever they saw a little more profession of strictness and distinctness of creed, a little more intellect, principle, and devotion, than was ordinary, thither they went, poor youths, like

St. Anthony when he first turned to God, for counsel
and encouragement ; and how, as this feeling, without
visible cause, mysteriously increased in the subjects of
that seat of learning, a whole class of teachers gradually
arose, unrecognised by its authorities, and rivals to the
teachers whom it furnished, and gained the hearts and
became the guides of the youthful generation, who found
no sympathy were they had a claim for it.   And then
moreover, you recollect, as well as I, how, as time went
on and that generation grew up and came into University
office themselves, then, from the memory of their own past
discomfort, they tried to mend matters, and to unite Rule
and Influence together, which had been so long severed,
and how they claimed from their pupils for themselves
that personal attachment which in their own pupillage
they were not invited to bestow ; and then, how in consequence a struggle began between the dry old red-
tapists, as in politics they are called, and—"

Here my friend, who had been unaccountably im-
patient for some time, fairly interrupted me.   " It seems
very rude," he said, " very inhospitable ; it is against
my interest ; perhaps you will stay the night ; but if
you must go, go at once you must, or you will lose the
train."   An announcement like this turned the current
of my thoughts, and I started up.   In a few seconds we
were walking, as briskly as elderly men walk, towards
the garden entrance.   Sorry was I to leave so abruptly
so sweet a place, so old and so dear to me ; sorry to
have disturbed it with controversy instead of drinking
in its calm.   When we reached the lofty avenue, from
which I entered, Richard shook my hand, and wished
me God-speed,

" portâque emittit eburnâ."

CHAPTER VII.

TAKING Influence and Law to be the two great principles of Government, it is plain that, historically speaking, Influence comes first, and then Law. Thus Orpheus preceded Lycurgus and Solon. Thus Deioces the Mede laid the foundations of his power in his personal reputation for justice, and then established it in the seven walls by which he surrounded himself in Ecbatana. First we have the " virum pietate gravem," whose word " rules the spirits and soothes the breasts " of the multitude ;—or the warrior ;—or the mythologist and bard ;—then follow at length the dynasty and constitution. Such is the history of society : it begins in the poet, and ends in the policeman.

Universities are instances of the same course : they begin in Influence, they end in System. At first, whatever good they may have done, has been the work of persons, of personal exertions ; of faith in persons, of personal attachments. Their Professors have been a sort of preachers and missionaries, and have not only taught, but have won over or inflamed their hearers. As time has gone on, it has been found out that personal influence does not last for ever ; that individuals get past their work, that they die, that they cannot always be depended on, that they change ; that, if they are to be the exponents of a University, it will have no abidance, no steadiness; that it will be great and small again, and will inspire no trust. Accordingly, system has of necessity been superadded to individual action; a University has been embodied in a constitution, it has exerted authority, it has been protected by rights and privileges, it has enforced discipline, it has developed itself into Colleges, and has admitted Monasteries into its territory. The details of this advance and consummation are of course different in different instances; each University has a career of its own; I have been stating the process in the logical, rather than in the historical order; but such it has been on the whole, whether in ancient or medieval times. Zeal began, power and wisdom completed: private enterprise came first, national or governmental recognition followed; first the Greek, then the Macedonian and Roman; the Athenian created, the Imperialist organized and consolidated. This is the subject I am going to enter upon to-day.

Now as to Athens, I have already shown what it did, and implied what it did not do; and I shall proceed to say something more about it. I have another reason for dwelling on the subject; it will lead me to direct attention to certain characteristics of Athenian opinion, which are not only to my immediate purpose, but will form an introduction to something I should like to say on a future occasion, if I could grasp my own thoughts, about the philosophical sentiments of the present age, their drift, and their bearing on a University. This is another matter; but I mention it because it is one out of several reasons which will set me on a course, in which I shall seem to be ranging very wide of my mark, while all the time I shall have a meaning in my wanderings.

Beginning then the subject very far back, I observe that the guide of life, implanted in our nature, discriminating right from wrong, and investing right with authority and sway, is our Conscience, which Revelation does but enlighten, strengthen, and refine. Coming from one and the same Author, these internal and external monitors of course recognize and bear witness to each other; Nature warrants without anticipating the Supernatural, and the Supernatural completes without superseding Nature. Such is the divine order of things; but man,—not being divine, nor over partial to so stern a reprover within his breast, yet seeing too the necessity of some rule or other, some common standard of conduct, if Society is to be kept together, and the children of Adam to be saved from setting up each for himself with every one else his foe,—as soon as he has secured for himself some little cultivation of intellect, looks about him how he can manage to dispense with Conscience, and find some other principle to do its work. The most plausible and obvious and ordinary of these expedients, is the Law of the State, human law; the more plausible and ordinary, because it really comes to us with a divine sanction, and necessarily has a place in every society or community of men. Accordingly it is very widely used instead of Conscience, as but a little experience of life will show us; "the law says this;" "would you have me go against the law?" is considered an unanswerable argument in every case; and, when the two come into collision, it follows of course that Conscience is to give way, and the Law to prevail.

Another substitute for Conscience is the rule of Expediency: Conscience is pronounced superannuated and retires on a pension, whenever a people is so far advanced in illumination, as to perceive that right and wrong can to a certain extent be measured and determined by the useful on the one hand, and by the hurtful on the other; according to the maxim, which embodies this principle, that " honesty is the best policy."

Another substitute of a more refined character is, the principle of Beauty :—it is maintained that the Beautiful and the Virtuous mean the same thing, and are convertible terms. Accordingly Conscience is found out to be but slavish ; and a fine taste, an exquisite sense of the decorous, the graceful, and the appropriate, this is to be our true guide for ordering our mind and our conduct, and bringing the whole man into shape. These are great sophisms, it is plain ; for, true though it be, that virtue is always expedient, always fair, it does not therefore follow that every thing which is expedient, and every thing which is fair, is virtuous. A pestilence is an evil, yet may have its undeniable uses ; and war, " glorious war," is an evil, yet an army is a very beautiful object to look upon ; and what holds in these cases, may hold in others ; so that it is not very safe or logical to say that Utility and Beauty are guarantees for Virtue.

However, there are these three principles of conduct, which may be plausibly made use of in order to dispense with Conscience ; viz., Law, Expedience, and Propriety ; and (at length to come to our point) the Athenians chose the last of them, as became so exquisite a people, and professed to practise virtue on no inferior consideration, but simply because it was so praiseworthy, so noble, and so fair. Not that they discarded Law, not that they had not an eye to their interest ; but they boasted that " grasshoppers " like them, old of race and pure of blood, could be influenced in their conduct by nothing short of a fine and delicate taste, a sense of honour, and an elevated, aspiring spirit. Their model man, like the pattern of chivalry, was a gentleman, καλοκἁγαθός ;—a word which has hardly its equivalent in the sterner language of Rome, where, on the contrary,

Vir bonus est quis?
Qui consulta patrum, qui leges juraque servat.

For the Romans deified Law, as the Athenians deified the Beautiful.

This being the state of the case, Athens was in truth a ready-made University. The present age, indeed, with that solidity of mind for which it is indebted to Christianity, and that practical character which has ever been the peculiarity of the West, would bargain that the True and Serviceable as well as the Beautiful should be made the aim of the Academic intellect and the business of a University ;—of course,—but the present age, and every age, will bargain for many things in its schools which Athens had not, when once we set about summing up her *desiderata:* Let us take her as she was, and I say, that a people so speculative, so imaginative, who throve upon mental activity as other races upon mental repose, and to whom it came as natural to think, as to a barbarian to smoke or to sleep, such a people were in a true sense born teachers, and merely to live among them was a cultivation of mind. Hence they took their place in this capacity forthwith, from the time that they emancipated themselves from the aristocratic families, with which their history opens. We talk of the " republic of letters," because thought is free, and minds of whatever rank in life are on a level. The Athenians felt that a democracy was but the political expression of an intellectual isonomy, and, when they had obtained it, and taken the Beautiful for their Sovereign, instead of king or tyrant, they came forth as the civilizers, not of Greece only, but of the European world.

6

A century had not passed from the expulsion of the
Pisistratidæ, when Pericles was able to call Athens the
" schoolmistress " of Greece. And ere it had well run out,
the old Syracusan, who, upon her misfortunes in Sicily,
pleaded in behalf of her citizens, conjured his fellow-
citizens, " in that they had the gift of Reason," to have
mercy upon those, who had opened their land, as "a
common school," to all men ; and he asks, " To what
foreign land will men betake themselves for liberal
education, if Athens be destroyed ?" And the story is
well known, when, in spite of his generous attempt, the
Athenian prisoners were set to work in the stone-quarries,
how that those who could recite passages from Euripides,
found this accomplishment serve them instead of ransom,
for their liberation. Such was Athens on the coast of
the Ægean and in the Mediterranean ; and it was hardly
more than the next generation, when her civilization was
conveyed by means of the conquests of Alexander into
the very heart of further Asia, and was the life of the
Greek kingdom which he founded in Bactriana. She
became the centre of a vast intellectual propagandism,
and had in her hands the spell of a more wonderful
influence than that semi-barbarous power which first
conquered and then used her. Wherever the Macedonian
phalanx held its ground, thither came a colony of her
philosophers ; Asia Minor and Syria were covered with
her schools, while in Alexandria her children, Theophrastus and Demetrius, became the life of the great
literary undertakings which have immortalized the name
of the Ptolemies.

Such was the effect of that peculiar democracy, in
which Pericles glories in his celebrated Funeral Oration.
It made Athens in the event politically weak, but it was
her strength as an ecumenical teacher and civilizer. The

love of the Beautiful will not conquer the world, but like the voice of Orpheus, it may for a while carry it away captive. Such is that " divine Philosophy," in the poet's words,

> " Not harsh and crabbed, as dull fools suppose,
> But musical, as is Apollo's lute,
> And a perpetual feast of nectared sweets,
> Where no crude surfeit reigns."

The Athenians then exercised Influence by discarding Law. It was their boast that they had found out the art of living well and happily, without working for it. They professed to do right, not from servile feeling, not because they were obliged, not from fear of command, not from belief of the unseen, but because it was their nature, because it was so truly pleasant, because it was such a luxury to do it. Their political bond was good will and generous sentiment. They were loyal citizens, active, hardy, brave, munificent, from their very love of what was high, and because the virtuous was the enjoy-able, and the enjoyable was the virtuous. They regulated themselves by music, and so danced through life.

Thus, according to Pericles, while, in private and personal matters, each Athenian was suffered to please himself, without any tyrannous public opinion to make him feel uncomfortable, the same freedom of will did but unite the people, one and all, in concerns of national interest, because obedience to the magistrates and the laws was with them a sort of passion, to shrink from dishonour an instinct, and to repress injustice an indul-gence. They could be splendid in their feasts and spectacles without extravagance, because the crowds whom they attracted from abroad, repaid them for the outlay ; and such large hospitality did but cherish in them a frank, unsuspicious, and courageous spirit, which better protected them than a pile of state secrets and exclusive laws. Nor did this joyous mode of life relax them, as it might relax a less noble race, for they were warlike without effort, and expert without training, and rich in resource by the gift of nature, and, after their fill of pleasure, they were only more gallant in the field, and more patient and enduring on the march. They cultivated the fine arts with too much taste to be expensive, and they studied the sciences with too much point to become effeminate ; debate did not blunt their energy, nor foresight of danger chill their daring ; but, as their tragic poet expresses it, "the loves were the attendants upon wisdom, and had a share in the acts of every virtue."

Such was the Athenian according to his own account of himself, and very beautiful is the picture ; very original and attractive ; very suitable, certainly, to a personage, who was to be the world-wide Professor of the humanities and the philosophic Missionary of mankind. Suitable, if he could be just what I have been depicting him, and nothing besides ; but, alas ! when we attentively consider what the above conception was likely in fact to turn out, as soon as it came to be carried into execution, we shall feel no surprise, on passing from panegyric to experience, that he looks so different in history, from what he promised to be in the glowing periods of the orator. The case, as I have already remarked, is very simple : if beautifulness was all that was needed to make a thing right, then nothing graceful and pleasant could be wrong ; and, since there is no abstract idea but admits of being embellished and dressed up, and made pleasant and graceful, it followed as a matter of course that any thing whatever is permissible. One sees at once, that, taking men as they are, the love of the Beautiful would be nothing short of the love of the Sensual ; nor was the anticipation falsified by the event : for in Athens genius and voluptuousness ever went hand in hand, and their literature, as it has come down to us, is no sample or measure of their actual mode of living.

Their literature indeed is of that serene and severe beauty, which has ever been associated with the word "classical ; " and it is grave and profound enough for ancient Fathers to have considered it a preparation for the gospel; but we are concerned here, not with the writings, but with the social life of Athens. I have been speaking of her as a living body, as an intellectual home, as the pattern school of the Professorial system ; and we now see where the hitch lay. She was of far too fine and dainty a nature for the wear and tear of life ;—she needed to be " of sterner stuff," if she was to aspire to the charge of the young and inexperienced. Not all the zeal of the teacher and devotion of the pupil, the thirst of giving and receiving, the exuberance of demand and supply, will avail for a University, unless some provision is made for the maintenance of authority and of discipline, unless the terrors of the Law are added to the persuasives of the Beautiful. Influence was not enough without command. This too is the reason why Athens, with all her high gifts, was at fault, not only as a University, but as an Empire. She was proud, indeed, of her imperial sway, in the season of her power, and ambitious of its extension ; but, in matter of fact, she was as ill adapted to reign in the cities of the earth, as to rule in its schools. In this world no one rules by mere love ; if you are but amiable, you are no hero ; to be powerful, you must be strong, and to have dominion you must have a genius for organizing. Macedon and

Rome were, as in politics, so in literature, the necessary complement of Athens.

Yet there is something so winning in the idea of Athenian life, which Pericles sets before us, that, acknowledging, as, alas! I must acknowledge, that that life was inseparable from the gravest disorders, in the world as it is, and much more in the pagan world, and that at best it is only ephemeral, if attempted, still, since I am now going to bid farewell to Athens and her schools, I am not sorry to be able to pay her some sort of compliment in parting. I think, then, her great orators have put to her credit a beautiful idea, which, though not really fulfilled in her, has literally and unequivocally been realized within the territory of Christianity. I am not speaking of course of the genius of the Athenians, which was peculiar to themselves, nor of those manifold gifts in detail, which have made them the wonder of the world, but of that profession of philosophical democracy, so original and so refined in its idea, of that grace, freedom, nobleness, and liberality of daily life, of which Pericles, in his oration, is specially enamoured; and, with my tenderness, on the one hand, for Athens (little as I love the radical Greek character), and my devotion to a particular Catholic Institution on the other, I have ever thought I could trace a certain resemblance between Athens, as contrasted with Rome, and the Oratory of St. Philip, as viewed in contrast with the Religious Orders.

All the creations of Holy Church have their own excellence and do their own service ; each is perfect in ts kind, nor can any one be measured against another in the way of rivalry or antagonism. We may admire one of them without disparaging the rest ; again, we may specify its characteristic gift, without implying thereby that it has not other gifts also. Whereas then, to take up the language which my friend Richard has put into my mouth, there are two great principles of action in human affairs, Influence and System, some ecclesiastical institutions are based upon System, and others upon Influence. Which are those which flourish and fulfil their mission by means of System? Evidently the Regular Bodies, as the very word "regular" implies; they are great, they are famous, they spread, they do exploits, in the strength of their Rule. They are of the nature of imperial states. Ancient Rome, for instance, had the talent of organization; and she formed a political framework to unite to herself and to each other the countries which she successively conquered. She sent out her legions all over the earth to secure and to govern it. She created establishments which were fitted to last for ever; she brought together a hundred nations into one, and she moulded Europe on a model, which it retains even now;—and this not by a sentiment or an imagination, but by wisdom of policy, and the iron hand of Law. Establishment is the very idea, which the name of Imperial Rome suggests. Athens, on the other hand, was as fertile, indeed, in schools, as Rome in military successes and political institutions; she was as metropolitan a city, and as frequented a capital, as Rome; she drew the world to her, she sent her literature into the world; but still men came and went, in and out, without constraint; and her preachers went to and fro, as they pleased; she sent out her missions by reason of her energy of intellect, and men came on pilgrimage to her from their love for philosophy.

Observe, I am all along directing attention, not to the mental gifts of Athens, which belonged to her nature, but to what is separable from her, her method and her instruments. I repeat, that, contrariwise to Rome, it was the method of Influence : it was the absence of rule, it was the action of personality, the intercourse of soul with soul, the play of mind upon mind, it was an admirable spontaneous force, which kept the schools of Athens going, and made the pulses of foreign intellects keep time with hers.

Now, I say, if there be an Institution in the Catholic Church, which in this point of view has caught the idea of this great heathen precursor of the Truth, and has made the idea Christian,—if it proceeds from one who has even gained for himself the title of the " Amabile Santo,"—who has placed the noblest aims before his children, yet withal the freest course ; who always drew them to their duty, instead of commanding, and brought them on to perform before they had yet promised ; who made it a man's praise that he " potuit transgredi, et non est transgressus, facere mala, et non fecit ; " who in his humility had no intention of forming any Congregation at all, but had formed it before he knew of it, from the beauty and the fascination of his own saintliness ; and then, when he was obliged to recognize it and put it into shape, shrank from the severity of the Regular, would have nothing to say to vows, and forbade propagation and dominion ; whose houses stand, like Greek colonies, independent of each other and complete in themselves ; whose subjects in those several houses are allowed, like Athenian citizens, freely to cultivate their respective gifts and to follow out their own mission ; whose one rule is Love, and whose own weapon Influence ;—I say, if all this is true of a certain Congregation in the Church, and if it so happens that that Congregation, in the person of one of its members, finds itself at the present moment in contact with the preparatory movements of

the establishment of a great University, then surely I
may trust, without fancifulness and without impertinence,
that there is a providential fitness discernible in the circumstance of the traditions of that Congregation flowing
in upon the first agitation of that design ; and, though
to frame, to organize, and to consolidate, be the imperial
gift of St. Dominic or St. Ignatius, and beyond his
range, yet a son of St. Philip Neri may aspire without
presumption to the preliminary task of breaking the
ground and clearing the foundations of the Future, of introducing the great idea into men's minds, and making
them understand it, and love it, and have hope in it, and
have faith in it, and show zeal for it ;—of bringing many
intellects to work together for it, and of teaching them to
understand each other, and bear with each other, and go on
together, not so much by rule, as by mutual kind feeling
and a common devotion,—after the conception and in
the spirit of that memorable people, who, though they
could bring nothing to perfection, were great (over and
above their supreme originality) in exciting a general interest, and in creating an elevated taste, in the various
subject-matters of art, science, and philosophy.

But here I am only in the middle of my subject, and
at the end of my paper ; so I must reserve the rest of
what I have to say for the next Chapter.

CHAPTER VIII.

MACEDONIAN AND ROMAN SCHOOLS:
DISCIPLINE.

LOOKING at Athens as the preacher and missionary of Letters, and as enlisting the whole Greek race in her work, who is not struck with admiration at the range and multiplicity of her operations? At first, the Ionian and Æolian cities are the principal scene of her activity; but, if we look on a century or two, we shall find that she forms the intellect of the colonies of Sicily and Magna Græcia, has penetrated Italy, and is shedding the light of philosophy and awakening thought in the cities of Gaul by means of Marseilles, and along the coast of Africa by means of Cyrene. She has sailed up both sides of the Euxine, and deposited her literary wares where she stopped, as traders nowadays leave samples of foreign merchandize, or as war steamers land muskets and ammunition, or as agents for religious societies drop their tracts or scatter their versions. The whole of Asia Minor and Syria resounds with her teaching; the barbarians of Parthia are quoting fragments of her tragedians; Greek manners are introduced and perpetuated on the Hydaspes and Acesines; Greek coins, lately come to light, are struck in the capital of Bactriana; and so charged is the moral atmosphere of the East with Greek civilization, that, down to this day, those tribes are said to show to most advantage, which can claim relation of place or kin with Greek colonies established there above two thousand years ago. But there is one city, which, though Greece and Athens have no longer any memorial in it, has in this point of view a claim, beyond the rest, upon our attention ; and that, not only from its Greek origin, and the memorable name which it bears, but because it introduces us to a new state of things, and is the record of an advance in the history of the education of the intellect ;—I mean, Alexandria.

Alexander, if we must call him a Greek, which the Greeks themselves would not permit, did that which no Greek had done before ; or rather, because he was no thorough Greek, though so nearly a Greek by descent and birthplace and by tastes, he was able, without sacrificing what Greece was, to show himself to be what Greece was not. The creator of a wide empire, he had talents for organization and administration, which were foreign to the Athenian mind, and which were absolutely necessary if its mission was to be carried out. The picture, which history presents of Alexander, is as beautiful as it is romantic. It is not only the history of a youth of twenty, pursuing conquests so vast, that at the end of a few years he had to weep that there was no second world to subjugate, but it is that of a beneficent prince, civilizing, as he went along, both by his political institutions and by his patronage of science. It is this union of an energetic devotion to letters with a genius for sovereignty, which places him in contrast both to Greek and Roman. Cæsar, with all his cultivation of mind, did not conquer in order to civilize, any more than Hannibal; he must add Augustus to himself, before he can be an Alexander. The royal pupil of Aristotle and Callisthenes started, where aspiring statesmen or generals end ; he professed to be more ambitious of a name for knowledge than for

power, and he paid a graceful homage to the city of intellect by confessing, when he was in India, that he was
doing his great acts to gain the immortal praise of the
Athenians. The classic poets and philosophers were his
recreation ; he preferred the contest of song to the palæs-
tra ; of medicine he had more than a theoretical knowledge ; and his ear for music was so fine, that Dryden's
celebrated Ode, legendary as may be its subject, only does
justice to its sensitiveness. He was either expert in
fostering, or quick in detecting, the literary tastes of those
around him; and two of his generals have left behind them
a literary fame. Eumenes and Ptolemy, after his death,
engaged in the honourable rivalry, the one in Asia Minor,
the other in Egypt, of investing the dynasties which they
respectively founded, with the patronage of learning and
of its professors.

Ptolemy, upon whom, on Alexander's death, devolved
the kingdom of Egypt, supplies us with the first great
instance of what may be called the establishment of
Letters. He and Eumenes may be considered the first
founders of public libraries. Some authors indeed allude
to the Egyptian king, Osymanduas, and others point to
Pisistratus, as having created a precedent for their imita-
tion. It is difficult to say what these pretensions are
exactly worth : or how far those personages are entitled
to more than the merit of a conception, which obviously
would occur to various minds before it was actually
accomplished. There is more reason for referring it to
Aristotle, who, from his relation to Alexander, may be
considered as the head of the Macedonian literary movement, and whose books, together with those of his wealthy
disciple, Theophrastus, ultimately came into the possession of the Ptolemies ; but Aristotle's idea, to whatever
extent he realized it, was carried out by the two Mace-

donian dynasties with a magnificence of execution, which kings alone could project, and a succession of ages secure. For the first time, a great system was set on foot for collecting together in one, and handing down to posterity, the oracles of the world's wisdom In the reign of the second Ptolemy the number of volumes rescued from destruction, and housed in the Alexandrian Library, amounted to 100,000, as volumes were then formed ; in course of time it grew to 400,000 ; and a second collection was commenced, which at length rose to 300,000, making, with the former, a sum total of 700,000 volumes. During Cæsar's military defence of Alexandria, the former of these collections was unfortunately burned ; but, in compensation, the library received the 200,000 volumes of the rival collection of the kings of Pergamus, the gift of Antony to Cleopatra. After lasting nearly a thousand years, this noblest of dynastic monuments was deliberately burned, as all the world knows, by the Saracens, on their becoming masters of Alexandria.

A library, however, was only one of two great conceptions brought into execution by the first Ptolemy ; and as the first was the embalming of dead genius, so the second was the endowment of living. Here again the Egyptian priests may be said in a certain sense to have preceded him ; moreover, in Athens itself there had grown up a custom of maintaining in the Prytaneum at the public cost, or of pensioning, those who had deserved well of the state, nay, their children also. This had been the privilege, for instance, conferred on the family of the physician Hippocrates, for his medical services at the time of the plague ; yet I suppose the provision of a home or residence was never contemplated in its idea. But as regards literature itself, to receive money for teaching, was considered to degrade it to an illiberal purpose, as had been felt in the instance of the Sophists; even the Pythian prize for verse, though at first gold or silver, became nothing more than a crown of leaves, as soon as a sufficient competition was secured. Kings, indeed, might lavish precious gifts upon the philosophers or poets whom they kept about them ; but such practices did not proceed on rule or by engagement, nor imply any salary settled on the objects of their bounty. Ptolemy, however, prompted, or at least encouraged, by the cele-brated Demetrius of Phalerus, put into execution a plan for the formal endowment of literature and science. The fact indeed of the possession of an immense library seemed sufficient to render Alexandria a University; for what could be a greater attraction to the students of all lands, than the opportunity afforded them of intellectual converse, not only with the living, but with the dead, with all who had any where at any time thrown light upon any subject of inquiry ? But Ptolemy determined that his teachers of knowledge should be as stationary and as permanent as his books ; so, resolving to make Alexandria the seat of a *Studium Generale*, he founded a College for its domicile, and endowed that College with ample revenues.

Here, I consider, he did more than has been com-monly done, till modern times. It requires considerable knowledge of medieval Universities to be entitled to give an opinion; as regards Germany, for instance, or Poland, or Spain ; but, as far as I have a right to speak, such an en-dowment has been rare down to the sixteenth century, as well as before Ptolemy. The University of Toulouse, I think, was founded in a College; so was Orleans ; so has been the Protestant University of Dublin ; other Universities have yearly salaries from the Government ; but even the University of Oxford to this day, viewed as a University, is a poor body. Its Professors have for the most part a scanty endowment and no house of residence ; and it subsists mainly on fees received from year to year from its members. Such too, I believe, is the case with the University of Cambridge. The University founded in Dublin in John the Twenty-second's time, fell for lack of funds. The University of Paris could not be very wealthy, even in the ninth century of its existence, or it would not have found it necessary to sell its beautiful Park or Pratum. As for ourselves at present, it is commonly understood, that we are starting with ample means already, while large contributions are still expected ; a sum equal perhaps to a third of what has already been collected is to be added to it from the United States ; as to Ireland herself, the overflowing, almost miraculous liberality of her poorest classes makes no anticipation of their prospective contributions extravagant. Well, any how, if money made a University, we might expect ours to last as long as the Ptolemies' ; and, I suppose, any one of us would be content that an institution, which he helped to found, should live through a thousand years.

But to return to the Alexandrian College. It was called the Museum,—a name since appropriated to another institution connected with the seats of science. Its situation affords an additional instance in corroboration of remarks I have already made upon the sites of Universities. There was a quarter of the city so distinct from the rest in Alexandria, that it is sometimes spoken of as a suburb. It was pleasantly situated on the water's edge, and had been set aside for ornamental buildings, and was traversed by groves of trees. Here stood the royal palace, here the theatre and amphitheatre ; here the gymnasia and stadium ; here the

famous Serapeum. And here it was, close upon the
Port, that Ptolemy placed his Library and College. As
might be supposed, the building was worthy of its purpose ; a noble portico stretched along its front, for
exercise or conversation, and opened upon the public
rooms devoted to disputations and lectures. A certain
number of Professors were lodged within the precincts,
and a handsome hall, or refectory, was provided for the
common meal. The Prefect of the house was a priest,
whose appointment lay with the government. Over the
Library a dignified person presided, who, if his jurisdiction extended to the Museum also, might somewhat answer to a medieval or modern Chancellor ; the first of
these functionaries being the celebrated Athenian who
had so much to do with the original design. As to the
Professors, so liberal was their maintenance, that a philosopher of the very age of the first foundation called the
place a " bread basket," or a " bird coop ;" yet, in spite
of accidental exceptions, so careful on the whole was
their selection, that even six hundred years afterwards,
Ammianus describes the Museum under the title of "the
lasting abode of distinguished men." Philostratus, too,
about a century before, calls it " a table gathering together celebrated men :" a phrase which merits attention,
as testifying both to the high character of the Professors,
and to the means by which they were secured. In some
cases, at least, they were chosen by *concursus* or competition, in which the native Egyptians are said sometimes to have surpassed the Greeks. We read too of
literary games or contests, apparently of the same
nature. As time went on, new Colleges were added to
the original Museum ; of which one was a foundation of
the Emperor Claudius, and called after his name.

It cannot be thought that the high reputation of these

foundations would have been maintained, unless Ptolemy
had looked beyond Egypt for occupants of his chairs ;
and indeed he got together the best men, wherever he
could find them. On these he heaped wealth and privileges; and so complete was their naturalization in their
adopted country, that they lost their usual surnames,
drawn from their place of birth, and, instead of being
called, for instance, Apion of Oasis, or Aristarchus of
Samothracia, or Dionysius of Thrace, received each
simply the title of " the Alexandrian." Thus Clement
of Alexandria, the learned father of the Church, was a
native of Athens.

A diversity of teachers secured an abundance of
students. " Hither," says Cave, " as to a public emporium of polite literature, congregated, from every
part of the world, youthful students, and attended the
lectures in Grammar, Rhetoric, Poetry, Philosophy,
Astronomy, Music, Medicine, and other arts and
sciences ; " and hence proceeded, as it would appear,
the great Christian writers and doctors, Clement, whom
I have just been mentioning, Origen, Anatolius, and
Athanasius. St. Gregory Thaumaturgus, in the third
century, may be added ; he came across Asia Minor
and Syria from Pontus, as to a place, says his name-
sake of Nyssa, " to which young men from all parts
gathered together, who were applying themselves to
philosophy."

As to the subjects taught in the Museum, Cave has
already enumerated the principal ; but he has not done
justice to the peculiar character of the Alexandrian
school. From the time that science got out of the
hands of the pure Greeks, into those of a power which
had a talent for administration, it became less theoretical, and bore more distinctly upon definite and

7

tangible objects. The very conception of an endowment is a specimen of this change. Without yielding the palm of subtle speculation to the Greeks, philosophy assumed a more masculine and vigorous character. Dreamy theorists, indeed, they could also show in still higher perfection than Athens, where there was the guarantee of genius that abstract investigation would never become ridiculous. The Alexandrian Neo-platonists certainly have incurred the risk of this imputation ; yet, Potamo, Ammonius, Plotinus, and Hierocles, who are to be numbered among them, with the addition perhaps of Proclus, in spite of the frivolousness and feebleness of their system, have a weight of character, taken together, which would do honour to any school. And the very circumstance that they originated a new philosophy is no ordinary distinction in the intellectual world : and that it was directly intended to be a rival and refutation of Christianity, while no great recommendation to it certainly in a religious judgment, marks the practical character of the Museum even amid its subtleties. So much for their philosophers : among their poets was Apollonius of Rhodes, whose poem on the Argonauts carries with it, in the very fact of its being still extant, the testimony of succeeding ages either to its merit, or to its antiquarian importance. Egyptian Antiquities were investigated, at least by the disciples of the Egyptian Manetho, fragments of whose history are considered to remain ; while Carthaginian and Etruscan had a place in the studies of the Claudian College. The Museum was celebrated, moreover, for its grammarians ; the work of Hephæstion *de Metris* still affords matter of thought to a living Professor of Oxford ; * and Aris-

---

* Dr. Gaisford, since dead. For the Alexandrian Grammarians, vid. Fabric. Bibl. Græc., t. vi., p. 353.

tarchus, like the Athenian Priscian, has almost become the nick-name for a critic.

Yet, eminent as is the Alexandrian school in these departments of science, its fame rests still more securely upon its proficiency in medicine and mathematics. Among its physicians is the celebrated Galen, who was attracted thither from Pergamus ; and we are told by a writer of the fourth century,* that in his time the very fact of a physician having studied at Alexandria, was an evidence of his science which superseded further testimonial. As to mathematics, it is sufficient to say, that, of four great ancient names, on whom the modern science is founded, three came from Alexandria. Archimedes indeed was a Syracusan ; but the Museum may boast of Apollonius of Perga, Diophantus, a native Alexandrian, and Euclid, whose country is unknown. Of these three, Euclid's services to Geometry are known, if not appreciated, by every school-boy ; Apollonius is the first writer on Conic Sections ; and Diophantus the first writer on Algebra. To these illustrious names, may be added, Eratosthenes of Cyrene, to whom astronomy has obligations so considerable ; Pappus ; Theon ; and Ptolemy, said to be of Pelusium, whose celebrated system, called after him the Ptolemaic, reigned in the schools till the time of Copernicus, and whose Geography, dealing with facts, not theories, is in repute still.

Such was the celebrated *Studium* or University of Alexandria ; for a while, in the course of the third and fourth centuries, it was subject to reverses, principally from war. The whole of the Bruchion, the quarter of the city in which it was situated, was given to the flames ; and, when Hilarion came to Alexandria, the

* Ammianus.

holy hermit, whose rule of life did not suffer him to lodge in cities, took up his lodgment with a few solitaries among the ruins of its edifices. The schools, however, and the library continued ; the library was reserved for the Caliph Omar's famous judgment ; as to the schools, even as late as the twelfth century, the Jew, Benjamin of Tudela, gives us a surprising report of what he found in Alexandria. "Outside the city," he says, a mode of speaking which agrees with what has been above said about the locality of the Museum, "is the Academy of Aristotle, Alexander's preceptor ; a handsome pile of buildings, which has twenty Colleges, whither students betake themselves from all parts of the world to learn his philosophy. The marble columns divide one College from another."

Though the Roman schools have more direct bearing on the subsequent rise of the medieval Universities, they are not so exact an anticipation of its type, as the Alexandrian Museum. They differ from the Museum, as being for the most part, as it would appear, devoted to the education of the very young, without any reference to the advancement of science. No list of writers or of discoveries, no local or historical authorities, can be adduced, from the date of Augustus to that of Justinian, to rival the fame of Alexandria ; we hear on the contrary much of the elements of knowledge, the Trivium and Quadrivium ; and the Law of the Empire provided, and the Theodosian Code has recorded, the discipline necessary for the students. Teaching and learning was a department of government ; and schools were set up and professors endowed, just as soldiers were stationed or courts opened, in every great city of the East and West. In Rome itself the seat of education was placed in the Capitol; ten chairs were appointed for Latin Grammar, ten for Greek; three for Latin Rhetoric, five for Greek; one, some say three, for Philosophy; two or four for Roman Law. Professorships of Medicine were afterwards added. Under Grammar (if St. Gregory's account of Athens in Roman times may be applied to the Roman schools generally), were included knowledge of language and metre, criticism, and history. Rome, as might be expected, and Carthage, were celebrated for their Latin teaching; Roman Law is said to have been taught in three cities only, Rome itself, Constantinople, and Berytus; but this probably was the restriction of a later age.

The study of grammar and geography was commenced at the age of twelve, and apparently at the private school, and was continued till the age of fourteen. Then the youths were sent to the public academy for oratory, philosophy, mathematics, and law. The course lasted five years; and, on entering on their twentieth year, their education was considered complete, and they were sent home. If they studied the law, they were allowed to stay, (for instance, in Berytus,) till their twenty-fifth year; a permission, indeed, which was extended in that city to the students in polite literature, or, as we should now say, in Arts.

The number of youths, who went up to Rome for the study of the Law, was considerable; chiefly from Africa and Gaul. Originally the Government had discouraged foreigners in repairing to the metropolis, from the dangers it naturally presented to youth; when their residence there became a necessary evil, it contented itself with imposing strict rules of discipline upon them. No youth could obtain admission into the Roman schools, without a certificate signed by the magistracy of his province. Next, he presented himself before the Magister Censûs, an official who was in the department of the Præfectus Urbis, and who, besides his ordinary duties, acted as Rector of the Academy. Next, his name, city, age, and qualifications were entered in a public register; and a specification, moreover, of the studies he proposed to pursue, and of the lodging-house where he proposed to reside. He was amenable for his conduct to the Censuales, as if they had been Proctors; and he was reminded that the eyes of the world were upon him, that he had a character to maintain, and that it was his duty to avoid clubs, of which the Government was jealous, riotous parties, and the public shows, which were of daily occurrence and of most corrupting nature. If he was refractory and disgraced himself, he was to be publicly flogged, and shipped off at once to his country. Those who acquitted themselves well, were reported to the Government, and received public appointments. The Professors were under the same jurisdiction as the students, and were sometimes made to feel it.

Of the schools planted through the Empire, the most considerable were the Gallic and the African, of which the latter had no good reputation, while the Gallic name stood especially high. Marseilles, one of the oldest of the Greek colonies, was the most celebrated of the schools of Gaul for learning and discipline. For this reason, and from its position, it drew off numbers, under the Empire, who otherwise would have repaired to Athens. It was here that Agricola received his education; "a school," says his biographer, "in which Greek politeness was happily blended and tempered with provincial strictness." The schools of Bourdeaux and Autun also had a high name; and Rheims received

the title of a new Athens. This appellation was also
bestowed upon the school of Milan. Besides these
countries, respectful mention is made of the schools of
Britain. As to Spain, the colonies there established are
even called, by one commentator on the Theodosian
code, "literary colonies ;" a singular title when Rome is
concerned; and, in fact, a considerable number of writers
of reputation came from Spain. Lucan, the Senecas,
Martial, perhaps Quintilian, Mela, Columella, and Hy-
ginus, are its contribution in the course of a century.

It will be seen that the Roman schools, as little as
Athens itself, answer to the precise idea of a modern
University. The Roman schools were for boys, or, at
least, *adolescentuli :* Agricola came to Marseilles when a
child, "parvulus." On the other hand, a residence at
Athens corresponded rather to seeing the world, as in
touring and travelling, and was often delayed till the
season of education was over. Cicero went thither,
after his public career had begun, with a view to his
health, as well as to his oratory. St. Basil had already
studied at the schools of Cæsarea and Cappadocia.
Sometimes young men on campaign, when quartered
near Athens, took the opportunity of attending her
schools. However, the case was the same with Rome
so far as regards the departments of jurisprudence and
general cultivation. We read both of Rusticus, the
correspondent of St. Jerome, and of St. Germanus of
Auxerre, coming to Rome, after attending the Gallic
schools ;—the latter expressly in order to study the law ;
the former, for the same general purpose as might take
a student to Athens, to polish and perfect his style of
conversation and writing.

All this suggests to us, what of course must ever be
borne in mind, that, while the necessities of human

society and the nature of the case are guarantees to us that such Schools of general education will ever be in requisition, still they will be modified in detail by the circumstances, and marked by the peculiarities, of the age to which they severally belong.

CHAPTER IX.

DOWNFALL AND REFUGE OF ANCIENT CIVILIZATION.
THE LOMBARDS.

THERE never was, perhaps, in the history of this tumultuous world, prosperity so great, so far-spreading, so lasting, as that which began throughout the vast Empire of Rome, at the time when the Prince of Peace was born into it. Preternatural as was the tyranny of certain of the Cæsars, it did not reach the mass of the population; and the reigns of the Five good Emperors, who succeeded them, are proverbs of wise and gentle government. The sole great exception to this universal happiness was the cruel persecution of the Christians; the sufferings of a whole world fell and were concentrated on them, and the children of heaven were tormented, that the sons of men might enjoy their revel. Their Lord, while His shadow brought peace upon earth, foretold that in the event He came to send "not peace but a sword;" and that sword was first let loose upon His own people. "Judgment commenced with the House of God;" and though, as time went on, it left Jerusalem behind, and began to career round the world and sweep the nations as it travelled on, nevertheless, as if by some paradox of Providence, it seemed at first, that truth and wretchedness had "met together," and sin and prosperity had "kissed one another." The more the heathens enjoyed themselves, the more they scorned,

hated, and persecuted their true Light and true Peace.
They persecuted Him, for the very reason that they had
little else to do ; happy and haughty, they saw in Him
the sole drawback, the sole exception, the sole hinder-
ance, to a universal, a continual sunshine ; they called
Him "the enemy of the human race:" and they felt
themselves bound, by their loyalty to the glorious and
immortal memory of their forefathers, by their traditions
of state, and their duties towards their children, to
trample upon, and, if they could, to stifle that teaching, which was destined to be the life and mould of a
new world.

But our immediate subject here is, not Christianity,
but the world that passed away ; and before it passed, it
had, I say, a tranquillity great in proportion to its former
commotions.   Ages of trouble terminated in two centuries of peace.   The present crust of the earth is said
to be the result of a long war of elements, and to have
been made so beautiful, so various, so rich, and so useful,
by the discipline of revolutions, by earthquake and
lightning, by mountains of water and seas of fire ; and
so in like manner, it required the events of two thousand years, the multiform fortunes of tribes and populations, the rise and fall of kings, the mutual collision of
states, the spread of colonies, the vicissitudes and the
succession of conquests, and the gradual adjustment and
settlement of innumerous discordant ideas and interests,
to carry on the human race to unity, and to shape and
consolidate the great Roman Power.

And when once those unwieldy materials were welded
together into one mass, what human force could split
them up again ? what "hammer of the earth" could
shiver at a stroke a solidity which it had taken ages to
form ?   Who can estimate the strength of a political

establishment, which has been the slow birth of time ? and what establishment ever equalled pagan Rome ? Hence has come the proverb, " Rome was not built in a day :" it was the portentous solidity of its power that forced the gazer back upon an exclamation, which was the relief of his astonishment, as being his solution of the prodigy. And, when at length it was built, Rome, so long in building, was " Eternal Rome :" it had been done once for all; its being was inconceivable before-hand, and its not being was inconceivable afterwards. It had been a miracle that it was brought to be ; it would take a second miracle that it should cease to be. To remove it from its place was to cast a mountain into the sea. Look at the Palatine Hill, penetrated, tra-versed, cased with brickwork, till it appears a work of man, not of nature ; run your eye along the cliffs from Ostia to Terracina, covered with the debris of masonry ; gaze around the bay of Baiæ, whose rocks have been made to serve as the foundations and the walls of palaces ; and in those mere remains, lasting to this day, you will have a type of the moral and political strength of the establishments of Rome. Think of the aqueducts making for the imperial city, for miles across the plain ; think of the straight roads stretching off again from that one centre to the ends of the earth ; consider the vast territory round about it strewn to this day with countless ruins ; follow in your imagination its suburbs, extending along its roads, for as much, at least in some directions, as forty miles ; and number up its continuous mass of population, amounting, as grave authors say, to almost six million ; and answer the question, how was Rome ever to be got rid of ? why was it not to progress ? why was it not to progress for ever ? where was that ancient civilization to end ? Such were the questionings and anticipations of thoughtful minds, not specially proud or fond of Rome. "The world," says Tertullian, "has more of cultivation every day, and is better furnished than in times of old. All places are opened up now ; all are familiarly known ; all are scenes of business. Smiling farms have obliterated the notorious wilderness ; tillage has tamed the forest land; flocks have put to flight the beasts of prey. Sandy tracts are sown ; rocks are put into shape ; marshes are drained. There are more cities now, than there were cottages at one time. Islands are no longer wild ; the crag is no longer frightful ; everywhere there is a home, a population, a state, and a livelihood." Such was the prosperity, such the promise of progress and permanence, in which the Assyrian, the Persian, the Greek, the Macedonian conquests had terminated.

Education had gone through a similar course of difficulties, and had a place in the prosperous result. First, carried forth upon the wings of genius, and disseminated by the energy of individual minds, or by the colonizing missions of single cities, Knowledge was irregularly extended to and fro over the spacious regions, of which the Mediterranean is the common basin. Introduced, in course of time, to a more intimate alliance with political power, it received the means, at the date of Alexander and his successors, both of its cultivation and its propagation. It was formally recognized and endowed under the Ptolemies, and at length became a direct object of the solicitude of the government under the Cæsars. It was honoured and dispensed in every considerable city of the Empire ; it tempered the political administration of the conquering people ; it civilized the manners of a hundred barbarian conquests; it gradually reconciled uncongenial, and associated distant countries, with each other; while it had ever ministered to the fine arts, it now proceeded to subserve the useful. It took in hand the reformation of the world's religion; it began to harmonize the legends of discordant worships; it purified the mythology by making it symbolical; it interpreted it, and gave it a moral, and explained away its idolatry. It began to develope a system of ethics, it framed a code of laws: what might not be expected of it, as time went on, were it not for that illiberal, unintelligible, fanatical, abominable sect of Galileans? If they were allowed to make play, and get power, what might not happen? There again Christians were in the way, as hateful to the philosopher, as to the statesman. Yet in truth it was not in this quarter that the peril of civilization lay: it lay in a very different direction, over against the Empire to the North and North-East, in a black cloud of inexhaustible barbarian populations: and when the storm mounted overhead and broke upon the earth, it was those scorned and detested Galileans, and none but they, the men-haters and God-despisers, who, returning good for evil, housed and lodged the scattered remnants of that old world's wisdom, which had so persecuted them, went forth valiantly to meet the savage destroyer, tamed him without arms, and became the founders of a new and higher civilization. Not a man in Europe now, who talks bravely against the Church, but owes it to the Church, that he can talk at all.

But what was to be the process, what the method, what the instruments, what the place, for sheltering the treasures of ancient intellect during the convulsion, of bridging over the abyss, and of linking the old world to the new? In spite of the consolidation of its power, Rome was to go, as all things human go, and vanish for ever. In the words of inspiration, "Great Babylon came in remembrance before God, and every island fled away, and the mountains were not found." All the fury of the elements was directed against it ; and, as a continual dropping wears away the stone, so blow after blow, and revolution after revolution, sufficed at last to heave up, and hurl down, and smash into fragments, the noblest earthly power that ever was. First came the Goth, then the Hun, and then the Lombard. The Goth took possession, but he was of noble nature, and soon lost his barbarism. The Hun came next ; he was irreclaimable, but did not stay. The Lombard kept both his savageness and his ground ; he appropriated to himself the territory, not the civilization of Italy, fierce as the Hun, and powerful as the Goth, the most tremendous scourge of Heaven. In his dark presence the poor remains of Greek and Roman splendour died away, and the world went more rapidly to ruin, material and moral, than it was advancing from triumph to triumph in the time of Tertullian. Alas ! the change between Rome in the hey-day of her pride, and in the agony of her judgment ! Tertullian writes while she is exalted ; Pope Gregory when she is in humiliation. He was delivering homilies upon the Prophet Ezekiel, when the news came to Rome of the advance of the Lombards upon the city, and in the course of them he several times burst out into lamentations at the news of miseries, which eventually obliged him to cut short his exposition.

"Sights and sounds of war," he says, "meet us on every side. The cities are destroyed ; the military stations broken up ; the land devastated ; the earth depopulated. No one remains in the country ; scarcely any inhabitants in the towns ; yet even the poor remains of human kind are still smitten daily and without intermission. Before our eyes some are carried away captive, some mutilated, some murdered. She herself, who once was mistress of the world, we behold how Rome fares : worn down by manifold and incalculable distresses, the bereavement of citizens, the attack of foes, the reiteration of overthrows, where is her senate ? where are her people ? We, the few survivors, are still the daily prey of the sword and of other innumerable tribulations. Where are they who in a former day revelled in her glory ? where is their pomp, their pride, their frequent and immoderate joy ?—youngsters, young men of the world, congregated here from every quarter, where they aimed at a secular advancement. Now no one hastens up to her for preferment ; and so it is with other cities also ; some places are laid waste by pestilence, others are depopulated by the sword, others are tormented by famine, and others are swallowed up by earthquakes."

These words, far from being a rhetorical lament, are but a meagre statement of some of the circumstances of a desolation, in which the elements themselves, as St. Gregory intimates, as well as the barbarians, took a principal part. In the dreadful age of that great Pope, a plague spread from the lowlands of Egypt to the Indies on the one hand, along Africa across to Spain on the other, till, reversing its course, it reached the eastern extremity of Europe. For fifty-two years did it retain possession of the infected atmosphere, and, in Constantinople, during three months, five thousand, and at length ten thousand persons, are said to have died daily. Many cities of the East were left without inhabitants ; and in several districts of Italy there were no labourers to gather either harvest or vintage. A succession of earthquakes accompanied for years this heavy calamity. Constantinople was shaken for above forty days. Two

hundred and fifty thousand persons are said to have
perished in the earthquake of Antioch, crowded, as the
city was, with strangers for the festival of the Ascension.
Berytus, the Eastern school of Roman jurisprudence,
called, from its literary and scientific importance, the eye
of Phœnicia, shared a similar fate. These, however,
were but local visitations. Cities are indeed the homes
of civilization, but the wide earth, with her hill and dale,
open plain and winding valley, is its refuge. The barbarian invaders, spreading over the country, like a flight
of locusts, did their best to destroy every fragment of
the old world, and every element of revival. Twenty-
nine public libraries had been founded at Rome ; but,
had these been destroyed, as in Antioch, or Berytus, by
earthquakes or by conflagration, yet a large aggregate
of books would have still survived. Such collections
had become a fashion and a luxury in the latter Empire,
and every colony and municipium, every larger temple,
every prætorium, the baths, and the private villas, had
their respective libraries. When the ruin swept across
the country, and these various libraries were destroyed,
then the patient monks had begun again, in their quiet
dwellings, to bring together, to arrange, to transcribe
and to catalogue ; but then again the new visitation of
the Lombards fell, and Monte Cassino, the famous
metropolis of the Benedictines, not to mention monasteries of lesser note, was sacked and destroyed.

Truly was Christianity revenged on that ancient civilization for the persecutions which it had inflicted on
Christianity. Man ceased from the earth, and his works
with him. The arts of life, architecture, engineering,
agriculture, were alike brought to nought. The waters
were let out over the face of the country ; arable and
pasture lands were drowned ; landmarks disappeared.

Pools and lakes intercepted the thoroughfares ; whole districts became pestilential marshes; the strong stream, or the abiding morass, sapped and obliterated the very site of cities. Here the mountain torrent cut a channel in the plain ; there it elevated ridges across it ; elsewhere it disengaged masses of rock and earth in its precipitous passage, and, hurrying them on, left them as islands in the midst of the flood. Forests overspread the land, in rivalry of the waters, and became the habitation of wild animals, of wolves, and even bears. The dwindled race of man lived in scattered huts of mud, where best they might avoid marauder, and pestilence, and inundation ; or clung together for mutual defence in cities, where wretched cottages, on the ruins of marble palaces, over-balanced the security of numbers by the frequency of conflagration.

In such a state of things, the very mention of educa-tion was a mockery, the very aim and effort to exist was occupation enough for mind and body. The heads of the Church bewailed a universal ignorance, which they could not remedy ; it was a great thing that schools re-mained sufficient for clerical education, and this educa-tion was only sufficient, as Pope Agatho informs us, to enable them to hand on the traditions of the Fathers, without scientific exposition or polemical defence. In that Pope's time, the great Council of Rome, in its letter to the Emperor of the East, who had asked for Episcopal legates of correct life and scientific knowledge of the Scriptures, made answer, that, if by science was meant knowledge of revealed truth, the demand could be sup-plied ; not, if more was required ; " since," continue the Fathers, " in these parts, the fury of our various heathen foes is ever breaking out, whether in conflicts, or in in-roads and rapine. Hence our life is simply one of

8

anxiety of soul and labour of body ; of anxiety, because
we are in the midst of the heathen; of labour, because the
maintenance, which used to come to us as ecclesiastics,
is at an end ; so that faith is our only substance, to live
in its possession our highest glory, to die for it our
eternal gain." The very profession of the clergy is the
knowledge of letters : if even these lost it, would others
retain it in their miseries, to whom it was no duty ?
And what then was the hope and prospect of the world
in the generations which were to follow ?

"What is coming ? what is to be the end?" Such was
the question, that weighed so heavily upon the august
line of Pontiffs, upon whom rested "the solicitude of all
the churches," and whose failure in vigilance and decision in that miserable time would had been the loss of
ancient learning, and the indefinite postponement of new
civilization. What could be done for art, science, and
philosophy, when towns had been burned up, and country
devastated ? In such distress, islands, or deserts, or the
mountain-top have commonly been the retreat, to which
in the last instance the hopes of humanity have been
conveyed. Thus the monks of the fourth century had
preserved the Catholic faith from the tyranny of Arianism
in the Egyptian desert ; and so the inhabitants of Lombardy had taken refuge from the Huns in the shallows
of the Adriatic ; so too just then the Christian Goths
were biding their time to revenge themselves on the
Saracens, in the mountains of Asturias. Where should
the Steward of the Household deposit the riches, which
his predecessors had inherited from Jew and heathen, the
things old as well as new, in an age, in which each succeeding century threatened them with woes worse than
the centuries which had gone before ! Pontiff after Pontiff
looked out from the ruins of the Imperial City, which

were to be his ever-lasting, ever-restless throne, if per-chance some place was to be found, more tranquil than his own, where the hope of the future might be lodged. They looked over the Earth, towards great cities and far provinces, and whether it was Gregory, or Vitalian, or Agatho, or Leo, their eyes had all been drawn in one direction, and fixed upon one quarter for that purpose,— not to the East, from which the light of knowledge had arisen, not to the West, whither it had spread,—but to the North.

High in the region of the North, beyond the just limits of the Roman world, though partly included in its range, so secluded and secure in their sea-encircled domain, that they have been thought to be the fabulous Hesperides, where heroes dwelt in peace, lay two sister islands,—whose names and histories, warned by my diminished space, I must reserve for another Chapter.

CHAPTER X.

THE TRADITION OF CIVILIZATION.

THE ISLES OF THE NORTH.

WHATEVER were the real causes of the downfall of the ancient civilization, its immediate instrument was the fury of the barbarian invasions, directed again and again against the institutions in which it was embodied. First one came down upon the devoted Empire, and then another.; and "that which the palmer worm left, the locust ate ; and what the locust left, the mildew destroyed." Nay, this succession of assaults did not merely carry on and finish the process of destruction, but rather undid the promise and actual prospect of recovery. In the interval between blow and blow, there was a direct tendency to a revival of what had been trodden down, and a restoration of what had been defaced ; and that, not only from any such reaction as might take place in the afflicted population itself, when the crisis was over, but from the incipient domestication of the conqueror, and the introduction of a new and vigorous element into the party and cause of civilization. The fierce soldier was vanquished by the captive of his sword and bow. The beauty of the southern climate, the richness of its productions, the material splendour of its cities, the majesty of the imperial organization, the spontaneous precision of a routine administration, the influence of religion upon the imagination and the affections, antiquity, rule, name, prescription, and territory, presented to him in visible and recognized forms,—in a word, the conservative power proper to establishments,— awed, overcame, and won, the sensitive and noble savage. "Order is heaven's first law," and bears upon it the impress of divinity; and it has an especial power over those minds which have had least experience of it. The Goth not only took pay, and sought refuge, from the Empire, but, still more, when, instead of dependent, he was lord and master, he found himself absorbed into and assimilated with the civilization, upon which he had violently thrust himself. Had he been left in possession, great revolutions certainly, but not dissolution, would have been the destiny of the social framework; and the tradition of science and of the arts of life would have been unbroken.

Thus, in the midst of the awful events which were then in progress, there were intervals of respite and of hope. The day of wrath seemed to be passing away; things began to look up, and the sun was on the point of coming out again. Statesmen, who watched the signs of the times, perhaps began to say, that at last they did think that the worst was over, and that there were good grounds for looking hopefully at the state of affairs. Adolphus, the successor of Alaric, took on himself the obligations of a Roman general, assumed the Roman dress, accepted the Emperor's sister in marriage, and opposed in arms the fiercer barbarians who had overrun Spain. The sons of Theodoric the Visigoth were taught Virgil and Roman Law in the schools of Gaul. Theodoric, the Ostrogoth, anxiously preserved the ancient monuments of Rome, and ornamented the cities of Italy with new edifices; he revived agriculture, promoted commerce, and patronized literature. But the

Goth was not to retain the booty which the Roman had been obliged to relinquish ; he had soon, in company with his former foe, to repel the Vandal, the Hun, or the Frank ; or, weakened from within, to yield to the younger assailants who were to succeed him. Then the whole work of civilization had to begin again—if indeed there was to be a new begining ; or rather there was not life enough left in its poor remains, to vivify the fresh mass of barbarism which fell heavily upon it, or even to save itself from a final extinction. As great Cæsar fell, not under one, but under twenty strokes ; so it was only by many a cleaving, many a shattering blow, " scalpri frequentis ictibus et tunsione plurimâ," that the existing fabric of the old world, to which Cæsar, more than any other, had given name and form, was battered down. It was the accumulation, the reiteration of calamities, in every quarter and through a long period, by " the rain falling, and the floods coming, and the winds blowing and breaking upon that house," that it fell, " and great was the fall thereof."

The judgments of God were upon the earth, and " the clouds returned after the rain ;" and as a thunder cloud careers around the sky, and condenses suddenly here or there, and repeats its violence when it seems to have been spent, so was it with the descent of the North upon the South. There was scarcely a province of the great Empire, but twice or thrice had to sustain attack, invasion, or occupation, from the barbarian. Till the termination of the reign of the Antonines, for a hundred and fifty years, the long peace continued, which the Prince of Peace brought with Him ; then a fitful century of cloud and sunshine, hope and fear, suspense and affliction ; till at length, just at the middle of the third century of our era, the trumpet sounded, and the time of visitation began. The tremendous period opened in a great pestilence, and in an eruption of the barbarians both on the East and on the West. The pestilence lasted for fifteen years ; and, though sooner brought to an end than that more awful pestilence in St. Gregory's day with which the season of judgment closed, yet in that fifteen years it made its way into every region and city of the Empire. Many cities were emptied ; Rome at one time lost 5,000 inhabitants daily, Alexandria lost half her population. As to the barbarians, the Franks on the West descended into Spain ; and the Goths on the East into Asia Minor.

Asia Minor had had a long peace of three hundred years, a phenomenon almost solitary in the history of the world, and difficult for the imagination to realize. Its cities were unwalled ; military duties had been abolished ; the taxes were employed on the public buildings and the well-being and enjoyments of life ; the face of the country was decorated and diversified by the long growth and development of vegetation, by the successive accumulations of art, and by the social memorials and reminiscences of nine peaceful generations. Its parks and groves, its palaces and temples, were removed further by a hundred years from the injuries of warfare, than England is now from the ravages of the Great Rebellion. Down came the Goths from Prussia, Poland, and the Crimea ; they sailed along the Euxine, ravaged Pontus and Bithynia, sacked the wealthy Trebizond and Chalcedon, and burned the imperial Nicæa and Nicomedia, and other great cities of the country ; then they fell upon Cyzicus and the cities on the coast, and finally demolished the famous temple of Diana at Ephesus, the wonder of the world. Then they passed over to the opposite continent, sacked Athens, and spread dismay and confusion, if not conflagration, through both upper Greece and the Peloponnese. At the same solemn era, the Franks fell upon Spain, and ran through the whole of it, destroying flourishing cities, whose ruins lay on the ground for centuries, nor stopped till they had crossed into Africa.

A second time, at a later date, was Spain laid waste by the Vandals and their confederates, with an utter desolation of its territory. Famine became so urgent, that human flesh was eaten; pestilence so rampant, that the wild beasts multiplied among the works of man. Passing on to Africa, these detestable savages cut down the very fruit-trees, as they went, in the wantonness of their fury; and the inhabitants of the plundered cities fled away with such property as they could save beyond sea. A new desolation of Africa took place two centuries later, when the Saracens passed in a contrary direction from Egypt into Spain.

Nor were the Greek and Asiatic provinces, more than the West, destined to be protected against successive invasions. Scarcely a hundred years had passed since the barbarian Goth had swept so fiercely each side of the Egean, when additional blows fell upon Europe and Asia from fresh enemies. In Asia the Huns poured down upon Cappadocia, Cilicia, and Syria, scaring the pagans of Antioch, and the monks and pilgrims of Palestine, silencing at once the melody of immodest song and of holy chant, till they came to the entrance of Egypt. In Europe it was the Goths again, who descended with fire and sword into Greece, desolated the rich lands of Phocis and Bœotia, destroyed Eleusis and its time-honoured superstitions, and passing into the Peloponnese, burned its cities and enslaved its population. About the same time the fertile and cultivated tract, stretching from the Euxine to the Adriatic, was devastated by the same reckless invaders, even to the destruction of the brute creation. Sixty years afterwards the same region was overrun by the still more terrible Huns, who sacked as many as seventy cities, and carried off their inhabitants. This double scourge, of which Alaric and Attila are the earlier and later representatives, travelled up the country northwards, and thence into Lombardy, pillaging, burning, exterminating, as it went along.

What Huns and Goths were to the South, such were Germans, Huns, and Franks to Gaul. That famous country, though in a less favoured climate, was as cultivated and happy as Asia Minor after its three centuries of peace. The banks of the Rhine are said to have been lined with villas and farms ; the schools of Marseilles, Autun, and Bordeaux, vied with those of the East, and even with that of Athens ; opulence had had its civilizing effect upon their manners, and familiarity with the Latin classics upon their native dialect. At the time that Alaric was carrying his ravages from Greece into Lombardy, the fierce Burgundians and other Germans, to the number of 200,000 fighting men, fell upon Gaul ; and, to use the words of a well-known historian, "the scene of peace and plenty was suddenly changed into a desert, and the prospect of the smoking ruins could alone distinguish the solitude of nature from the work of man." The barbarian torrent, sweeping away cities and inhabitants, spread from the banks of the Rhine to the Atlantic and the Pyrenees. Fifty years later a great portion of the same region was devastated with like excesses by the Huns ; and in the intervals between the two visitations, destructive inroads, or rather permanent occupations, were effected by the Franks and Burgundians.

As to Italy, with Rome as a centre, its multiplied

miseries are too familiarly known to require illustration.
I need not enlarge upon the punishments inflicted on it
by German, Goth, Vandal, Hun, and Byzantine, who in
those same centuries overspread the country, or upon the
destruction of cities, villas, monasteries, of every place
where literature might be stored, or civilization transmitted to posterity. Barbarians occupied the broad
lands of nobles and senators ; mercenary bands infested
its roads, and tyrannized in its towns and its farms ;
even the useful arts were gradually forgotten, and the
ruins of its cities sufficed for the remnant of its citizens.
Such was the state of things, when, after the gleam of
prosperity and hope which accompanied the Gothic
ascendency, at length the Lombards came down in the
age of St. Gregory, a more fatal foe than any before, to
complete the desolation of the garden of Europe.

Encompassed then by such calamities, present and
hereditary, through such a succession of centuries and in
such a multitude of countries, where should the Roman
Pontiff look for a refuge of learning, sacred and profane,
when the waters were out all over the earth ? What
place shall he prepare, what people shall he choose, with
a view to a service, the more necessary in proportion as
it was difficult ? I know where it must be ; doubtless
in the old citadel of science, which hitherto had been
safe from the spoiler,—in Alexandria. The city and
country of the Ptolemies was inviolate as yet ; the Huns
had stopped on its eastern, the Vandals at its western
boundary ; and though Athens and Rhodes, Carthage
and Madaura, Cordova and Lerida, Marseilles and
Bordeaux, Rheims and Milan, had been overrun by the
barbarian, yet the Museum, the greatest of all schools,
and the Serapeum, the largest of all libraries, had recovered from the civil calamities which had pressed upon

them in a past century, and were now far away from the
Lombard, who was the terror of the age. It would have
been a plausible representation in the age of St. Gregory
and his immediate successors, if human wisdom had been
their rule of judgment, that they must strengthen their
alliance, since they could not with ambitious and
schismatical Constantinople, at least with Alexandria.
Yet to Alexandria they did not turn, and in fact, before
another century had passed, Alexandria itself was taken,
and her library burned by an enemy, more hostile to religion, if not to philosophy, even than the Lombard.
The instinctive sagacity of Popes, when troubled about
the prospective fortunes of the human race, did not look
for a place of refuge to a city which had done great
services to science and literature in its day, but was soon
to fall for ever.

The weak and contemptible things of this world are
destined to bring to nought and to confound the strong
and noble. High up in the North, above the continent
of Europe, lay two sister islands, ample in size, happy in
soil and climate, and beautiful in the face of the country.
Alas! that the passions of man should alienate from one
another, those whom nature and religion had bound together! So far away were they from foreign foes, that
one of them the barbarians had never reached, and though
a solitary wave of their invasion has passed over the
other, it was not destined to be followed by a second for
some centuries. In those days the larger of the two
was called Britannia, the lesser Hibernia. The latter
was then the seat of a flourishing Church, abounding
in the fruits of sanctity, learning, and zeal; the former, at least its southern half, had formed part of the
Empire, had partaken both of its civilization and its
Christianity, but had lately been occupied, with the ex-

termination of its population, by the right wing of the
great barbaric host which was overrunning Europe. I
need but allude to a well-known history ; we all recollect
how some of those pagan invaders of Britain were brought
for sale in the slave-market at Rome, and were taken as
samples of their brethren by the great Saint so often
mentioned in these pages, who succeeded at length in
buying the whole race, not for any human master, but
for Christ.

St. Gregory, who, amid his troubles at Rome, engaged
in this sacred negotiation, was led by his charity towards
a particular people, to do a deed which resulted in sur-
passing benefits on the whole of Christendom. Here
lay the answer to the prayers and questionings of himself and other holy Popes, and the solution of the great
problem which had so anxiously perplexed their minds.
The old world was to pass away, and its wealth and
wisdom with it ; but these two islands were to be the
storehouse of the past and the birthplace of the future.
A divine purpose ruled his act of love towards the
Anglo-Saxon race ; or, if we ascribe it to the special
prescience proper to Popes, then we may say that it was
inspired by what he saw already realized in his own day,
in the instance of the remarkable people planted from
time immemorial on the sister island. For the Celt, it
cannot be denied, preceded the Anglo-Saxon, not only
in his Christianity, but in his cultivation and custody of
learning, religious and secular, and again in his special
zeal for its propagation ; and St. Gregory, in evangeliz-
ing England, was but following the example of St.
Celestine. Let us on this point hear the words of an
historian, who has high claims on the respect and gratitude of this generation :—

" During the sixth and seventh centuries," says Dr.

Döllinger, "the Church of Ireland stood in the full beauty of its bloom. The spirit of the gospel operated amongst the people with a vigorous and vivifying power; troops of holy men, from the highest to the lowest ranks of society, obeyed the counsel of Christ, and forsook all things, that they might follow Him. There was not a country of the world, during this period, which could boast of pious foundations or of religious communities equal to those that adorned this far distant island. Among the Irish, the doctrines of the Christian Religion were preserved pure and entire; the names of heresy or of schism were not known to them; and in the Bishop of Rome they acknowledged and venerated the Supreme Head of the Church on earth, and continued with him, and through him with the whole Church, in a never interrupted communion. The schools in the Irish cloisters were at this time the most celebrated in all the West; and in addition to those which have been already mentioned, there flourished the Schools of St. Finian of Clonard, founded in 530, and those of Cataldus, founded in 640. Whilst almost the whole of Europe was desolated by war, peaceful Ireland, free from the invasions of external foes, opened to the lovers of learning and piety a welcome asylum. The strangers, who visited the island, not only from the neighbouring shores of Britain, but also from the most remote nations of the Continent, received from the Irish people the most hospitable reception, a gratuitous entertainment, free instruction, and even the books that were necessary for their studies. Thus in the year 536, in the time of St. Senanus, there arrived at Cork, from the Continent, fifteen monks, who were led thither by their desire to perfect themselves in the practices of an ascetic life under Irish directors, and to study the Sacred Scriptures in the school established near that city. At a later period, after the year 650, the Anglo-Saxons in particular passed over to Ireland in great numbers for the same laudable purposes. On the other hand, many holy and learned Irishmen left their own country to proclaim the faith, to establish or to reform monasteries in distant lands, and thus to become the benefactors of almost every nation in Europe."

Such was St. Columba, who is the Apostle of the Northern Picts in the sixth century; such St. Fridolin in the beginning of the same century, who, after long labours in France, established himself on the Rhine; such the far-famed Columbanus, who, at its end, was sent with twelve of his brethren to preach in France, Burgundy, Switzerland, and Lombardy, where he died. All these great acts and encouraging events had taken place, ere yet the Anglo-Saxon race was converted to the faith, or at least while it was still under education for its own part in extending it; and thus in the contemporary or previous labours of the Irish the Pope found an encouragement, as time went on, boldly to prosecute that conversion and education of the English, which was beginning with such good promise,—and not only in the labours of the Irish missionaries elsewhere, for in England itself, as the writer I have quoted intimates, they had already commenced their evangelical work.

"The foundation of many of the English sees," he says, "is due to Irishmen; the Northumbrian diocese was for many years governed by them, and the abbey of Lindisfarne, which was peopled by Irish monks and their Saxon disciples, spread far around it its all-blessing influence. These holy men served God and not the world; they possessed neither gold nor silver, and

all that they received from the rich, passed through
their hands into the hands of the poor. Kings and
nobles visited them from time to time, only to pray in
their churches, or to listen to their sermons ; and as
long as they remained in the cloisters, they were content with the humble food of the brethren. Wherever
one of these ecclesiastics or monks came, he was received by all with joy; and whenever he was seen
journeying across the country, the people streamed
around him to implore his benediction and to hearken
to his words. The priests entered the villages only to
preach or to administer the sacraments ; and so free
were they from avarice, that it was only when compelled by the rich and noble, that they would accept
lands for the erection of monasteries. Thus has Bede
described the Irish bishops, priests, and monks of
Northumbria, although so displeased with their custom
of celebrating Easter. Many Anglo-Saxons passed
over to Ireland, where they received a most hospitable
reception in the monasteries and schools. In crowds,
numerous as bees, as Aldhelm writes, the English went
to Ireland, or the Irish visited England, where the
Archbishop Theodore was surrounded by Irish scholars.
Of the most celebrated Anglo-Saxon scholars and
saints, many had studied in Ireland ; among these were
St. Egbert, the author of the first Anglo-Saxon mission
to the pagan continent, and the blessed Willebrod, the
Apostle of the Frieslanders, who had resided twelve
years in Ireland. From the same abode of virtue and
of learning, came forth two English priests, both named
Ewald, who in 690, went as messengers of the gospel
to the German Saxons, and received from them the
crown of martyrdom. An Irishman, Mailduf, founded,
in the year 670, a school, which afterwards grew into

the famed Abbey of Malmesbury; among his scholars was St. Aldhelm, afterwards Abbot of Malmesbury, and first bishop of Sherburne or Salisbury, and whom, after two centuries, Alfred pronounced to be the best of the Anglo-Saxon poets."

The seventh and eighth centuries are the glory of the Anglo-Saxon Church, as are the sixth and seventh of the Irish. As the Irish missionaries travelled down through England, France, and Switzerland, to lower Italy, and attempted Germany at the peril of their lives, converting the barbarian, restoring the lapsed, encouraging the desolate, collecting the scattered, and founding churches, schools, and monasteries, as they went along; so, amid the deep pagan woods of Germany and round about, the English Benedictine plied his axe and drove his plough, planted his rude dwelling and raised his rustic altar upon the ruins of idolatry, and then settling down as a colonist upon the soil, began to sing his chants and to copy his old volumes, and thus to lay the slow but sure foundations of the new civilization. Distinct, nay antagonistic, in character and talent, the one nation and the other, Irish and English, the one more resembling the Greek, the other the Roman, open from the first perhaps to jealousies as well as rivalries, they consecrated their respective gifts to the Almighty Giver, and, labouring together for the same great end, they obliterated whatever there was of human infirmity in their mutual intercourse by the merit of their common achievements. Each by turn could claim preëminence in the contest of sanctity and of learning. In the schools of science England has no name to rival Erigena in originality, or St. Virgil in freedom of thought; nor among its canonized women any saintly virgin to compare with St. Bridget; nor, although it has 150 saints in its calendar, can it pretend to equal that Irish multitude which the Book of Life alone is large enough to contain. Nor can Ireland, on the other hand, boast of a doctor such as St. Bede, or of an Apostle equal to St. Boniface, or of a Martyr like St. Thomas,—or of so long a catalogue of royal devotees as that of the thirty male or female Saxons who in the course of two centuries resigned their crowns, or as the roll of twenty-three kings, and sixty queens and princes, who, between the seventh and the eleventh centuries, gained a place among the saints. Yet, after all, the Irish, whose brilliancy of genius has sometimes been considered, like the Greek, to augur fickleness and change, have managed to persevere to this day in the science of the saints, long after their ancient rivals have lost the gift of faith.

But I am not writing a history of the Church, nor of England or Ireland ; but tracing the fortunes of literature. When Charlemagne arose upon the Continent, the special mission of the two islands was at an end ; and accordingly Ragnor Lodbrog with his Danes then began his descents upon their coasts. Yet they were not superseded, till they had formally handed over the tradition of learning to the schools of France, and had written their immortal names on one and the same page of history. The Anglo-Saxon Alcuin was the first Rector, and the Irish Clement the second, of the Studium of Paris. In the same age the Irish John was sent to found the school of Pavia ; and, when the heretical Claudius of Turin exulted over the ignorance of the devastated Churches of the Continent, and called the Synod of Bishops, who summoned him, "a congregation of asses," it was no other than the Irish Dungall, a monk of St. Denis, who met and overthrew the presumptuous railer.

9

CHAPTER XI.

A CHARACTERISTIC OF THE POPES.

ST. GREGORY THE GREAT.

DETACHMENT, as we know from spiritual books, is a rare and high Christian virtue; a great Saint, St. Philip Neri, said that, if he had a dozen really detached men, he should be able to convert the world. To be detached is to be loosened from every tie which binds the soul to the earth, to be dependent on nothing sublunary, to lean on nothing temporal; it is to care simply nothing what other men choose to think or say of us, or do to us; to go about our own work, because it is our duty, as soldiers go to battle, without a care for the consequences; to account credit, honour, name, easy circumstances, comfort, human affections, just nothing at all, when any religious obligation involves the sacrifice of them. It is to be as reckless of all these goods of life on such occasions, as under ordinary circumstances we are lavish and wanton, if I must take an example, in our use of water,—or as we make a present of our words without grudging to friend or stranger,—or as we get rid of wasps or flies or gnats, which trouble us, without any sort of compunction, without hesitation before the act, and without a second thought after it.

Now this "detachment" is one of the special ecclesiastical virtues of the Popes. They are of all men most exposed to the temptation of secular connections; and, as history tells us, they have been of all men least subject to it. By their very office they are brought across every form of earthly power; for they have a mission to high as well as low, and it is on the high, and not the low, that their maintenance ordinarily depends. Cæsar ministers to Christ; the framework of society, itself a divine ordinance, receives such important aid from the sanction of religion, that it is its interest in turn to uphold religion, and to enrich it with temporal gifts and honours. Ordinarily speaking, then, the Roman Pontiffs owe their exaltation to the secular power, and have a great stake in its stability and prosperity. Under such circumstances, any men but they would have had a strong leaning towards what is called "Conservatism;" and they have been, and are, of course Conservatives in the right sense of the word; that is, they cannot bear anarchy, they think revolution an evil, they pray for the peace of the world and the prosperity of all Christian States, and they effectively support the cause of order and good government. The name of Religion is but another name for law on the one hand, freedom on the other; and at this very time, who are its professed enemies, but Socialists, Red Republicans, Anarchists, and Rebels? But a Conservative, in the political sense of the word, commonly signifies something else, which the Pope never is, and cannot be. It means a man who is at the top of the tree, and knows it, and means never to come down, whatever it may cost him to keep his place there. It means a man who upholds government and society and the existing state of things,—not because it exists,—not because it is good and desirable, because it is established, because it is a benefit to the population, because it is full of promise for the future,—but rather because he himself is well off in consequence of it, and because to take care of number one is his main political principle.   It means a man who defends religion, not for religion's sake, but for the sake of its accidents and externals ; and in this sense Conservative a Pope can never be, without a simple betrayal of the dispensation committed to him.   Hence at this very moment the extreme violence against the Holy See, of the British legislature and constituency, and their newspapers and other organs, mainly because it will not identify the cause of civil government with its own, because, while it ever benefits this world, it ever contemplates the world unseen.

So much, however, is intelligible enough ; but there is a more subtle form of Conservatism, by which ecclesiastical persons are much more likely to be tempted and overcome, and to which also the Popes are shown in history to be superior.   Temporal possessions and natural gifts may rightly be dedicated to the service of religion; however, since they do not lose their old nature by being invested by a new mission or quality, they still possess the pabulum of temptation, and may be fatal to ecclesiastical " detachment."   To prefer the establishment of religion to its purity, is Conservatism, though in a plausible garb.   It was once of no uncommon occurrence for saintly Bishops, in the time of famine or war, to break up the Church plate and sell it, in order to relieve the hungry or to redeem the captives by the sums which it brought them.   Now this proceeding was not unfrequently urged against them in their day as some great offence; but the Church has always justified them. Here we see, as in a typical instance, both the wrong Conservatism, of which I am speaking, and its righteous repudiation.   This fault is an over-attachment to the ecclesiastical establishment, as such;—to the seats of its power, to its holy places, its sanctuaries, churches, and palaces,

—to its various national hierarchies, with their several prescriptions, privileges, and possessions,—to traditional lines of policy, precedent, and discipline,—to rules and customs of long standing. But a great Pontiff must be detached from everything save the deposit of faith, the tradition of the Apostles, and the vital principles of the divine polity. He may use, he may uphold, he may and will be very slow to part with, a hundred things which have grown up, or taken shelter, or are stored, under the shadow of the Church ; but, at bottom, and after all, he will be simply detached from pomp and etiquette, secular rank, secular learning, schools and libraries, Basilicas and Gothic cathedrals, old ways, old alliances, and old friends. He will be rightly jealous of their loss, but still he will "know nothing but" Him whose Vicar he is ; he will not stake his fortunes, he will not rest his cause, upon any one else :—this is what he will do, and what he will not do, as in fact the great Popes of history have shown, in their own particular instances, on so many and various occasions.

Take the early Martyr-Popes, or the Gregories and the Leos ; whether they were rich or poor, in power or in persecution, they were simply detached from every earthly thing save the Rock of Peter. This was their adamantine foundation, their starting-point in every enterprise, their refuge in every calamity, the point of leverage by which they moved the world. Secure in this, they have let other things come and go, as they would ; or have deliberately made light of what they had, in order that they might gain what they had not. They have known, in the fulness of an heroic faith, that, while they were true to themselves and to their divinely appointed position, they could not but "inherit the earth," and that, if they lost ground here, it was only to make progress elsewhere. Old men usually get fond of old habits; they cannot imagine, understand, relish any thing to which they are not accustomed. The Popes have been old men; but, wonderful to say, they have never been slow to venture out upon a new line, when it was necessary, and had ever been looking about, sounding, exploring, taking observations, reconnoitring, attempting, even when there was no immediate reason why they should not let well alone, as the world would say, or even when they were hampered with difficulties at their door so great, that you would think that they had no time or thought to spare for anything in the distance. It is but a few years ago that a man of eighty, of humble origin, the most Conservative of Popes, as he was considered, with disaffection and sedition upheaving his throne, was found to be planning missions for the interior of Africa, and, when a moment's opportunity was given him, made the most autocratical of Emperors, the very hope of Conservatives, the very terror of Catholics, quail beneath his glance. And, thus independent of times and places, the Popes have never found any difficulty, when the proper moment came, of following out a new and daring line of policy (as their astonished foes have called it), of leaving the old world to shift for itself and to disappear from the scene in its due season, and of fastening on and establishing themselves in the new.

I am led to this line of thought by St. Gregory's behaviour to the Anglo-Saxon race, on the break-up of the old civilization. I am not mentioning our people for their own sake, but because they furnish an instance of that remarkable trait in the character of Popes, of which I have been speaking. One would have thought that in the age of St. Gregory, a Pope had enough to do in living on from day to day, without troubling himself about the future ; that, with the Lombard at his doors, he would not have had spirit to set about converting the English ; and that, if he was anxious about the preservation of learning, he would have looked elsewhere than to the Isles of the North, for its refuge in the evil day. Why, I repeat, was it not easier, safer, and more feasible for him to have made much of the prosperous, secure, and long established schools of Alexandria, when the enemy went about him plundering and burning ? He was not indeed on the best terms with Constantinople ; Antioch was exposed to other enemies, and had suffered from them already ; but Alexandria was not only learned and protected, but was a special ally of the Holy See ; yet Alexandria was put aside for England and Ireland.

With what pertinacity of zeal does Gregory send his missionaries to England ! with what an appetite he waits for the tidings of their progress ! with what a relish he dwells over the good news, when they are able to send it ! He wrote back to Augustine in words of triumph :—" ' Gloria in excelsis Deo,' " he says, " ' et in terrâ pax hominibus bonæ voluntatis !' for the Grain of corn died and was buried in the earth, that It might reign with a great company in Heaven,—by whose death we live, by whose weakness we are strengthened, by whose sufferings we escape suffering, by whose love we are seeking in Britain brothers whom we know not of, by whose gift we find those whom, not knowing, we were seeking. Who can describe the joy, which was caused in the hearts of all the faithful here, on the news that the English nation, by the operation of the grace of the Omnipotent God, and by your labours, my brother, had been rescued from the shades of error and overspread with the light of holy faith! If on one penitent there is great joy in heaven, what, think we, does it become, when a whole people has turned from its error, and has betaken itself to faith, and condemned the evil it has done by repenting of the doing! Wherefore in this joy of Heaven and Angels, let me say once more the very Angels' words, 'Gloria in excelsis Deo, et in terrâ pax hominibus bonæ voluntatis.'"

What were these outer barbarians to Gregory? how could they relieve him or profit him? What compensation could they make for what the Church was then losing, or might lose in future? Yet he corresponds with their king and queen, urges them to complete what they had so happily begun, reminds Bertha of St. Helena, and what St. Helena did for the Romans, and Ethelbert, of the great Constantine; informs them of the satisfaction which their conversion had given to the Imperial Court at Constantinople, and sends them sacred presents from the Apostle Peter. Nay he cannot keep from talking of these savages, apropos of anything whatever, for they have been running in his head from the day he first saw them in the slave market; and he makes the learned Church of Alexandria the special partner of his joy upon this contemptible victory. The Patriarch Eulogius had been telling him of his own success in reclaiming the heretics of Alexandria, and he sends him a piece of good news in return:—"As I am well aware," he says, "that in the midst of your own good deeds, you rejoice in those of others, I will repay you for the kindness of your tidings by telling you something of the same sort." And then he goes on to speak of the conversion of the English, "who are situated in a corner of the world," as if their gain was comparable to that of the educated and wealthy persons whom Eulogius had been reconciling to the Church. Nay, lest he should take too much credit for his own success, and grow vain upon it, he attributes it to the prayers of the Alexandrians, or at least of their Bishop, all that way off, as if the Angles and Jutes were anything at all to the city of the Ptolemies! "On Christmas Day," he says, "more than 10,000 of them were baptized. I tell you of it, that you may know, that, while your words avail for your own people, your prayers avail for the ends of the earth. For you are by prayer where you are not, while you manifest yourself by holy labours where you are."

Time went on, and the Popes showed less and less disposition to cling to past associations, or to confide in existing establishments, or to embarrass themselves in political engagements. When they were in trouble, their old friends could not, or would not, help them. Rome was almost deserted ; no throng of pilgrims mounted to the threshold of the Apostles ; no students flocked to the schools. The Pope sat in the Lateran desolate, till at length news was brought him that one foreigner had made his appearance. Whence did he come ? from the north ; from beyond the sea ; he was one of those barbarians whom his Holiness's predecessor, Gregory of blessed memory, had converted. The pilgrim came, and he went. An interval, and then, I think, a second pilgrim-student came : and who was he ? Why, he was an Englishman too. A fact to remember ! one of these young barbarians is worth a thousand of those time-servers of Constantinople. Our predecessor must have acted under some special guidance, when, at the beginning of this century, he set his heart upon the worshippers of Thor and Woden ! So, when a vacancy occurs in the see of Canterbury, Pope Vitalian determines to place in it a man of his own choosing, one whom so faithful a people deserves. The Irish, says the Pope, have done much for England, but teachers it still needs. Moreover, local teaching, even the best, and though saints be its organs, is apt to have something in it of local flavour, and needs from time to time to be refreshed from the founts of apostolical tradition. We will pick out, says he, the best specimens of learning and science, which the length and breadth of southern Christendom can furnish, and send them thither, uniting the excellence of different lands, under the immediate sanction of Rome. In this eclecticism, he did but follow St. Gregory himself, who, when Augustine represented to him, that, while faith was one, customs were so various, made answer, "I wish that, wherever you find anything especially pleasing to Almighty God, whether in the Roman, or Gallic, or any other Church, you would be at pains to select it, and introduce it into the English Church, as yet new in the faith."

This line of proceeding in ecclesiastical matters was carried on by Vitalian into the province of learning. The Greek colonies of Syria and Asia Minor, and the Roman settlements upon the African coast, had been, almost from their first formation, flourishing schools of education ; and now that they were perishing under the barbarism of the Saracens, they were abandoned, by such professors and students as remained, for the cities of Italy. In a convent near Naples lived Adrian, an African ; at Rome there was a monk, named Theodore, from Tarsus in Cilicia ; both of them were distinguished for their classical, as well as their ecclesiastical attainments; and while Theodore had been educated in Greek usages, Adrian represented the more congenial and suitable traditions of the West. Of these two, Theodore, at the age of sixty-six, was made Primate of England, while Adrian was placed at the head of the monastery of Canterbury. Passing through France, in their way to their post of duty, they delayed there a while at the command of the Pope, to accustom themselves to the manners of the North ; and at length they made their appearance in England, with a collection of books, Greek classics, and Gregorian chants, and whatever other subjects of study may be considered to fill up the interval between those two. They then proceeded to found schools of secular, as well as of sacred learning throughout the south of the island ; and we are assured by St. Bede, that many of their scholars were as well acqainted with Latin and Greek, as with their native tongue. One of these schools in Wiltshire, as the legend goes, was, on that account, called "Greeklade," since corrupted into Cricklade, and, migrating afterwards to Oxford, was one of the first elements of its University. Meanwhile, one of those Saxon pilgrims, who had been so busy at Rome, having paid, it is said, as many as five visits to the Apostles, went up to the north of the country. Before the coming of the two foreign teachers, Benedict Biscop had been Abbot of Canterbury ; but, making way for Adrian, he took himself and his valuable library, the fruit of his travels, to Wearmouth in Northumberland, where he founded a Church and monastery.

These details are not out of place in the history of Universities ; but I introduce them here as illustrating a point, much to be remarked, in the character of the Popes. It is a common observation of Protestants, that, curiously enough, the Holy See is weakest at home when it is strongest abroad, and they derive some consolation to themselves, I do not know what, from the fact. So it is ; this weakness is an alleviation of the annoyance which they feel at the sight of a world succumbing to the See of Peter. They say, that after all, if the world has its mortifications, Peter, on the other hand, has his discomforts too. True, the gates of hell do not prevail against him, but then he is driven about from place to place, thrown into prison, and, if he escapes the sword of Herod, it is only that Nero may inflict upon him the more cruel death of crucifixion. What then is Peter's but a hollow power, which profits the possessor nothing, though it be ecumenical ? Does it secure him health, strength, wealth, comfort, ease, that he is revered by millions whom he never saw ? He inherits the earth, but is not certain of a roof to sleep under, or a grave to be buried in. How is he better off, because his name is mentioned in Mass in the Brazils, and his briefs are read in the Churches of Cochin China ?

This taunt does but supply a boast to the Catholic, and has a moral for the philosopher. Certainly Popes are unlike any other old and infirm men that ever were. To clutch at what is within their reach, to keep tight hold of what they have, to believe what they see, to care that things should last their own time, to let posterity shift for itself, to hate disturbance and turmoil, to compound for present peace, to be sceptical about improvements, to be averse to new plans, in a word, to live in sense, not in imagination, is the characterstic of old statesmen, old lawyers, and old traders. They cannot throw their minds into new ideas ; they cannot realize the views of others ; they cannot move out of their life-long position, nor advance one inch towards any other. Were such a person,—sound, safe, sensible, sagacious, experienced,—at the elbow of Pope Gregory, or his successors of the seventh century, he would have advised him to fall back upon Constantinople, to come to an understanding with the Imperial Court, to link his fortunes with those of an effete civilization, and to allow the encroachments of an ambitious hierarchy ; as to Franks, and Frisons, and Westphalians, and Saxons, and Burgundians, and Visigoths, and Scots, to leave them to themselves. I need not take an imaginary instance ; not many years have passed since a *Nuncio* of the Holy See passed through England in his way from Portugal to Rome, and had an interview with a great warrior now no more, a man of preternatural sagacity in his own sphere of thought,—which was not Catholic and divine. When the ecclesiastic in question asked the great man's advice what the then Pope's policy should be, the Duke abruptly replied, " Let him catch hold of the coat-tail of Austria, and hang on as hard as he can." Yes, and the able statesmen of each age would have said the same to Gregory the First, to the Second, the Third, and the Seventh, as well as to Gregory the Sixteenth,—to Julius, Silverian, and Martin ; they would have counselled the Vicar of Christ a safe and pleasant course, " fallentis semita vitæ," which would have ended in some uninhabitable desert, or some steep precipice, far from the haunts of man.

When Pius the Ninth, foiled in his attempt to better the civil condition of his states, from the worthlessness both of his materials and his instruments, was a fugitive and exile at Gaeta, the Protestant public jeered and mocked at him, as one whose career was over and whose candle was put out. Yet he has but supplied a fresh and the latest instance, later there cannot be, of the heroic detachment of Popes, and has carried down the tradition of St. Peter into the age of railroads and newspapers. But we are entering upon a new part of the subject, which our present limits will not admit, and which we cannot perhaps treat without freedom.

CHAPTER XII.

MORAL OF THAT CHARACTERISTIC OF THE POPES.
PIUS THE NINTH.

A GREAT personage, within the last fifteen years, sent his advice to the Pope "to make sure of the coat-tail of Austria, and hold on." Austria is a great and religious power ; she inherits the prerogatives of the German Empire and the titles of the Cæsars. There must ever be relations of a very peculiar kind between the Holy See and the Holy Roman Empire. Nevertheless, when the time came for taking advantage of his advice, the Pope did just the reverse. He made light of this master of political wisdom, and showed his independence of Austria ;—not that he did not honour Austria, but that he honoured the Rock of Peter more. And what has been the consequence ? he has simply gained by his fidelity to his position. Austria has been far more truly the friend and protector, the child and servant of the Pope than before ; she has repealed the Josephine statutes, so injurious to the Church, and has opened her territories to the full religious influences of the Holy See. Here is an instance of what I have called "ecclesiastical detachment," and of its working.

Again, a revolution breaks out in Europe, and a deep scheme is laid to mix up the Pope in secular politics of a contrary character. He is to be the head of Italy, to range himself against the sovereigns of Europe, and to carry all things before him in the name of Religion. He steadily refuses to accept the insidious proposal ; and at length he is driven out of his dominions, because, while he would ameliorate their condition, he would do so as a Father and a Prince, and not as the tool of a conspiracy. However, not many months pass, and the party of disorder is defeated, and he goes back to Rome again. Rome is his place ; but it is little to him whether he is there or away, compared with the duty of fidelity to his Trust.

Once more, the power which restores him to his country, presumes ; and insists upon his modelling his temporal polity upon the unecclesiastical principles of a foreign code. France, too, as Austria, is a great Catholic power ; the eldest-born of the Church ; the representative of the coming civilization, as Austria is the heir of the past ; but France was not likely to gain for the Code of a dead Emperor, what that Emperor, in the plenitude of his living genius and authority, could not compass for it. The Pope refuses to subject himself to France, as he had refused to subject himself to Austria ; and what is the consequence? It is the old story ; a new Emperor arises, with the name, and without the religious shortsightedness, of his great predecessor. He has the wisdom to run a race with Austria in doing honour to the Church, and France professes Catholicity with an ardour unknown to her since the reign of Louis the Fourteenth.

These are times of peculiar difficulty and delicacy for the Church. It is not as in the middle ages, or as in the ante-Nicene period, when right and wrong were boldly marked out, and there was a broad line between them, and little chance of mistaking one for the other. In such times detachment was another name for faith ;

it was scarcely a virtue, substantive and *sui generis ;* for attachment to any temporal possession or advantage then was practically nothing else than apostasy. Things are otherwise now ; it has not, therefore, fallen to the lot of many Popes, to have such opportunities as Pius the Ninth, of resisting temptation, of resigning himself to the political weakness incident to the Holy See, of falling back calmly upon its traditionary principles, of rejecting the arguments for innovating upon its true position, and in consequence of attaining so rapid a triumph after deplorable reverses. When Pius was at Gaeta and Portici, the world laughed on hearing that he was giving his attention to the theological bearings of the doctrine of the Immaculate Conception. Little fancying what various subject-matters fall all at once under a Pope's contemplation, and are successively carried out into effect, as circumstances require ; little dreaming of the intimate connexion of these matters with each other, even when they seem most heterogeneous ; or that a belief touching the Blessed Virgin might have any influence upon the fortunes of the Holy See ; the wise men of the day concluded from the Pope's Encyclical about that doctrine, that he had, what they called, given up politics in disgust, and had become a harmless devotee or a trifling school-divine. But soon they heard of other acts of the Holy Father ; they heard of his interposition in the East ; of his success in Spain ; of his vigilant eye directed towards Sardinia and Switzerland in his own neighbourhood, and towards North and South America in another hemisphere ; of his preachers spreading through Germany ; of his wonderful triumphs, already noticed, in Austria and France ; of his children rising as if out of the very earth in England ; and of their increasing moral strength in Ireland, in proportion

to her past extraordinary sufferings ; of the hierarchies of
England and Holland, and of the struggle going forward
on the Rhine ; and then they exchanged contempt for
astonishment and indignation, saying that it was intolerable that a potentate who could not keep his own, and
whose ease and comfort at home were not worth a
month's purchase, should be so blind to his own interests
as to busy himself with the fortunes of Religion at the
ends of the earth.

And an additional feeling arose, which it is more to
our purpose to dwell upon, They were not only angry,
but they began to fear. It may strike one at first with
surprise, that, in the middle of the nineteenth century,
in an age of professed light and liberality, so determined
a spirit of persecution should have arisen, as we experience it, in these countries, against the professors of the
ancient faith. Catholics have been startled, irritated,
and depressed, at this unexpected occurrence ; they have
been frightened, and have wished to retrace their steps ;
but after all, far from suggesting matter for alarm or
despondency, it is nothing more or less than a confession
on the part of our adversaries, how strong we are, and
how great our promise. It is the expression of their
profound misgiving that the Religion which existed long
before theirs, is destined to live after it. This is no
mere deduction from their acts ; it is their own avowal.
They have seen that Protestantism was all but extinct
abroad ; they have confessed that its last refuge and fortress was in England ; they have proclaimed aloud, that,
if England was supine at this moment, Protestantism
was gone. Twenty years ago England could afford, as
much in contempt as in generosity, to grant to Catholics
political emancipation.* Forty or fifty years ago it was

* It is not meant that contempt was the feeling towards Ireland at the

a common belief in her religious circles, that the great Emperor, with whom she was at war, was raised up to annihilate the Popedom. But from the very grave of Pius the Sixth, and from the prison of Pius the Seventh, from the very moment that they had an opportunity of showing to the world their familiarity with that ecclesiastical virtue of which I have said so much, the Catholic movement began. In proportion to the weakness of the Holy See at home, became its influence and its success in the world. The Apostles were told to be prudent as serpents, and simple as doves. It has been the simplicity of the Sovereign Pontiffs which has been their prudence. It is their fidelity to their commission, and their detachment from all secular objects, which has given them the possession of the earth.

I am not pursuing the line of thought which has engaged me in my last chapter and my present without a drift. It bears directly upon the subject which leads me to write at all ; and it has an important bearing, intelligible even to the historian and philosopher, so that reason and experience would be able to extort from him what faith could not obtain. Even a pagan ought to be able to prophecy that our University is destined for great things. I look back at the early combats of Popes Victor and Stephen ; I go on to Julius and Celestine, Leo and Gregory, Boniface and Nicholas ; I pass along the Middle Ages, down to Paul the Third and Pius the Fifth ; and thence to the two Popes of the same name, who occupy the most eventful fifty years, since Christianity was; and I cannot shut my eyes to the fact, that the Sovereign Pontiffs have had a gift, proper to them-

time, which influenced Sir Robert Peel, or of the Government of the day, but that it was the feeling of the Peelite and Whig parties towards Catholicism as such. *Vide* infr. ch. xix. p. 231.

selves, of understanding what is good for the Church, and what Catholic interests require. And in the next place, I find that this gift exercises itself in an absolute independence of secular politics, and a detachment from every earthly and temporal advantage, and pursues its end by uncommon courses, and by unlikely instruments, and by methods of its own. I see that it shines the brightest, and is the most surprising in its results, when its possessors are the weakest in this world and the most despised ; that in them are most vividly exemplified the Apostle's words, in the most beautiful and most touching of his Epistles, " We have this treasure in earthen vessels, that the excellency may be of the power of God, and not of us ; as needy, yet enriching many, as having nothing, and possessing all things."

I get these two points of history well into my mind ; and then I shut my book, and look at the world before my eyes. I see an age of transition, the breaking up of the old and the coming in of the new ; an old system shattered some sixty years ago, and a new state of things scarcely in its rudiments as yet, to be settled perhaps some centuries after our time. And it is a special circumstance in these changes, that they extend beyond the past historical platform of human affairs ; not only is Europe broken up, but other continents are thrown open, and the new organization of society aims at embracing the world. It is a day of colonists and emigrants ;— and, what is another most pertinent consideration, the language they carry with them is English, which consequently, as time goes on, is certain, humanly speaking, to extend itself into every part of the world. It is already occupying the whole of North America, whence it threatens to descend upon South ; already is it the language of Australia, a country large enough in the course of centuries to rival Europe in population; already it has become the speech of a hundred marts of commerce, scattered over the East, and, even where not the mother tongue, it is at least the medium of intercourse between nations. And, lastly, though the people who own that language is Protestant, a race preëminently Catholic has adopted it, and has a share in its literature; and this Catholic race is, at this very time, of all tribes of the earth, the most fertile in emigrants both to the West and the South. These are the manifest facts of the day, which would be before our eyes, whether the Pope had anything to say to them or no. The English language and the Irish race are overrunning the world.

When then I consider what an eye the Sovereign Pontiffs have for the future ; and what an independence in policy and vigour in action have been the characteristics of their present representative ; and what a flood of success, mounting higher and higher, has lifted up the Ark of God from the beginning of this century ; and then, that the Holy Father has definitely put His finger upon Ireland, and selected her soil as the seat of a great Catholic University, to spread religion, science, and learning, wherever the English language is spoken; when I take all these things together,—I care not what others think, I care not what others do, God has no need of men,—oppose who will, shrink who will, I know and cannot doubt that a great work is begun. It is no great imprudence to commit oneself to a guidance which never yet has failed ; nor is it surely irrational or fanatical to believe, that, whatever difficulties or disappointments, reverses or delays, may be our lot in the prosecution of the work, its ultimate success is certain, even though it seemed at first to fail,—just as the greatest measures in former times have been the most tardy in execution, as Athanasius triumphed though he passed away before Arianism, and Hildebrand died in exile, that his successors might enter into his labours.

CHAPTER XIII.

SCHOOLS OF CHARLEMAGNE.

PARIS.

AS nations are inscrutably brought within the sacred fold, and inscrutably cast without it, so are they used, while within it, in this way or that, according to the supreme will and for the greater glory of Him, who has brought them into being from some common ancestor, and holds them together by unity of government or by traditionary ideas. One Catholic nation is high in the world, another low ; one rises and expands into an Empire, another is ever in the position of subject or even dependent. England and Ireland were, in the darkest age of Christian history, the conservators of sacred and profane knowledge : not, however, for any merit of their own, but according to the good pleasure of their Maker : and, when the time came, in His counsels, for the revival of learning on the Continent, then He dispensed with their ministry, and put them aside. It is a remarkable fact, to which I have already alluded, that the appearance of the Danes off the coasts of England and Ireland, the destroyers in both islands of religion and science, synchronizes with the rise of Charlemagne, the founder of modern civilization.

Christianity, which hitherto might be considered as a quality superinduced upon the face of society, now became the element, out of which society grew into shape and reached its stature. The Church had battled with the Roman Empire, and had eventually vanquished it; but, while she succeeded in teaching it the new song of the Saints, she did not demand of it that flexibility of the organs of speech which only exists in the young. It was the case of an old man learning a foreign tongue; its figure, gait, attitudes, and gestures, and in like manner its accent, belonged to an earlier time. Up to the point at which a change was imperative, its institutions were suffered to remain just as they had been in paganism; christianized just so far as to enable them to work christian-wise, however cumbrously or circuitously. And as to the system of education in particular, I suppose the primary, or, as they may be better called, the grammar schools, as far as they were not private speculations, were from first to last in the hands of the State; state-institutions, first of pagan, then of mixed education. I do not mean to say that there are no traces in Christian antiquity of a higher pattern of education, in which religion and learning were brought together,—as in the method of teaching which St. Basil and St. Gregory brought into Asia Minor from Alexandria, and in the Benedictine Schools of Italy; but I am speaking of what the Christian Empire did, and again of what the Church exacted from it. She for the most part confined herself to the education of the clergy, and their ecclesiastical education; the laity and secular learning seem to have been still, more or less, in the charge of the State;—not, however, as if this were the best way of doing things, as the attempts I have spoken of bore testimony, but, because she found things in a certain state, and used them as best she could. Her aim was to make the Empire Christian, not to revolutionize it; and, without a revolution of society, the typical form of a Christian polity could not have been given to the institutions of Rome. But, when society was broken up, and had to be constructed over again, the case was different; it would have been as preposterous, under such circumstances, not to build it up upon Catholicity, as it would have been to attempt to do so before. Henceforth, as all government, so all education, was to be founded on Revealed Truth. Secular teaching was to be united to sacred ; and the Church had the supervision both of lay students and of profane learning.

The new state of things began in the Frankish Empire; but it is observable how Rome after all strikes the key note of the movement. Charlemagne indeed betook himself to the two Islands of the North for a tradition ; Alcuin, an Englishman, was at the head of his educational establishments; he came to France, not with sacred learning only, but with profane ; he set up schools for laity as well as clergy ; but whence was it that he in turn got the tradition which he brought ? His history takes us back to that earlier age, when Theodore of Tarsus, Primate of England, brought with him thither from Rome the classics, and made Greek and Latin as familiar to the Anglo-Saxons as their native tongue. Alcuin was the scholar of Bede and Egbert ; Egbert was educated in the York school of Theodore, and Bede in that of Benedict Biscop and of John precentor of the Vatican Basilica. Here was the germ of the new civilization of Europe, which was to join together what man had divided, to adjust the claims of Reason and of Revelation, and to fit men for this world while it trained them for another. Charlemagne has the glory of commencing this noble work ; and, whether his school at Paris be called a University or not, he laid down principles of which a University is the result, in that he aimed at educating all classes, and undertook all subjects of teaching.

In the first place, however, he turned his attention to the Episcopal Seminaries, which seem to have been institutions of the earliest times of Christianity, though they had been in great measure interrupted amid the dissolution of society consequent upon the barbarian inroads, as various passages in these Essays have already suggested. His restoration lasted for four centuries, till Universities rose in their turn, and indirectly interfered with the efficiency of the Seminaries, by absorbing them into the larger institution. This inconvenience was set right at a later period by the Council of Trent, whose wise regulations were in turn the objects of the jealousy of the Josephism of the last century, which used or rather abused the University system to their prejudice. The present policy of the Church in most places has been to return to the model both of the first ages and of Charlemagne.

To these Seminaries he added, what I have spoken of as his characteristic institution, grammar and public schools, as preparatory both to the Seminaries and to secular professions. Not that they were confined to grammar, for they recognized the *trivium* and *quadrivium*; but grammar, in the sense of literature, seems to have been the principle subject of their teaching. These schools were established in connexion with the Cathedral or the Cloister; and they received ecclesiastics and the sons of the nobility, though not to the exclusion of the poorer class.

Charlemagne probably did not do much more than this; though it was once the custom to represent him as the actual founder of the University of Paris. But great creations are not perfected in a day; without doing everything which had to be done, he did many things, and opened the way for more. It will throw light upon his position in the history of Christian education, to

quote a passage from the elaborate work of Bulæus, on
the University of Paris, though he not unnaturally claims
the great Emperor as its founder, maintaining that he
established, not only the grammar or public schools
already mentioned, but the higher *Studia Generalia.*
This assumption, well founded or not, will not make his
account less instructive, if, as I have supposed, Charlemagne certainly introduced ideas and principles, of which
the University was the result.

"It is observable," says Bulæus, "that Charles, in
seeking out masters, had in view, not merely the education of his own family, but of his subjects generally,
and of all lovers of the Christian Religion ; and wished
to be of service to all students and cultivators of the
liberal arts. It is indeed certain that he sought out
learned men and celebrated teachers from all parts of the
world, and induced them to accept his invitation by rewards and honours, on which Alcuin lays great stress.
'I was well aware, my Lord David,' he says, 'that it has
been your praiseworthy solicitude ever to love and to
extol wisdom ; and to exhort all men to cultivate it, nay,
to incite them by means of prizes and honours ; and out
of divers parts of the world to bring together its lovers
as the helpers of your good purpose ; among whom you
have taken pains to secure even me, the meanest slave
of that holy wisdom, from the extremest boundaries of
Britain.'

"It is evident hence, that Charles's intention was not
to found any common sort of schools, such, that is, as
would have required only a few instructors, but public
schools, open to all, and possessing all kinds of learning.
Hence the necessity of a multiplicity of Professors, who
from their number and the remoteness of their homes
might seem a formidable charge, not only to the court,

or to one city, but even to his whole kingdom. Such is the testimony of Eginhart, who says : 'Charles loved foreigners and took great pains to support them; so that their number was a real charge, not to the Palace alone, but even to the realm. Such, however, was his greatness of soul, that the burden of them was no trouble to him, because even of great inconveniences the praise of munificence is a compensation.'

" Charles had in mind to found two kinds of schools, less and greater. The less he placed in Bishops' palaces, canons' cloisters, monasteries, and elsewhere ; the greater, however, he established in places which were public, and suitable for public teaching ; and he intended them, not only for ecclesiastics, but for the nobility and their children, and on the other hand for poor scholars too ; in short, for every rank, class, and race.

" He seems to have had two institutions before his mind, when he contemplated this object; the first of them was the ancient schools. Certainly, a man of so active and inquiring a mind as Charles, with his intercourse with learned persons and his knowledge of mankind, must have been well aware that in former ages these two kinds of schools were to be found everywhere ; the one kind few in number, public, and of great reputation, possessed moreover of privileges, and planted in certain conspicuous and central sites. Such was the Alexandrian in Egypt, the Athenian in Greece ; such under the Roman Emperors, the schools of Rome, of Constantinople, of Berytus, which are known to have been attended by multitudes, and amply privileged by Theodosius, Justinian, and other princes ; whereas the other kind of schools, which were far more numerous, were to be found up and down the country, in cities, towns, villages, and were remarkable neither in number of students nor in name.

" The other pattern which was open to Charles was to be found in the practice of monasteries, if it really existed there. The Benedictines, from the very beginning of their institution, had applied themselves to the profession of literature, and it has been their purpose to have in their houses two kinds of school, a greater or a less, according to the size of the house ; and the greater they wished to throw open to all students, at a time when there were but few laymen at all who could teach, so that externs, seculars, laymen, as well as clerics, might be free to attend to them. However, true as it was that boys, who were there from childhood intrusted to the monks, bound themselves by no vow, but could leave when they pleased, marry, go to court, or enter the army, still a great many of the cleverest of them were led, either by the habits which they acquired from their intercourse with their teachers, or by their persuasion, to embrace the monastic life. And thus, while the Church in consequence gained her most powerful supports, the State, on the other hand, was wanting in men of judgment, learning, and experience, to conduct its affairs. This led very frequently to kings choosing monks for civil administration, because no others were to be found capable of undertaking it.

" Charles then, consulting for the common good, made literature in a certain sense secular, and transplanted it from the convents to the royal palace ; in a word, he established in Paris a Universal School like that at Rome.

" Not that he deprived Monks of the license to teach and profess, though he certainly limited it, from a clear view that that variety of sciences, human and profane, which secular academies require, is inconsistent with the profession and devotion of ascetics ; and accordingly, in conformity to the spirit of their institute, it was his wish that the lesser schools should be set up or retained in the Bishops' palaces and monasteries, while he prescribed the subjects which they were to teach. The case was different with the schools which are higher and public, which, instead of multiplying, he confined to certain central and celebrated spots, not more than to three in his whole empire—Paris, and in Italy, Pavia and Bologna."

Such certainly was the result, in which his reforms ended, even though they did not reach it ; and they may be said to have directly tended to it, considering that it was their characteristic, in contrast with the previous schools, to undertake the education of laity as well as clergy, and secular studies as well as religious. But, after all, it was not in an Emperor's power, though he were Charlemagne, to carry into effect in any case, by the resources peculiar to himself, so great an idea as a University. Benefactors and patrons may supply the framework of a Studium Generale ; but there must be a popular interest and sympathy, a spontaneous coöperation of the many, the concurrence of genius, and a spreading thirst for knowledge, if it is to live. Centuries passed before these conditions were supplied, and then at length about the year 1200 a remarkable intellectual movement took place in Christendom ; and to it must be ascribed the development of Universities, out of the public or grammar schools, which I have already described. No such movement could happen, without the rise of some deep and comprehensive philosophy ; and, when it rose, then the existing Trivium and Quadrivium became the subjects, and the existing seats of learning the scene, of its victories ; and next the curiosity and enthusiasm, which it excited, attracted larger and larger numbers to places which were hitherto but local centres of education. Such a gathering of students, such a systematizing of knowledge, are the notes of a University.

The increase of members and the multiplication of sciences both involved changes in the organization of the Schools of Charlemagne; and of these the increase of members came first. Hitherto there had been but one governor over the students, who were but few at the most, and came from the neighbourhood; but now the academic body was divided into Nations, according to the part of Europe from which they joined it, and each Nation had a head of its own, under the title of Procurator or Proctor. There were traces of this division, as we have seen in a former Chapter, in Athens; where the students were arranged under the names of Attic, Oriental, Arab, and Pontic, with a protector for each class. In like manner, in the University of Paris, there were four nations, first, the French, which included the middle and south of France, Spain, Italy, and Greece; secondly, the English, which, besides the two British islands, comprehended Germany and Scandinavia; thirdly, the Norman; and fourthly, the Picards, who carried with them the inhabitants of Flanders and Brabant. Again, in the University of Vienna, there were also four nations,—Austria, the Rhine, Hungary, and Bohemia. Oxford recognized only two Nations; the north English, which comprehended the Scotch; and the South English, which comprehended the Irish and Welsh. The Proctors of the Nations both governed and represented them; the double office is still traceable, unless the recent Act of Parliament has destroyed it, in the modern constitution of Oxford, in which the two Proctors on the one hand represent the Masters of

Arts in the Hebdomadal Board, and on the othei have in their hands the discipline of the University.

And as Nations and their Proctors arose out of the metropolitan character of a University, to which students congregated from the farthest and most various places, so are Faculties and Deans of Faculties the consequence of its encyclopedic profession. According to the idea of the institutions of Charlemagne, each school had its own teacher, who was called Rector, or Master. In Paris, however, where the school was founded in St. Genevieve's, the Chancellor of that Church became the Rector, and he kept his old title of Chancellor in his new office. Elsewhere the head of the University was called Provost. However, it was not every one who would be qualified to profess even the Seven Sciences, of which the old course of instruction consisted, though the teaching was only elementary, and to become the Rector, Chancellor, or Provost, of the University ; but, when these sciences became only parts of a whole system of instruction, which demanded in addition a knowledge of philosophy, scholastic theology, civil and canon law, medicine, natural history, and the Semitic languages, no one person was equal to the undertaking. The Rector fell back from the position of a teacher to that of a governor ; and the instruction was divided among a board of Doctors, each of whom represented a special province in Science. This is the origin of Deans of Faculties ; and, inasmuch as they undertook among themselves one of those departments of academical duty, which the Chancellor or Rector had hitherto fulfilled, they naturally became his Council. In some places the Proctors of the Nations were added. Thus, in Vienna the Council consisted of the Four Deans of Faculties, and the Four Proctors.

As Nations preceded Faculties, we may suppose that Degrees, which are naturally connected with the latter, either did not enter into the original provisions of a University, or had not the same meaning as afterwards. And this seems to have been the case. At first they were only testimonials that a resident was fit to take part in the public teaching of the place ; and hence, in the Oxford forms still observed, the Vice-Chancellor admits the person taking a degree to the " lectio " of certain books. Degrees would not at that time be considered mere honours or testimonials, to be enjoyed by persons who at once left the University and mixed in the world. The University would only confer them for its own purposes ; and to its own subjects, for the sake of its own subjects. It would claim nothing for them external to its own limits ; and, if so, only used a power obviously connate with its own existence. But of course the recognition of a University by the State, not to say by other Universities, would change the import of degrees, and, since such recognition has commonly been granted from the first, degrees have seldom been only what they were in their original idea ; but the formal words by which they are denoted, still preserve its memory. As students on taking degrees are admitted " legere et disputare," so are they called " Magistri," that is, of the *schools ;* and " Doctors," that is, teachers, or in some places " Professors," as the letters S.T.P. show, used instead of D.D.

It will be observed that the respective distributions into Faculties and into Nations are cross-divisions. Another cross-division, on which I shall not now enter, is into Colleges and Halls.

I conclude by enumerating the characteristic distinctions, laid down by Bulæus, between the public or grammar schools founded by Charlemagne, and the Universities into which eventually some of them grew, or, as he would say, which Charlemagne also founded.

First, he says, they differ from each other *ratione disciplinæ*. The Scholæ Minores only taught the Trivium (*viz.*, Grammar, Logic, Rhetoric,) and the Quadrivium, (*viz.*, Geometry, Astronomy, Arithmetic, and Music,) the seven liberal Arts ; whereas the Scholæ Majores added Medicine, Law, and Theology.

Next, *ratione loci ;* for the Minores were many and everywhere, but the Majores only in great cities, and few in number. I have already remarked on the physical and social qualifications necessary for a place which is to become the seat of a great school of learning : Bulæus observes, that the Muses were said to inhabit mountains, Parnassus or Helicon, spots high and healthy and secured against the perils of war, and that the Academy was a grove; though of course he does not forget that the place must be accessible too, and in the highway of the world. "That the city of Paris," he says, "is ample in size, largely frequented, healthy and pleasant in site, there can be no doubt." Frederic the Second spoke the general sentiment, when he gave as a reason for establishing a University at Naples, the convenience of the sea coast and the fertility of the soil. We are informed by Matamorus, in his account of the Spanish Universities,* that Salamanca was but the second site of its University, which was transferred thither from Palencia on account of the fertility of the neighbourhood, and the mildness of its climate. And Mr. Prescott speaks of Alcala being chosen by Cardinal Ximenes as the site for his celebrated foundations, because " the salubrity of the air, and the sober, tranquil complexion of the scenery, on the beautiful

---

* Hispan. Illustr. t. 2, p. 801.

11

borders of the Henares, seemed well suited to academic study and meditation."

The third difference between the greater and lesser schools lies *ratione fundatorum.* Popes, Emperors, and Kings, are the founders of Universities ; lesser authorities in Church and State are the founders of Colleges and Schools.

Fourthly, *ratione privilegiorum.* The very notion of a University, I believe, is, that it is an institution of privilege. I think it is Bulæus who says, " Studia Generalia cannot exist without privileges, any more than the body without the soul. And in this all writers on Universities agree." He reduces those privileges to two heads, " Patrocinium" and " Præmium ; " and these, it is obvious, may be either of a civil or an ecclesiastical nature. There were formerly five Universities endowed with singular privileges : those of Rome, of Paris, of Bologna, of Oxford, and of Salamanca ; but Antony à Wood quotes an author who seems to substitute Padua for Rome in this list.

Lastly, the greater and lesser schools differ *ratione regiminis.* The head of a College is one ; but a University is a " respublica litteraria."

CHAPTER XIV.

SUPPLY AND DEMAND:
THE SCHOOLMEN.

IT is most interesting to observe how the foundations of the present intellectual greatness of Europe were laid, and most wonderful to think that they were ever laid at all. Let us consider how wide and how high is the platform of our knowledge at this day, and what openings in every direction are in progress,—openings of such promise, that, unless some convulsion of society takes place, even what we have attained, will in future times be nothing better than a poor beginning; and then on the other hand, let us recollect that, seven centuries ago, putting aside revealed truths, Europe had little more than that poor knowledge, partial and uncertain, and at best only practical, which is conveyed to us by the senses. Even our first principles now are beyond the most daring conjectures then; and what has been said so touchingly of Christian ideas as compared with pagan, is true in its way and degree of the progress of secular knowledge also in the seven centuries I have named.

> "What sages would have died to learn,
> [Is] taught by cottage dames."

Nor is this the only point in which the revelations of science may be compared to the supernatural revelations of Christianity. Though sacred truth was delivered once for all, and scientific discoveries are progressive, yet there is a great resemblance in the respective histories of Christianity and of Science. We are accustomed to point to the rise and spread of Christianity as a miraculous fact, and rightly so, on account of the weakness of its instruments, and the appalling weight and multiplicity of the obstacles which confronted it. To clear away those obstacles was to move mountains ; yet this was done by a few poor, obscure, unbefriended men, and their poor, obscure, unbefriended followers. No social movement can come up to this marvel, which is singular and archetypical, certainly ; it is a divine work, and we soon cease to admire it in order to adore. But there is more in it than its own greatness to contemplate ; it is so great as to be prolific of greatness. Those whom it has created, its children who have become such by a supernatural power, have imitated, in their own acts, the dispensation which made them what they were ; and, though they have not carried out works simply miraculous, yet they have done exploits sufficient to bespeak their own unearthly origin, and the new powers which had come into the world. The revival of letters by the energy of Christian ecclesiastics and laymen, when everything had to be done, reminds us of the birth of Christianity itself, as far as a work of man can resemble a work of God.

Two characteristics, as I have already had occasion to say, are generally found to attend the history of Science:—first, its instruments have an innate force, and can dispense with foreign assistance in their work ; and secondly, these instruments must exist and must begin to act, before subjects are found who are to profit by their action. In plainer language, the teacher is strong, not in the patronage of great men, but in the intrinsic value and attraction of what he has to communicate ; and next, he must come forward and advertise himself, before he can gain hearers. This I have expressed before, in saying that a great school of learning lived in demand and supply, and that the supply must be before the demand. Now, what is this but the very history of the preaching of the Gospel ? who but the Apostles and Evangelists went out to the ends of the earth without patron, or friend, or other external advantage which could insure their success ? and again, who among the multitude they enlightened, would have called for their aid unless they had gone to that multitude first, and offered to it blessings which up to that moment it had not heard of ? They had no commission, they had no invitation, from man ; their strength lay neither in their being sent, nor in their being sent for ; but in the circumstances that they had that with them, a divine message, which they knew would at once, when it was uttered, thrill through the hearts of those to whom they spoke, and make for themselves friends in any place, strangers and outcasts as they were when they first came. They appealed to the secret wants and aspirations of human nature, to its laden conscience, its weariness, its desolateness, and its sense of the true and the divine ; nor did they long wait for listeners and disciples, when they announced the remedy of evils which were so real.

Something like this were the first stages of the process by which in medieval Christendom the structure of our present intellectual elevation was carried forward. From Rome as from a centre, as the Apostles from Jerusalem, went forth the missionaries of knowledge, passing to and fro all over Europe ; and, as metropolitan sees were the record of the presence of Apostles, so did Paris, Pavia, and Bologna, and Padua, and Ferrara, Pisa and Naples, Vienna, Louvain, and Oxford, rise into Universities at the voice of the theologian or the philosopher. Moreover, as the Apostles went through labours untold, by sea and land, in their charity to souls ; so, if robbers, shipwrecks, bad lodging, and scanty fare are trials of zeal, such trials were encountered without hesitation by the martyrs and confessors of science. And as Evangelists had grounded their teaching upon the longing for happiness natural to man, so did these securely rest their cause on the natural thirst for knowledge : and again as the preachers of Gospel peace had often to bewail the ruin which persecution or dissension had brought upon their flourishing colonies, so also did the professors of science often find or flee the ravages of sword or pestilence in those places, which they themselves perhaps in former times had made the seats of religious, honourable, and useful learning. And lastly, as kings and nobles have fortified and advanced the interests of the Christian faith without being necessary to it, so in like manner we may enumerate with honour Charlemagne, Alfred, Henry the First of England, Joan of Navarre, and many others, as patrons of the schools of learning, without being obliged to allow that those schools could not have progressed without such countenance.

These are some of the points of resemblance between the propagation of Christian truth and the revival of letters ; and, to return to the two points, to which I have particularly drawn attention, the University Professor's confidence in his own powers, and his taking the initiative in the exercise of them, I find both these distinctly recognized by Mr. Hallam in his history of Literature. As to the latter point, he says, "The schools of Charlemagne were designed to lay the basis of a learned education,

for which there was at that time no sufficient desire" :—
that is, the supply was prior to the demand. As to the
former : "In the twelfth century," he says, "the *impetuosity* with which men *rushed* to that source of what
they deemed wisdom, the great University of Paris,
*did not depend upon academical privileges or eleemosynary
stipends,* though these were undoubtedly very effectual
in keeping it up. The University *created patrons, and
was not created by them*":—that is, demand and supply
were all in all.

A story of the age of Charlemagne will serve in
illustration. We are told that two wandering Irish
students were brought by British traders to the coast of
France. There, observing the eagerness with which
those hawkers of perishable merchandize were surrounded by the populace, they imitated them by crying
out, "Who wants wisdom ? here is wisdom on sale ! this
is the store for wisdom !" till a sensation was created, and
they were sent for and taken into favour by the great
Emperor.

The professors of Greece and Rome, though pursuing
the same course, had an easy time of it, compared with
the duties, which, at least in the earlier periods or in
certain localities, fell upon the medieval missionaries of
knowledge. The pagan teachers might indeed be told
to quit the city, whither they had come, on their outrag-
ing its religious sentiments or arousing its political
jealousy ; but still they were received as superior beings
by the persons in immediate contact with them, and
what they lost in one place they regained in another.
On the contrary, as the cloister alone gave birth to the
revivers of knowledge, so the cloister alone prepared them
for their work. There was nothing selfish in their aim,
nothing cowardly in their mode of operation. It was

generosity which sent them out upon the public stage ; it was ascetic practice which prepared them for it. Afterwards, indeed, they received the secular rewards of their exertions ; but even then the general character of the intellectual movement remained as before. " The Doctors," says Fleury in his Discourses, " being sure of finding in a certain town occupation with recompense for their labours, established themselves there of their own accord ; and students, in like manner, sure to find there good masters with all the commodities of life, assembled there in crowds from all parts, even from distant countries. Thus they came to Paris from England, from Germany and all the North, from Italy, from Spain."

Bec, a poor monastery of Normandy, set up in the eleventh century by an illiterate soldier, who sought the cloister, soon attracted scholars to its dreary clime from Italy, and transmitted them to England. Lanfranc, after-wards Archbishop of Canterbury, was one of these, and he found the simple monks so necessitous, that he opened a school of logic to all comers, in order, says William of Malmesbury, " that he might support his needy monas-tery by the pay of the students." The same author adds, that " his reputation went into the most remote parts of the Latin world, and Bec became a great and famous Academy of letters." Here is an instance of a commencement without support, without scholars, in order to attract scholars, and in them to find support. William of Jumièges, too, bears witness to the effect, powerful, sudden, wide spreading, and various, of Lanfranc's advertisement of himself. The fame of Bec and Lanfranc, he says, quickly penetrated through the whole world ; and " clerks, the sons of dukes, the most esteemed masters of the Latin schools, powerful laymen, high nobles, flocked to him." What words can more strikingly attest the enthusiastic character of the movement which he began, than to say that it carried away with it all classes ; rich as well as poor, laymen as well as ecclesiastics, those who were in that day in the habit of despising letters, as well as those who might wish to live by them ?

It was about a century after Lanfrac that from this same monastery of Bec came forth another Abbot, and he another Lombard, to begin a second movement, in a new science, in these same northern regions, especially in England. This was the celebrated Vacarius, or Bacalareus, who from the proximity of his birthplace to Bologna, seems to have gained that devotion to the study of the Law which he ultimately kindled in Oxford. Lanfranc had lectured in logic; Vacarius lectured in law. Bologna, which is celebrated in history for its cultivation of this august science, was one of the earliest, if not the earliest, of Universities, as far as historical evidence is to decide the question. Its University was commenced a little later than the first years of the School of Bec ; and affords us an observable instance, first, of the self-originating, independent character of the scientific movement, —then, of the influence and attraction it exerted on the people,—and lastly, of the incidental difficulties through which it slowly advanced in the course of many years to its completion. There Irnerius, or Warner, according to Muratori, is found at the end of the eleventh century, and opened a school of civil law. In the next century canon law was added; in the first years of the thirteenth, the school of grammar and literature ; and a few years later, those of theology and medicine. Fifty years later, it had ten thousand students under its teaching, numbers of whom had come all across sea and mountain from England; so strong and encompassing was the sentiment.

And as Englishmen at that time sought Italy, so in turn, I say, did Vacarius a native of Italy, seek England. Selden completes the parallel between him and Lanfranc, by making him Archbishop of Canterbury, after which he retired again to Bec.   However, to England he came, and to Oxford; and there, he effected a revolution in the studies of the place, and that on the special ground of the definite drift and direct usefulness of the science in which he was a proficient.   As in the case of Lanfranc, not one class of persons, but "rich and poor," says Wood, "gathered around him."   The professors of Arts were thrown into the shade.   Their alarm was increased by the rival zeal with which the medical science was prosecuted, and the aspect of things got in course of years so threatening, that the Holy See was obliged to interfere.   If knowledge is power, it also may be honour and wealth; hence the couplet, expressive of the feeling of the day,

> " Dat Galenus opes, dat Justinianus honores,
>   Sed Genus et Species, cogitur ire pedes."

It was indeed the Faculty of Arts which constituted the staple, as it may be called, of a University; Arts, as seems to be commonly allowed, constituted a University; and by Arts are understood the studies comprised in the Trivium and Quadrivium, that is, (as I have said before), Grammar, Rhetoric, Logic, Arithmetic, Geometry, Astronomy, and Music.   These were inherited from the ancient world, and were the foundation of the system which was then in course of formation. But the life of Universities lay in the new sciences, not indeed superseding, but presupposing Arts, viz., those of

Theology, Law, Medicine, and in subordination to them, of Metaphysics, Natural History, and the languages. I have been speaking of the law movement, as it may be called ; now, about the same time that Vacarius came to Oxford, Robert Pullus or Pulleyne came thither too from Exeter, just about the time of St. Anselm, and gave the same sort of impulse to biblical learning, which Vacarius gave to law. "From his teaching," says the Osney Chronicle, "the Church both in England and in France gained great profit." Leland says, that he lectured daily, "and left no stone unturned to make the British youth flourish in the sacred tongues." "Multitudes" are said to have come to hear him, and his fame spread to Rome, whither Pope Innocent the Second sent for him. Celestine the Second made him a Cardinal, and Lucius the Second his Chancellor. He was an intimate friend of St. Bernard's, and his influence extended to Cambridge as well as to Paris.

At Cambridge the intellectual movement had already commenced, and with similar phenomena in its course. These points, indeed, are so enveloped in obscurity, and on the other hand have so intimate a bearing on the sensibilities, now as keen as ever, of rival schools, that I, who look on philosophically, a member neither of Cambridge nor of Oxford nor of Paris, "turbantibus æquora ventis," find it necessary to state that, in what I shall say, I am determining nothing to the prejudice of the antiquity or precedence of any of those seats of learning. I take the account given us by Peter of Blois, merely as a *specimen* of the way in which the present fabric of knowledge was founded and reared, as a picture in miniature of the great medieval revival, whatever becomes of its historical truth. As a mere legend, it is sufficient for my purpose ; for historical legends and fictions are made according to what is probable, and after the pattern of precedents.

The author, then, to whom I have referred, says, that Jeoffred, or Goisfred, had studied at Orleans ; thence he came to Lincolnshire, and became Abbot of Croyland ; whence he sent to his manor of Cotenham, near Cambridge, four of his French fellow-students and monks, one of them to be Professor of sacred learning, the rest teachers in Philosophy, in which they were excellently versed. At Cambridge they hired a common barn, and opened it as a School of the high Sciences. They taught daily. By the second year the number of hearers was so great, from town and country, "that not the biggest house and barn that was," says Wood, "nor any church whatsoever, sufficed to hold them." They accordingly divided off into several schools, and began an arrangement of classes, some of which are enumerated. "Betimes in the morning, brother Odo, a very good grammarian and satirical poet, read grammar to the boys, and those of the younger sort, according to the doctrine of Priscian ;" at one o'clock "a most acute and subtle Sophist taught the elder sort of young men Aristotle's Logic ;" at three o'clock, "brother William read a lecture on Tully's Rhetoric and Quintilian's Flores ;"—such was the beginning of the University of Cambridge. And " Master Gislebert upon every Sunday and Holyday, preached the Word of God to the people ;"—such was the beginning of its University Church.

It will be observed, that in these accounts, Scripture comment is insisted on, and little or nothing is said of Theology, properly so called. Indeed, it was not till the next (the thirteenth) century, that Theology took that place, which Law assumed about a century before

it. Then it was that the Friars, especially the Dominicans, were doing as much for Theology, as Irnerius,
Vacarius, and the Bolognese Professors did for Law.
They raised it (if I may so speak of what is divine) to
the dignity of a science. " They had such a succinct
and delightful method," says Wood, speaking of them
at Oxford, " in the whole course of their discipline, quite
in a manner different from the sophistical way of the
Academicians, that thereby they did not only draw to
them the Benedictines and Carthusians, to be sometimes their constant auditors, but also the Friars of St.
Augustine."

Here we have another exemplification of the same
great principles of the movement which we have noticed
elsewhere; its teachers came from afar, and they depended, not on kings and great men for their support,
but on the enthusiasm they created. " The reputation
of the school of Paris," says Fleury, " increased consider-
ably at the commencement of the twelfth century under
William of Champeaux and his disciples at St. Victor's.
At the same time Peter Abelard came thither and taught
them with great *éclat* the humanities and the Aristotelic
philosophy. Alberic of Rheims taught there also; and
Peter Lombard, Hildebert, Robert Pullus, the Abbot
Rupert, and Hugh of St. Victor; Albertus Magnus
also, and the Angelic Doctor." How few of these professors at Paris were fellow-countrymen! Albert was
from Germany, St. Thomas from Naples, Peter Lombard from Novara, Robert Pullus from Exeter in England. The case had been the same three centuries
before in the same great school. Charlemagne brought
Peter of Pisa from Pavia for Grammar; Alcuin from
England for Rhetoric and Logic; Theodore and Benedict from Rome for Music; John of Melrose, who was

afterwards at the head of the schools at Pavia, and Claudius Clemens, two Scots, from Ireland. Ireland, indeed, contributed a multitude of teachers to the continental schools, and the more, because, great as was the fame of its earlier schools, it had now no University of its own. The names of its professors have not commonly been preserved, though Erigena and Scotus by their very titles show their origin : but we find that, when the Emperor Frederick the Second would set up the University of Naples, he sent all the way to Ireland for the learned Peter to be its first Rector ; and an author, quoted in Bulæus, speaks of "the whole of Ireland, with its *family* of philosophers, despising the dangers of the sea," and migrating to the south. Such was the famous Richard of St. Victor, whose very title marks his connexion with the great school of Paris.

There is a force in the words, "despising the dangers of the sea." We in this degenerate age sometimes shrink from the passage between Holyhead and Kingstown, when duty calls for it ; yet before steam-boats, almost before seaworthy vessels, we find those zealous scholars, both Irish and English, voluntarily exposing themselves to the winds and waves, from their desire of imparting and acquiring knowledge. Not content with one teacher, they went from place to place, according as in each there was preëminence in a particular branch of knowledge. We have in St. Athanasius's life of St. Antony a beautiful account of the diligence with which the young hermit went about " like the bee," as his great biographer says, in quest of superiority in various kinds of virtue. From one holy man, he says (I quote from memory), the youth gained courtesy and grace, from another gentleness, from another mortification, from another humility ; and in a similar way did the knights errant of science go about, seeking indeed sometimes rivals to encounter, but more frequently patterns and instructors to follow. As then the legendary St. George or St. Denys wandered from place to place to achieve feats of heroism, as St. Antony or Sulpicius Severus went about on pilgrimage to holy hermits, as St. Gregory Nazianzen visited Greece, or St. Jerome traversed Europe, and became, the one the most accomplished theologian, the other the first Biblical scholar of his age, so did the medieval Doctors and Masters go the round of Universities in order to get the best instruction in every school.

The famous John of Salisbury (as Mr. Sharon Turner tells us) went to Paris for the lectures of Abelard just on the death of Henry the First, and with him he studied logic. Then for dialectics he went to Alberic and to the English Robert for two years. Then for three years to William de Conchia for grammar; afterwards to Richard Bishop for a renewed study of grammar and logic, going on to the Quadrivium; and to the German Harduin. Next he restudied rhetoric, which he had learned from Theodoric, and more completely from Father Elias. Meanwhile, he supported himself by teaching the children of noble persons, and became intimate with Adam, an Englishman, a stout Aristotelian, and returned to logic with William of Soissons and Gilbert. Lastly, he studied theology with Robert Pulleyne or Pullus, already mentioned, and Simon de Poissy. Thus he passed as many as twelve years. Better instances, however, than his, as introducing a wider extent of travel, are those already referred to, of St. Thomas, or Vacarius, or Lanfranc, or St. Anselm, or John of Melrose.

The ordinary course of study, however, lay between

the schools of Paris and Oxford, in which was almost centered the talent of the age, and which were united by the most intimate connexion. Happy age, whatever its other inconveniences, happy so far as this, that religion and science were then a bond of union, till the ambition of monarchs and the rivalry of race dissolved it! Wood gives us a list of thirty-two Oxford professors of name, who in their respective times went to teach in Paris, among whom were Alexander Hales, and the admirable St. Edmund, afterwards Archbishop of Canterbury,—St. Edmund, who, as St. Anselm and St. Thomas, shows us how sanctity is not inconsistent with preëminence in the schools. On the other hand, Bulæus recites the names of men, even greater, viewed as a body, who went from Oxford to Paris, not to teach, but to be taught ; such as St. Thomas of Canterbury, St. Richard, St. Gilbert of Sempringham, Giraldus Cambrensis, Gilbert the Universal, Haimo, Richard de Barry, Nicholas Breakspeare, afterwards Pope, Nekam, Morley, and Galfredus de Vinsalfe. So intimate, or to use the word, so *thick* were Paris and Oxford at this time, as to give occasion to this couplet,

> " Et procul et propius jam Francus et Anglicus æquè,
> Norunt Parisiis quid feceris, Oxoniæque."

And this continued till the time of Edward the Third, when came the wretched French wars and the Lollards, and then adieu to familiar intercourse down to this day.

I have not found the number of students in Paris; but from what I have said, one is led to expect two things of it, first, that it would be very great, next, that it would be very variable : and these inferences are confirmed by what is told us of the numbers at Oxford. In that University we read of Scotch, Irish, Welsh, French, Spanish, German, Bohemian, Hungarian, and Polish Students ; and, when it is considered, as a modern writer tells us, that they would bring with them, or require for their uses, a number of dependents in addition, such as parchment-preparers, bookbinders, stationers, apothecaries, surgeons, and laundresses, it may be understood that the whole number of matriculated persons was sometimes even marvellous, and as fluctuating in a long period as excessive at particular dates. We are told that there were in Oxford in 1209 three thousand members of the University, in 1231 thirty thousand, in 1263 fifteen thousand, in 1350 between three and four thousand, and in 1360 six thousand. This ebbing and flowing, moreover, suggests what it is all along very much to my purpose to observe, and on which, if I have the opportunity, I shall have more to say presently ; first, that the zeal for study and knowledge is sufficient indeed in itself for the being of a University ; but secondly, that it is not sufficient for its well being, or what is technically called its *integrity*.

The era of the French wars, which put an end to this free intercourse of France and England, seems for various reasons to have been the beginning of a decline in the ecumenical greatness of Universities. They lost some advantages, they gained others ; they became national bodies ; they gained much in the way of good order and in comfort ; they became rich and honourable establishments. Each age has its own character and its own wants : and we trust that in each a loving Providence shapes the institutions of the Church as they may best subserve the objects for which she has been sent into the world. We cannot tell exactly what the Catholic University ought to be at this era ; doubtless neither the

University of Scotus, nor that of Gerson, in matters of detail ; but, if we keep great principles before us, and feel our way carefully, and ask guidance from above for every step we take, we may trust to be able to serve the cause of truth in our day and according to our measure, and in that way which is most expedient and most profitable, as our betters did in ages past and gone.

CHAPTER XV.

PROFESSORS AND TUTORS.

I MAY seem in the foregoing Chapter to have relapsed into the tone of thought which created some surprise when I was speaking of Athens and the Sophists; and my good friend Richard, the Epicurean, may be upon me again, for my worship, as he will consider it, of the intellect, and my advocacy of the Professorial System. This is an additional call on me to go forward with my subject, if I can do so without wearying the reader. I say "without wearying," for I beg to assure him, if he has not already found it out for himself, that it is very difficult for any one to discuss points of ancient usage or national peculiarity, as I am doing, and to escape the dry, dull tone of an antiquarian. This is so acknowledged an inconvenience, that every now and then you find an author attempting to evade it by turning his book of learned research into a novel or a poem. I will say nothing of Thalaba or Kehama, though the various learning displayed in the notes appended to those pleasing fables, certainly suggests the idea, that the poetry may have grown out of the notes, instead of the notes being the illustration of the poetry. However, I believe it is undoubted, that Morier converted his unsaleable quarto on Persia into his amusing Hadji Baba; while Palgrave has poured out his medieval erudition by the channels of Friar Bacon and Marco Polo, and Bekker has insinuated archeology in the persons of Charicles and Gallus. Were I to attempt to do the same, whether for the grouping of facts or the relief of abstract discussion, I have reason to believe I should not displease men of great authority and judgment; but for success in such an undertaking there would be demanded a very considerable stock of details, and no small ability in bringing them to bear on principles, and working them up into a narrative. On the whole, then, I prefer to avail myself, both as counsel and as comfort, of the proverb, "Si gravis, brevis;" and to make it a point, that, weary as my reader may be, he shall not have time to go to sleep. And to-day especially, since I mean to be particularly heavy in the line of abstract discussion, I mean also to be particularly short.

I purpose, then, to state here what is the obvious safeguard of a University from the evils to which it is liable if left to itself, or what may be called, to use the philosophical term, its *integrity*. By the "integrity" of anything is meant a gift superadded to its nature, without which that nature is indeed complete, and can act, and fulfil its end, but does not find itself, if I may use the expression, in easy circumstances. It is in fact very much what easy circumstances are in relation to human happiness. This reminds me of Aristotle's account of happiness, which is an instance in point. He specifies two conditions, which are required for its integrity; it is indeed a state of *mind*, and in its nature independent of externals, yet he goes on (inconsistently we might say, till we make the distinction I am pointing out), he goes on, I say, after laying down that "man's chief good is an energy of the soul according to virtue," to add, "besides this, *throughout the greater part of life*,—for, as neither one swallow, nor one day, makes a spring, so neither does one day, nor a short time, make a man blessed and happy." Here then is one condition, which in some sense may be said to fall under the notion of "integrity ;" but, whether this be so or not, a second condition, which he proceeds to mention, seems altogether to answer to it. After repeating that "happiness is the best and most noble and most delightful of energies according to virtue," he adds : "at the same time *it seems to stand in need of external goods*, for it is impossible, or at least not easy, to perform praiseworthy actions without external means, for many things are performed, as it were by instruments, by friends, and wealth, and political power. But men deprived of some things, as of noble birth, fine progeny, a fine form, have a flaw in their happiness ; for he is not altogether capable of happiness, who is deformed in his body, or of mean birth, or deserted and childless ; and still less so, perhaps, if he have vicious children, or if they were dear and dutiful, and have died. Therefore it seems to demand such prosperity as this ; whence some arrange good fortune in the same class with happiness ; but others virtue."

This then is how we may settle the dispute which my Epicurean introduced, and which has been carried on at intervals in the British Universities for the last fifty years. It began in the pages of the Edinburgh Review, which at that time might in some sense be called the organ of the University of Edinburgh. Twenty years later, if my memory does not play me false, it was renewed in the same quarter ; then it was taken up at Cambridge, and lately it was going on briskly between some of the most able members of the University of Oxford. Now what has been the point of dispute between the combatants ? This,—whether a University should be conducted on the system of Professors, or on the system of Colleges and College Tutors. By a College was understood something more than the Museum of Alexandria, or such corporations among ourselves, as are established for Medicine, Surgery, Engineering, or Agriculture. It was taken to mean a place of residence for the University student, who would there find himself under the guidance and instruction of Superiors and Tutors, bound to attend to his personal interests, moral and intellectual. The party of the North and of progress have ever advocated the Professorial system, as it has been called, and have pointed in their own behalf to the practice of the middle ages and of modern Germany and France; the party of the South and of prescription have ever stood up for the Tutorial or collegiate system, and have pointed to Protestant Oxford and Cambridge, where it has almost or altogether superseded the Professorial. Now I have on former occasions said enough to show that I am for both views at once, and think neither of them complete without the other. I admire the Professor, I venerate the College. The Professorial system fulfils the strict idea of a University, and is sufficient for its *being*, but it is not sufficient for its *well-being*. Colleges constitute the *integrity* of a University.

This view harmonizes with what I said in a former Chapter, about Influence and Law; for though Professors may be and have been utterly without personal weight and persuasiveness, and Colleges utterly forgetful of moral and religious discipline, still, taking a broad view of history, we shall find that Colleges are to be accounted the maintainers of order, and Universities the centres of movement. It coincides, too, with what I have lately said in a Treatise on University Education,* in which a *Studium Generale* is considered first in its own nature, then as it

* Discourses on the Scope and Nature of University Education.

exists within the pale of Catholicism. "It is," I there say, "a place of teaching universal knowledge. Such is a University in its *essence* and independently of its relation to the Church. But, practically speaking, it cannot fulfil its object duly without the Church's assistance, or the Church is necessary for its *integrity ;* not that its main characters are changed by this incorporation ; it still has the office of intellectual education ; but the Church steadies it in the performance of that office." I say this passage coincides with the statements I have been making, because Colleges are the direct and special instruments, which the Church *uses* in a University, for the attainment of her sacred objects,—as other passages of the same Volume incidentally teach.

Let us then bring the real state of the case before our minds. A University is "a school of knowledge of every kind, consisting of teachers and learners from every quarter." Two or three learned men, with little or no means, make their way to some great city. They come with introductions to the Bishop, if there is no University there yet, and receive his sanction, or they get the necessary leave, and then on their own responsibility they open a school. They may, or they may not be priests ; but, any how, they are men of correct principles, in earnest, set on their work, and not careful of their own ease and interest. They do not mind where they lodge, or how they live, and their learning, zeal, and eloquence soon bring hearers to them, not only natives, but strangers to the place, travelling thither from considerable distances, on the report of the teachers who have there congregated. If the professors have but scanty means, the pupils have not more abundant ; and, in spite of their thirst for knowledge, whatever it may be, they cannot have the staidness and gravity of character, or the self-command, which years and experience have given to their teachers. They have difficulty in finding food or lodging, and are thrown upon shifts, and upon the world, for both the one and the other.

Now, it must be an extraordinary devotion to science which can save them from the consequences of a trial such as this. They lodge in garrets or cellars, or they share a room with others; they mix with the inhabitants of the place, who, if not worse, at least will not be better than the run of mankind. A man must either be a saint or an enthusiast to be affected in no degree by the disadvantages of such a mode of living. There are few people whose minds are not unsettled on being thrown out of habits of regularity ; few who do not suffer, when withdrawn from the eye of those who know them, or from the scrutiny of public opinion. How often does a religious community complain, on finding themselves in a new home, of the serious inconvenience, in a spiritual point of view, which attaches to the mere circumstance that they have not an habitation suited to the rule which they are bound to observe ! Without elbow room, without order, without tranquillity, they grieve to find that recollection and devotion have not fair play. What, then, will be the case with a number of youths of unformed minds, so little weaned from the world that their very studies are perhaps the result of their ambition, and who are under no definite obligation to be better than their neighbours, only bound by that general Christian profession, which those neighbours share with them ? The excitement of novelty or emulation does not last long ; and then the mind is commonly left a prey to its enemies, even when there is no disarrangement of daily life such as I have been describing. It is not to be expected that the Professor, whom they attend, necessitous himself, can exercise a control over such a set of pupils, even if he has any jurisdiction, or can bring his personal influence to bear upon any great number of them; or that he can see them beyond the hours in which the schools are open, or, indeed, can do much more than deliver lectures in their presence. It is certain then, that, in proportion to the popularity, whether of the Professor or the place itself, granting there will be numerous exceptions to the contrary, a mob of lawless youths will gradually be formed, after the pattern of the rioters whom Eunapius encountered and St. Basil escaped, at Athens. Nor will the state of things be substantially different, even if we suppose that, instead of the indigence I have described, the frequenters of the schools have a competency for their maintenance ; much less, if they have superfluity of means.

To these disorders, which are of certain occurrence, others may easily be added. A popular Professor will be carried away by his success, and, in proportion as his learning is profound, his talents ready, and his elocution attractive, will be in danger of falling into some extravagance of doctrine, or even of being betrayed into heresy. The teacher has his own perils, as well as the taught ; there are in his path such enemies as the pride of intellect, the aberrations of reasoning, and the intoxication of applause. The very advantages of his position are his temptation. I have spoken in a former Chapter of the superiority of oral instruction to books, in the communication of knowledge ; the following passage from an able controversialist of the day, which is intended to illustrate that superiority, incidentally suggests to us also, that, first, the speaker may suffer from the popularity of his gift, and, then, the hearer from its fascination.

" While the type," he says, " is so admirable a contrivance for perpetuating knowledge, it is certainly more expensive, and in some points of view less effective as a means of communication, than the lecture. The type is a poor substitute for the human voice. It has no means of arousing, moderating, and adjusting the attention. It has no emphasis except Italics, and this meagre notation cannot finely graduate itself to the need of the occasion. It cannot in this way mark the heed which should be specially and chiefly given to peculiar passages or words. It has no variety of manner and intonation, to show by their changes how the words are to be accepted, or what comparative importance is to be attached to them. It has no natural music to take the ear, like the human voice ; it carries with it no human eye to range, and to rivet the student when on the verge of truancy, and to command his intellectual activity by an appeal to the courtesies of life. Half the symbolism of a living language is thus lost, when it is committed to paper ; and that symbolism is the very means by which the forces of the hearer's mind can be best economized or most pleasantly excited. The lecture, on the other hand, as delivered, possesses all these instruments to win, and hold, and harmonize attention ; and above all, it imparts to the whole teaching a human character, which the printed book can never supply. The Professor is the science or subject, vitalized and humanized in the student's presence. He sees him kindle into his subject ; he sees reflected and exhibited in him, his manner, and his earnestness, the general power of the science to engage, delight, and absorb a human intelligence. His natural sympathy and admiration attract or impel his tastes and feelings and wishes for the moment into the same currents of feeling, and his mind is naturally and rapidly and insensibly strung and attuned to the strain of truth which is offered to him."*

It needs not this elegant panegyric of an Oxford Professor to inform us of the influence which eloquence can exert over an audience; I quote it rather for its able analysis of that influence. I quote it, because it forcibly suggests to the mind how fitted the talent is, first to exalt the possessor in his own eyes, and then through him to mislead his hearers. I will *cap* it, if I may use the expression, with the following histories or legends of the thirteenth century;—"Simon of Tournay, a famous Parisian doctor, one day proved in a lecture by such powerful arguments, the divinity of Christianity, that his school burst out into admiration of his ability. On this he cried out, 'Ha, good Jesus; I could, if I chose, refute Thee quite as well.'" The story goes on to say that he was instantly struck dumb. A disciple of Silo, a professor of theology, died; after a while he returned to his master from the grave, invested in a cope of fire, inscribed all over with philosophical theses. A drop of his sweat fell upon the professor's hand, and burned it through. This cope lay on him as a punishment for intellectual pride."†

Considerations such as this, are sufficiently suggestive of the dangers of the Professorial system; it is obvious, however, to mention one additional evil. We are supposing a vast influx and congregation of young men, their own masters, in a strange city, from countries various, of different traditions, politics, and manners, and which have often been at war with each other. And they have come to attend lecturers, whom they are to choose out of a number of able men, themselves of various countries

* Professor Vaughan
† Vide Fr. Dalgairns's article in the British Critic, Jan. 1843.

and characters too. Some of these professors are their own countrymen respectively, others are not; and all of them are more or less in rivalry one with another, so far as their department of teaching is the same. They will have their respective gatherings, their respective hostilities; many will puff them, many run them down; their countrymen, for the sake of "la belle France," or "merry England," will range themselves on their side, and fight in their behalf. Squabbles, conflicts, feuds, will be the consequence; the peace of the University will be broken, the houses will be besieged, the streets will be impassable. Accustomed to brawls with each other, they are not likely to be peaceable with any third party; they will find themselves a match for the authority of Chancellor and Rector; nor will they scruple at compromising themselves with the law, or even with the government; nay, with the Church, if her authorities come in their way; with the townspeople of course—a sort of ready-made opponent. The bells of St. Mary's and St. Martin's will ring; out will rush from their quarters the academic youth; and the smart blackguard of the city, and the stout peasant from the neighbourhood, will answer to the challenge. The worse organized is a country, the greater of course will be the disorder; intolerable of course in the middle ages; in times such as these, the magistracy or police would to a very considerable extent keep under such manifestations; yet, in Germany, we are told that at least duels and party skirmishes are not uncommon, and even within the very home and citadel of Order, town-and-gown rows are not yet matters of history in the English Universities.

Now, I have said quite enough for the purpose of showing that, taking human nature as it is, the thirst of knowledge and the opportunity of quenching it, though these be the real life of a great school of philosophy and science, will not be sufficient in fact for its establishment; that they will not work to their ultimate end, which is the attainment and propagation of truth, unless surrounded by influences of a different sort, which have no pretension indeed to be the essence of a University, but are conservative of that essence. The Church does not think much of any "wisdom," which is not "*desursum*," that is, revealed; nor unless, as the Apostle proceeds, it is "primum quidem *pudica*, deinde *pacifica*." These may be called the three vital principles of the Christian student, faith, chastity, love; because their contraries, viz., unbelief or heresy, impurity, and enmity, are just the three great sins against God, ourselves, and our neighbour, which are the death of the soul :—now, these are also just the three imputations which I have been bringing against the incidental action of what may be called the Professorial system.

And lastly, obvious as are the deficiencies of that system, as obvious surely is its remedy, as far as human nature admits of one. I have been saying that regularity, rule, respect for others, the eye of friends and acquaintances, the absence from temptation, external restraints generally, are of first importance in protecting us against ourselves. When a boy leaves his home, when a peasant leaves his country, his faith and morals are in great danger, both because he is in the world, and also because he is among strangers. The remedy, then, of the perils which a University presents to the student, is to create within it homes, "altera Trojæ Pergama," such as those, or better than those, which he has left behind. Small communities must be set up within its precincts, where his better thoughts will find countenance, and his good resolutions support ; where his waywardness will be restrained, his heedlessness forewarned, and his prospective deviations anticipated. Here, too, his diligence will be steadily stimulated ; he will be kept up to his aim ; his progress will be ascertained, and his week's work, like a labourer's, measured. It is not easy for a young man to determine for himself whether he has mastered what he has been taught ; a careful catechetical training, and a jealous scrutiny into his power of expressing himself and of turning his knowledge to account, will be necessary, if he is really to profit from the able Professors whom he is attending ; and all this he will gain from the College Tutor.

Moreover, it has always been considered the wisdom of lawgivers and founders, to find a safe outlet for natural impulses and sentiments, which are sure to be found in their subjects, and which are hurtful only in excess ; and to direct, and moderate, and variously influence what they cannot extinguish. The story is familiarly told, when a politician was advocating violently repressive measures upon some national crisis, of a dissentient friend who was present, proceeding to fasten down the lid of the kettle, which was hissing on his fire, and to stop up its spout. Here, in like manner, the subdivision of the members of a University, while it breaks up the larger combination of parties, and makes them more manageable, answers also the purposes of providing a safe channel for national, or provincial, or political feeling, and for a rivalry which is wholesome when it is not inordinate. These small societies, pitted, as it were, one against another, give scope to the exertion of an honourable emulation ; and this, while it is a stimulus on the literary exertions of their respective members, is changed from a personal and self-ish feeling, into a desire for the reputation of the body.

Patriotic sentiment, too, here finds its home ; one college has a preponderance of members from one race or district, another from another ; the "Nations" no longer fight on the academic scene, like the elements in chaos ; they are submitted to a salutary organization ; and the love of country, without being less intense, becomes purer, and more civilized, and more religious.

My object at present is not to prove what I have been saying, either by argument or from history, but to suggest views to the reader which he will pursue for himself. It may be said that small bodies may fall into a state of decay or irregularity, as well as large. It is true ; but that is not the question ; but whether in themselves smaller bodies of students are not easier to manage on the long run, than large ones. I should not like to do either, but, if I must choose between the two, I would rather drive four-in-hand, than the fifty wild cows which were harnessed to the travelling wagon of the Tartars.

CHAPTER XVI.

THE STRENGTH AND WEAKNESS OF UNIVERSITIES.
ABELARD.

WE can have few more apposite illustrations of at once the strength and weakness of what may be called the University principle, of what it can do and what it cannot, of its power to collect students, and its impotence to preserve and edify them, than the history of the celebrated Abelard. His name is closely associated with the commencement of the University of Paris; and in his popularity and in his reverses, in the criticisms of John of Salisbury on his method, and the protest of St. Bernard against his teaching, we read, as in a pattern specimen, what a University professes in its essence, and what it needs for its "integrity." It is not to be supposed, that I am prepared to show this here, as fully as it might be shown; but it is a subject so pertinent to the general object of these Essays, that it may be useful to devote even a few pages to it.

The oracles of Divine Truth, as time goes on, do but repeat the one message from above which they have ever uttered, since the tongues of fire attested the coming of the Paraclete; still, as time goes on, they utter it with greater force and precision, under diverse forms, with fuller luminousness, and a richer ministration of thought, statement, and argument. They meet the varying wants, and encounter the special resistance of each successive age ; and, though prescient of coming errors and their remedy long before, they cautiously reserve their new enunciation of the old Truth, till it is imperatively demanded. And, as it happens in kings' cabinets, that surmises arise, and rumours spread, of what is said in council, and is in course of preparation, and secrets perhaps get wind, true in substance or in direction, though distorted in detail ; so too, before the Church speaks, one or other of her forward children speaks for her, and, while he does anticipate to a certain point what she is about to say or enjoin, he states it incorrectly, makes it error instead of truth, and risks his own faith in the process. Indeed, this is actually one source, or rather concomitant, of heresy, the presence of some misshapen, huge, and grotesque foreshadow of true statements which are to come. Speaking under correction, I would apply this remark to the heresy of Tertullian or of Sabellius, which may be considered a reaction from existing errors, and an attempt, presumptuous, and therefore unsuccessful, to meet them with those divinely-appointed correctives which the Church alone can apply, and which she will actually apply, when the proper moment comes. The Gnostics boasted of their intellectual proficiency before the time of St. Irenæus, St. Athanasius, and St. Augustine ; yet, when these doctors made their appearance, I suppose they were examples of that knowledge, true and deep, which the Gnostics professed. Apollinaris anticipated the work of St Cyril and the Ephesine Council, and became a heresiarch in consequence ; and, to come down to the present times, we may conceive that writers, who have impatiently fallen away from the Church, because she would not adopt their views, would have found, had they but trusted her, and waited, that she knew how to profit by them, though she never could have need to borrow

13

her enunciations from them; for their writings contained, so to speak, truth *in the ore*, truth which they themselves had not the gift to disengage from its foreign concomitants, and safely use, which she alone could use, which she would use in her destined hour, and which became their stone of stumbling simply because she did not use it faster. Now, applying this principle to the subject before us, I observe, that, supposing Abelard to be the first master of scholastic philosophy, as many seem to hold, we shall have still no difficulty in condemning the author, while we honour the work. To him is only the glory of spoiling by his own self-will what would have been done well and surely under the teaching and guidance of Infallible Authority.

Nothing is more certain, than that some ideas are consistent with one another, and others inconsistent; and, again, that every truth must be consistent with every other truth;—hence, that all truths of whatever kind form into one large body of Truth, by virtue of the consistency between one truth and another, which is a connecting link running through them all. The science which discovers this connection, is logic; and, as it discovers the connection when the truths are given. so, having one truth given and the connecting principle, it is able to go on to ascertain the other. Though all this is obvious, it was realized and acted on in the middle age with a distinctness unknown before; all subjects of knowledge were viewed as parts of one vast system, each with its own place in it, and from knowing one, another was inferred. Not indeed always rightly inferred, because the art might be less perfect than the science, the instrument than the theory and aim; but I am speaking of the principle of the scholastic method, of which Saints and Doctors were the teachers;—such

I conceive it to be, and Abelard was the ill-fated logician who had a principal share in bringing it into operation.

Others will consider the great St. Anselm and the school of Bec, as the proper source of Scholasticism ; I am not going to discuss the question ; any how, Abelard, and not St. Anselm, was the Professor at the University of Paris, and it is of Universities that I am speaking ; any how, Abelard illustrates the strength and the weakness of the principle of advertising and communicating knowledge for its own sake, which I have called the University principle, whether he is, or is not, the first of scholastic philosophers or scholastic theologians. And, though I could not speak of him at all without mentioning the subject of his teaching, yet, after all, it is of him and of his teaching itself, that I am going to speak, whatever that might be which he actually taught.

Since Charlemagne's time the schools of Paris had continued, with various fortunes, faithful, as far as the age admitted, to the old learning, as other schools else-where, when, in the eleventh century, the famous school of Bec began to develop the powers of logic in forming a new philosophy. As the inductive method rose in Bacon, so did the logical in the médieval schoolmen ; and Aristotle, the most comprehensive intellect of Antiquity, as the one who had conceived the sublime idea of mapping the whole field of knowledge, and subjecting all things to one profound analysis, became the presiding master in their lecture halls. It was at the end of the eleventh century that William of Champeaux founded the celebrated Abbey of St. Victor under the shadow of St. Geneviève, and by the dialectic methods which he introduced into his teaching, has a claim to have commenced the work of forming the University out of the Schools of Paris. For one at least, out of the two characteristics of a University, he prepared the way ; for, though the schools were not public till after his day, so as to admit laymen as well as clerks, and foreigners as well as natives of the place, yet the logical principle of constructing all sciences into one system, implied of course a recognition of all the sciences that are comprehended in it. Of this William of Champeax, or de Campellis, Abelard was the pupil ; he had studied the dialectic art elsewhere, before he offered himself for his instructions ; and, in the course of two years, when as yet he had only reached the age of twenty-two, he made such progress, as to be capable of quarrelling with his master, and setting up a school for himself.

This school of Abelard was first situated in the royal castle of Melun ; then at Corbeil, which was nearer to Paris, and where he attracted to himself a considerable number of hearers. His labours had an injurious effect upon his health ; and at length he withdrew for two years to his native Britanny. Whether other causes coöperated in this withdrawal, I think, is not known ; but, at the end of the two years, we find him returning to Paris, and renewing his attendance on the lectures of William, who was by this time a monk. Rhetoric was the subject of the lectures he now heard; and after awhile the pupil repeated with greater force and success his former treatment of his teacher. He held a public disputation with him, got the victory, and reduced him to silence. The school of William was deserted, and its master himself became an instance of the vicissitudes incident to that gladiatorial wisdom (as I may style it) which was then eclipsing the old Benedictine method of the Seven Arts. After a time, Abelard found his reputation sufficient to warrant him in setting up a school himself on Mount St. Geneviève ; whence he waged incessant war against the unwearied logician, who by this time had rallied his forces to repel the young and ungrateful adventurer who had raised his hand against him.

Great things are done by devotion to one idea; there is one class of geniuses, who would never be what they are, could they grasp a second. The calm philosophical mind, which contemplates parts without denying the whole, and the whole without confusing the parts, is notoriously indisposed to action; whereas single and simple views arrest the mind, and hurry it on to carry them out. Thus, men of one idea and nothing more, whatever their merit, must be to a certain extent narrow-minded; and it is not wonderful that Abelard's devotion to the new philosophy made him undervalue the Seven Arts out of which it had grown. He felt it impossible so to honour what was now to be added, as not to dishonour what existed before. He would not suffer the Arts to have their own use, since he had found a new instrument for a new purpose. So he opposed the reading of the Classics. The monks had opposed them before him; but this is little to our present purpose; it was the duty of men, who abjured the gifts of this world on the principle of mortification, to deny themselves literature just as they would deny themselves particular friendships or figured music. The doctrine which Abelard introduced and represents was founded on a different basis. He did not recognize in the poets of antiquity any other merit than that of furnishing an assemblage of elegant phrases and figures; and accordingly he asks why they should not be banished from the city of God, since Plato banished them from his own commonwealth. The *animus* of this language is clear, when we turn to the pages of John of Salisbury and Peter of Blois, who were champions of the ancient learning. We find them complaining that the careful "getting up," as we now call it, "of books," was growing out of fashion. Youths once studied critically the text of poets or philosophers; they got them by heart; they analyzed their arguments; they noted down their fallacies; they were closely examined in the matters which had been brought before them in lecture; they composed. But now, another teaching was coming in; students were promised truth in a nutshell; they intended to get possession of the sum-total of philosophy in less than two or three years; and facts were apprehended, not in their substance and details, by means of living and, as it were, personal documents, but in dead abstracts and tables. Such were the reclamations to which the new Logic gave occasion.

These, however, are lesser matters; we have a graver quarrel with Abelard than that of his undervaluing the Classics. As I have said, my main object here is not what he taught, but why and how, and how he lived. Now it is certain, his activity was stimulated by nothing very high, but something very earthly and sordid. I grant there is nothing morally wrong in the mere desire to rise in the world, though Ambition and it are twin sisters. I should not blame Abelard merely for wishing to distinguish himself at the University; but when he makes the ecclesiastical state the instrument of his ambition, mixes up spiritual matters with temporal, and aims at a bishopric through the medium of his logic, he joins together things incompatible, and cannot complain of being censured. It is he himself, who tells us, unless my memory plays me false, that the circumstance of William of Champeaux being promoted to the see of Chalons, was an incentive to him to pursue the same path with an eye to the same reward. Accordingly, we next hear of his attending the theological lectures of a certain master of William's, named Anselm, an old man, whose school was situated at Laon. This person had a great reputation in his day ; John of Salisbury, speaking of him in the next generation, calls him the doctor of doctors ; he had been attended by students from Italy and Germany ; but the age had advanced since he was in his prime, and Abelard was disappointed in a teacher, who had been good enough for William. He left Anselm, and began to lecture on the prophet Ezekiel on his own resources.

Now came the time of his great popularity, which was more than his head could bear ; which dizzied him, took him off his legs, and whirled him to his destruction. I spoke in my foregoing Chapter of those three qualities of true wisdom, which a University, absolutely and nakedly considered, apart from the safeguards which constitute its integrity, is sure to compromise. Wisdom, says the inspired writer, is *desursum*, is *pudica*, is *pacifica*, " from above, chaste, peaceable." We have already seen enough of Abelard's career to understand that his wisdom, instead of being " pacifica," was ambitious and contentious. An Apostle speaks of the tongue both as a blessing and as a curse. It may be the beginning of a fire, he says, a " Universitas iniquitatis ; " and alas ! such did it become in the mouth of the gifted Abelard. His eloquence was wonderful ; he dazzled his contemporaries, says Fulco, " by the brilliancy of his genius, the sweetness of his eloquence, the ready flow of his language, and the subtlety of his knowledge." People came to him from all quarters ;—from Rome, in spite of mountains and robbers ; from England, in spite of the sea ; from Flanders and Germany ; from Normandy, and the remote districts of France ; from Angers and

Poitiers ; from Navarre by the Pyrenees, and from Spain, besides the students of Paris itself ; and among those, who sought his instructions now or afterwards, were the great luminaries of the schools in the next generation. Such were Peter of Poitiers, Peter Lombard, John of Salisbury, Arnold of Brescia, Ivo, and Geoffrey of Auxerre. It was too much for a weak head and heart, weak in spite of intellectual power ; for vanity will possess the head, and worldliness the heart, of the man, however gifted, whose wisdom is not an effluence of the Eternal Light.

True wisdom is not only "pacifica," it is "pudica ; " chaste as well as peaceable. Alas for Abelard ! a second disgrace, deeper than ambition, is his portion now. The strong man,—the Samson of the schools in the wildness of his course, the Solomon in the fascination of his genius,—shivers and falls before the temptation which overcame that mighty pair, the most excelling in body and in mind.

> Desire of wine, and all delicious drinks,
> Which many a famous warrior overturns,
> Thou couldst repress ; nor did the dancing ruby
> Sparkling outpour'd, the flavour or the smell,
> Or taste that cheers the heart of gods and men,
> Allure thee from the cool crystalline stream.
> But what avail'd this temperance, not complete,
> Against another object more enticing ?
> What boots it at one gate to make defence,
> And at another to let in the foe,
> Effeminately vanquished ?

In a time when Colleges were unknown, and the young scholar was commonly thrown upon the dubious hospitality of a great city, Abelard might even be thought careful of his honour, that he went to lodge with an old ecclesiastic, had not his host's niece Eloisa lived with him. A more subtle snare was laid for him than beset the heroic champion or the all-accomplished monarch of Israel; for sensuality came upon him under the guise of intellect, and it was the high mental endowments of Eloisa, who became his pupil, speaking in her eyes, and thrilling on her tongue, which were the intoxication and the delirium of Abelard. . . . .

He is judged, he is punished ;—but he is not reclaimed. True wisdom is not only "pacifica," not only "pudica ; " it is "desursum" too. It is a revelation from above ; it knows heresy as little as it knows strife or licence. But Abelard, who had run the career of earthly wisdom in two of its phases, now is destined to represent its third.

It is at the famous Abbey of St. Denis that we find him languidly rising from his dream of sin, and the suffering that followed. The bad dream is cleared away ; clerks come to him, and the Abbot,—begging him to lecture still, for love now, as for gain before. Once more his school is thronged by the curious and the studious ; but at length a rumour spreads, that Abelard is exploring the way to some novel view on the subject of the Most Holy Trinity. Wherefore is hardly clear, but about the same time the monks drive him away from the place of refuge he had gained. He betakes himself to a cell, and thither his pupils follow him. "I betook myself to a certain cell," he says, "wishing to give myself to the schools, as was my custom. Thither so great a multitude of scholars flocked, that there was neither room to house them, nor fruits of the earth to feed them," such was the enthusiasm of the student, such the attraction of the teacher, when knowledge was advertised freely, and its market opened.

Next he is in Champagne, in a delightful solitude near Nogent in the diocese of Troyes. Here the same phenomenon presents itself, which is so frequent in his history. "When the scholars knew it," he says, "they began to crowd thither from all parts ; and, leaving other cities and strongholds, they were content to dwell in the wilderness. For spacious houses they framed for themselves small tabernacles, and for delicate food they put up with wild herbs. Secretly did they whisper among themselves : 'Behold, the whole world is gone out after him !' When, however, my Oratory could not hold even a moderate portion of them, then they were forced to enlarge it, and to build it up with wood and stone." He called the place his Paraclete, because it had been his consolation.

I do not know why I need follow his life further. I have said enough to illustrate the course of one, who may be called the founder, or at least the first great name, of the Parisian Schools. After the events I have mentioned he is found in Lower Britanny ; then, being about forty-eight years of age, in the Abbey of St. Gildas ; then with St. Geneviève again. He had to sustain the fiery eloquence of a Saint, directed against his novelties ; he had to present himself before two Councils ; he had to burn the book which had given offence to pious ears. His last two years were spent at Clugni on his way to Rome. The home of the weary, the hospital of the sick, the school of the erring, the tribunal of the penitent, is the city of St. Peter. He did not reach it ; but he is said to have retracted what had given scandal in his writings, and to have made an edifying end. He died at the age of sixty-two, in the year of grace 1142.

In reviewing his career, the career of so great an intellect so miserably thrown away, we are reminded of the famous words of the dying scholar and jurist, which are a lesson to us all : " Heu, vitam perdidi, operosè nihil agendo." A happier lot be ours !

CHAPTER XVII.

THE ANCIENT UNIVERSITY OF DUBLIN.

THE most prominent distinction between the primitive and the medieval schools, as I have already many times said, was, that the latter had a range and system in their subjects and the manner of their teaching, which were unknown to the former. The primitive schools, for instance, lectured from Scripture with the comments of the Fathers ; but the medieval schools created the science of theology. The primitive schools collected and transmitted the canonical rules and traditions of the Church ; the medieval schools taught the science of canon law. And so as regards secular studies, the primitive schools professed the three sciences of grammar, rhetoric, and logic, which make up the Trivium, and the four branches of the mathematics, arithmetic, geometry, astronomy, and music, which make up the Quadrivium. On the other hand, the medieval schools recognized philosophy as a science of sciences, which included, located, connected, and used all kinds and modes of knowledge ; they enlarged the sphere and application of logic ; and they added civil law, natural history, and medicine to the curriculum. It followed, moreover, from this, that while, on the one hand, they were led to divide their work among a number of Professors, they opened their doors on the other to laity as well as clergy, and to foreigners as well as natives.

Of schools founded on this magnificent idea and answering to a profession so comprehensive and so engrossing, there could be but a few specimens ; for instance, Paris, Oxford, and Bologna. These, too, owed their characteristic splendour in no small measure to the zeal and learning of the Friars, especially the Dominicans ; accordingly, their great era was the thirteenth century. But various causes came into operation to modify the University type, as I have described it, or at least its applications and manifestations, when that century had passed away. The first movements of new agents, both in the physical and social world, are commonly more energetic and more successful than those which follow ; and this remark includes both Universities themselves, and the religious bodies which were their prominent supporters. New orders of religion commonly achieve their greatest works in their first fervour. The very success too of the experiment would tend to impair the University type by multiplying copies of it ; for an imperial power (and a University was such in the intellectual world) must be solitary to be imperial. As, then, the utility of the new schools was recognized, they became more numerous and their respective territories less extensive. Moreover, it was natural, that, as country after country woke up into existence and assumed an individuality, each in turn should desire a University of its own, that is, an institution indigenous and national. Peace between states could not always be maintained ; the elements were beyond the traveller's control ; and a safe-conduct did not secure the pilgrim scholar from bandits and pirates. The mutual divergence and distinctive formation of languages and of national character, national histories, national pride, national antipathies, would all carry forward the course of events in the same direction ; and the Collegiate system, of which I shall presently speak, coöperated in making a University a local institution, and in embodying it among the establishments of the nation. Hence it came to pass, that Oxford, for instance, in course of time, was not exactly the Oxford of the thirteenth century. Not that the great and primary idea of a University was not sufficiently preserved ; it was still a light set upon a hill, or a sort of ecumenical doctor on all subjects of knowledge, human and divine ; but it was directed and coloured by the political and social influences to which it was accidentally exposed. This change began about the commencement of the fourteenth century ; however, I am not going to dwell upon it here ; for the foregoing reference to it is only introductory to a short notice, which I propose now to give, of the ancient University of Dublin or of Ireland, set up at this very era,—a subject to which the mind naturally reverts just at this moment, when we are now on the point of laying down the rudiments of its revival or reconstruction upon the old foundations, on a grander scale, and, as we trust and believe, with a happier prospect for the future.

If by " University " is meant a large national School, conducted on the basis of the old Roman education, it was impossible that such should not have existed in a people so literary as the Irish, from the very time that St. Patrick brought among them Christianity and civilization. Accordingly, we hear of great seats of learning of this description in various parts of the country. The school of Armagh is said at one time to have numbered as many as seven thousand students ; and tradition assigns a University town to the locality where the Seven Churches still preserve the memory of St. Kevin. Foreigners, at least Anglo-Saxons, frequented such schools, and, so far, they certainly had a University character ; but that they offered to their pupils more than the glosses on the sacred text and the collections of canons, and the Trivium and the Quadrivium, which were the teaching of the schools of the Continent, it is difficult to suppose; or that the national genius for philosophizing, which afterwards anticipated or originated the scholastic period, should at this era have come into exercise. When that period came, the Irish, so far having its characteristic studies already domiciled among them, were forced to go abroad for their prosecution. They went to Paris or to Oxford for the living traditions, which are the ordinary means by which religion and morals, science and art, are diffused over communities, and propagated from land to land. In Oxford, indeed, there was from the earliest time even a street called "Irishman's Street," and the Irish were included there under the "Nation" of the Southern English; but they gained what they sought in that seat of learning, at the expense of discomforts which were the serious drawback of the first age of Universities. Lasting feuds and incessant broils marked the presence of Irish, Welsh, Scotch, English, and French in one place, at a time when the Collegiate System was not formed. To this great evil was added the very circumstance that home was far away, and the danger of the passage across the channel; which would diminish the number, while it illustrated the literary zeal, of the foreign students. And an additional source of discontent was found in the feeling of incongruity, that Ireland, with her literary antecedents, should be without a University of her own; and, moreover, as time went on, in the feeling which existed at Rome, in favour of the multiplication of such centres of science and learning.

Another perfectly distinct cause was in operation, to which I was just now referring. The Dominicans, and other Orders of the age, had had a preëminent place in the history of the Universities of Paris and Oxford, and had done more than any other teachers to give the knowledge taught in them their distinctive form. When then these Orders came into Ireland, it was only to be expected that they should set about the same work there, which had marked their presence in England and France. Accordingly, at the end of the thirteenth century, the question of a University in Ireland had been mooted, and its establishment was commenced in the first years of the fourteenth.

This was the date of the foundation of the Universities of Avignon and Perugia, which was followed by that of Cahors, Grenoble, Pisa, and Prague. It was the date at which Oxford in consequence lost its especial preëminence in science ; and it was the date, I say, at which the University of Dublin was projected and begun. In 1311 or 1312, John Lech or Leach, Archbishop of Dublin, obtained of Clement the Fifth a brief for the undertaking ; in which, as is usual in such documents, the Pope gives the reasons which have induced him to decide upon it. He begins by setting forth the manifold, or rather complex, benefits of which a University is the instrument ; as father of the faithful, he recognizes it as his office to nurture learned sons, who, by the illumination of their knowledge, may investigate the divine law, protect justice and truth, illustrate the faith, promote good government, teach the ignorant, confirm the weak, and restore the fallen. This office he is only fulfilling, in receiving favourably the supplication of his venerable brother, John de Lecke, who has brought before him the necessities of his country, in which, as well as in Scotland, Man, and Norway, the countries nearest to Ireland, a " Universitas Scholarum," or " Generale Studium," is not to be found ;—the consequence being, that though there are in Ireland some doctors and bachelors in theology, and other graduates in grammar, these are, after all, few in comparison of the number which the country might fairly produce. The Pope proceeds to express his desire, that from the land itself should grow up men skilled and fruitful in the sciences, who would make it to be a well-watered garden, to the exaltation of the Catholic faith, the honour of Mother Church, and the advantage of the faithful population. And with this view he erects in Dublin a *Studium Generale* in every science and faculty, to continue for " perpetual times."

And, I suppose no greater benefit could have been projected for Ireland at that date, than such a bond of union and means of national strength, as an Irish University. But the parties, who had originated the undertaking, had also to carry it out : and at the moment of which I am speaking, by the fault neither of Prelate nor laity, nor by division, nor by intemperance or jealousy, nor by wrong-headedness within the fold, nor by malignant interference from without, but by the will of heaven and the course of nature, the work was suspended ;—for John de Lecke fell ill and died the next year, and his successor, Alexander de Bicknor, was not in circumstances to take up his plans at the moment, where de Lecke had left them.

Seven years passed ; and then Bicknor turned his mind to their prosecution. Acting under the authority of the brief of Clement, and with the sanction and confirmation of the reigning Pontiff, John the Twenty-second, he published an instrument, in which he lays down on his own authority the provisions and dispositions which he had determined for the nascent University. He addresses himself to " the Masters and Scholars of our

University," and that "with the consent and assent of our chapters of Holy Trinity and St. Patrick." I think I am correct in saying, though I write without book, that he makes no mention of a Rector. If not, the Chancellor probably, whom he does mention, took his place, or was his synonyme, as in some other Universities. This Chancellor the Regent Masters were to have the privilege of choosing, with a *proviso* that he was a "Doctor in sacrâ paginâ," or in "jure canonico," with a preference of members of the two chapters. He was to take the oath of fidelity to the Archbishop. The Regent Masters elected the Proctors also, who were two in number, and who supplied the place of the Chancellor in his absence. The Chancellor was invested with jurisdiction over the members of the University, and had a court, to which causes belonged in which they were concerned. There was, moreover, a University chest, supplied by means of the fines which were the result of his decisions. Degrees were to be conferred upon certificate of the Masters of the Faculty, in which the candidate was proceeding. Statutes were to be passed by the Chancellor, in council of Masters Regent and Non-regent, subject to the confirmation of the Archbishop. The Schools of the Friars Preachers (or Dominicans) and of the Minorites (or Franciscans) were recognized in their connection with the University, the Archbishop reserving to himself the right of appointing a Lecturer in Holy Scripture.

Such was the encouraging and hopeful start of the University ; the Dean of St. Patrick was advanced to the Doctorate in Canon Law, and was created its first Chancellor; its first Doctors in Theology were two Dominicans and one Franciscan. The Canons of the Cathedral seem to have been its acting members, and

14

filled the offices of a place of education without pre-
judicing their capitular duties. However, it soon appeared that there was somewhere a hitch, and the work
did not make progress. It has been supposed with
reason, that under the unhappy circumstances of the
time, the University could not make head against the
necessary difficulties of a commencement. Another
and more definite cause which is assigned for the
failure, is the want of funds. The Irish people were
poor, and unable to meet the expenses involved in the
establishment of a great seat of learning, at a time when
other similar institutions already existed. The time
had passed when Universities grew up out of the enthusiasm of teachers and the curiosity and eagerness of
students; or, if these causes still were in operation, they
had been directed and flowed in upon seats of learning
already existing in other countries. It was the age of
national schools, of colleges and endowments; and,
though the civil power appeared willing to take its part
in endowments in furtherance of the new undertaking,
it did not go much further than to enrich it now
and then with a stray lectureship, and wealthy prelates
or nobles were not forthcoming in that age, capable of
conceiving and executing works in the spirit of Ximenes
two centuries afterwards in Spain.

Yet down to the very time of Ximenes, and beyond
it, continual and praiseworthy efforts were made, on the
part both of the Church and of the State, to accomplish
a work which was important in proportion to its difficulty. In 1358 the clergy and scholars of Ireland represented to Edward the Third the necessity under which
they lay of cultivating theology, canon law, and the other
clerical sciences, and the serious impediments in the
way of these studies which lay in the expense of travel

and the dangers of the sea to those who had no University of their own. In answer to this request, the king seems to have founded a lectureship in theology; and he indirectly encouraged the University schools by issuing his letters-patent, giving special protection and safe-conduct to English as well as Irish, of whatever degree, with their servants and attendants, their goods and habiliments, in going, residing, and returning. A few years later, in 1364, Lionel, Duke of Clarence, founded a preachership and lectureship in the Cathedral, to be held by an Augustinian.

A further attempt in behalf of a University was made a century later. In 1465, the Irish Parliament, under the presidency of Thomas Geraldine, Earl of Desmond, Vicegerent of George, Duke of Clarence, Lieutenant of the English King, had erected a University at Drogheda, and endowed it with the privileges of the University of Oxford. This attempt, however, in like manner was rendered abortive by the want of funds; but it seems to have suggested a new effort in favour of the elder institution at Dublin, which at this time could scarcely be said to exist. Ten years after the Parliament in question, the Dominican and other friars preferred a supplication to Pope Sixtus the Fourth, in which they represent that in Ireland there is no University to which Masters, Doctors of Law, and Scholars may resort; that it is necessary to go to England at a great expense and peril; and consequently they ask for leave to erect a University in the metropolitan city. The Pope granted their request, and, though nothing followed, the attempt is so far satisfactory, as evidencing the perseverance of the Irish clergy in aiming at what they felt to be a benefit of supreme importance to their country.

Nor was this the last of such attempts, nor were the

secular behind the regular clergy in zeal for a University. As late as the reign of Henry the Seventh, in the year 1496, Walter Fitzsimon, Archbishop of Dublin, in provincial Synod, settled an annual contribution to be levied for seven years in order to provide salaries for the Lecturers. And, though we have no record, I believe, of the effect of this measure, yet, when the chapter was reëstablished in the reign of Philip and Mary, the allusion made in the legal instrument to the loss which the youthful members of society had sustained in its suppression, may be taken to show, that certain scholastic benefits had resulted from its stalls though the education which they provided was not of that character which the name of a University demanded.

Times are changed since these attempts were made ; and, while the causes no longer exist which operated in their failure, the object towards which they were directed has attained a moment, both in itself and in its various bearings, which could never have been predicted in the fourteenth or the sixteenth century. Ireland is no longer the conquered possession of a foreign king ; it is, as in the primitive times, the centre of a great Catholic movement and of a world-wide missionary enterprise. Nor does the Holy See simply lend an ear to the project of others : it originates the undertaking.

CHAPTER XVIII.

COLLEGES THE CORRECTIVE OF UNIVERSITIES.

OXFORD.

COLLEGES, and Colleges for the advancement of science, were not altogether a medieval idea. To say nothing else, it is obvious to refer to the Museum of the Ptolemies at Alexandria, of which I spoke in an earlier Chapter. The Saracens too founded Colleges for learned education at Cordova, Granada, and Malaga; and these obtained a great reputation. Yet it is an idea, which has been brought out and familiarized in history, and recognized in political institutions, and completed in its parts, during the era of Universities, with a fulness which almost allows us to claim it as belonging to the new civilization. By a College, I suppose, is meant, not merely a body of men living together in one dwelling, but belonging to one establishment. In its very notion, the word suggests to us position, authority, and stability; and again, these attributes presuppose a foundation; and that foundation consists either in public recognition, or in the possession of revenues, or in some similar advantage. If two or three individuals live together, the community is not at once called a College; but a charter, or an endowment, some legal *status*, or some ecclesiastical privilege, is necessary to erect it into the Collegiate form. However, it does, I suppose, imply a community or *convitto* too ; and, if so, it must be of a certain definite size : for, as soon as it exceeds in point of numbers, non-residence may be expected to follow. It is then a household, and offers an abode to its members, and requires or involves the same virtuous and paternal discipline which is proper to a family and home. Moreover, as no family can subsist without a mainte- nance, and as children are dependent on their homes, so it is not unnatural that an endowment, which is, as I have said, suggested by the very idea of a College, should ordinarily be necessary for its actual carrying out. Still more necessary are buildings, and buildings of a prominent character ; for, whereas every family must have its dwelling, a family which has a recognized and official existence, must live in a sort of public building, which satisfies the eye, and is the enduring habitation of an enduring body.

This view of a College, which I have not been attempt- ing to prove but to delineate, suggests to us the objects which a College is adapted to fulfil in a University. It is all, and does all, which is implied in the name of home. Youths, who have left the paternal roof, and travelled some hundred miles for the acquisition of knowledge, find an "altera Troja" and "simulata Pergama" at the end of their journey and in their place of temporary sojourn. Home is for the young, who know nothing of the world, and who would be forlorn and sad, if thrown upon it. It is the refuge of helpless boyhood, which would be famished and pine away, if it were not main- tained by others. It is the providential shelter of the weak and inexperienced, who have still to learn how to cope with the temptations which lie outside of it. It is the place of training for those who are not only ignorant, but have not yet learned how to learn, and who have to

be taught, by careful individual trial, how to set about
profiting by the lessons of a teacher. And it is the
school of elementary studies, not of advanced ; for such
studies alone can boys at best apprehend and master.
Moreover, it is the shrine of our best affections, the bosom
of our fondest recollections, a spell upon our after life, a
stay for world-weary mind and soul, wherever we are cast,
till the end comes. Such are the attributes or offices of
home, and like to these, in one or other sense and measure, are the attributes and offices of a College in a University.

We may consider, historically speaking, that Colleges
were but continuations, *mutatis mutandis*, of the schools
which preceded the rise of Universities. These schools
indeed were monastic or at least clerical, and observed a
religious or an ecclesiastical rule ; so far they were not
simple Colleges, still they were devoted to study, and, at
least sometimes, admitted laymen. They had two
courses of instruction going on at once, attended by the
inner classes and the outer ; of which the latter were
filled by what would now be called *externs*. Thus even
in that early day the school of Rheims educated a certain number of noble youths; and the same arrangement
is reported of Bec also.

And in matter of fact these monastic schools remained
within the limits of the University, when it was set up,
as they had been before, only of course more exclusively
religious ; for, as soon as the reception of laymen was
found to be a part of the academical idea, the monasteries
seemed to be relieved of the necessity of receiving lay
students within their walls. At first, those Orders only
would have a place in the University which were already
there ; but in process of time nearly every religious fra-
ternity found it its interest to provide a College for its

own subjects, and to have representatives in the Academical body.   Thus in Paris, as soon as the Dominicans and Franciscans had thrown themselves into the new system, and had determined that their vocation did not hinder them from taking degrees, the Cistercians, under the headship of an Englishman, founded a College near St. Victor's ; and the Premonstrants followed their example. The Carmelites, being at first at a distance from St. Geneviève, were planted by a king of France close under her hill.   The Benedictines were stationed in the famous Abbey of St. German, near the University Pratum ; the monks of Cluni and of Marmoutier had their respective houses also, and the former provided lecturers within their walls for the students.   And in Oxford, in like manner, the Benedictines founded Durham Hall for their monks of the North of England, and Gloucester Hall for their monks of the South, on the respective sites of the present Trinity and Worcester Colleges.   The Carmelites (to speak without book,) were at Beaumont, the site of Henry the First's palace ; and St. John's and Wadham Colleges are also on the sites of monastic establishments.   Besides these, there were in Oxford houses of Dominicans, Franciscans, Cistercians, and Augustinians.

These several foundations, indeed, are of very different eras; but, looking at the course of the history as a whole, we shall find that such houses as were monastic preceded the rest.   And if the new changes had stopped there, lay education would have suffered, not gained, by the rise of Universities ; for it had the effect of multiplying, indeed, monastic halls, but of shutting their doors against all but monks more rigidly than before.   The solitary strangers, who came up to Paris or Oxford from a far country, must have been stimulated by a most uncommon thirst for knowledge, to persevere in spite of the discouragements by which they were surrounded. Some attempt indeed was made by the Professors to meet so obvious and so oppressive an evil. The former scholastic type had recognized one master, and one only, in a school, who professed in consequence the whole course of instruction without any assistant Tutors. The tradition of this system continued ; and led in many instances to the formation of halls, inns, courts, or hostels, as they were variously called. That is, the Professor of the school kept house, and boarded his pupils. Thus we read of Torald schools in Oxford in the reign of Henry the Third, which had belonged previously to one Master Richard Bacum, who had fitted up a large tenement, partly for lodging house, partly for lecture rooms. In like manner, early in the twelfth century, Theobald had as many as from sixty to a hundred scholars under his tuition, for whom he would necessarily be more or less answerable. A similar custom was pointed out in Athens, in an early Chapter of these sketches, where it was the occasion of a great deal of rivalry and canvassing between the Professorial housekeepers, each being set upon obtaining as many lodgers as possible. And apparently a similar inconvenience had to be checked at Paris in the thirteenth century, though, whatever might be that incidental inconvenience, the custom itself, under the circumstances of the day, was as advantageous to the cause of study, as it was natural and obvious.

But still lodging keepers, though Professors, must be paid, and how could poor scholars find the means of fulfilling so hard a condition ? And the length of time then required for a University course hindered an evasion of its difficulties by such shifts and expedients, as serve for passing a mere trying crisis, or weathering a threatening

season.   The whole course, from the termination of the
grammatical studies to the licentiate, extended originally through twenty years ; though afterwards it was
reduced to ten.   If we are to consider the six years of
the course in Arts to have been in addition to this long
space, the residence at the University is no longer a
sojourn at the seat of learning, but becomes a sort of
naturalization, yet without offering a home.

  The University itself has little or no funds, to meet
the difficulty withal.   At Oxford, it had no buildings of
its own, but rented such as were indispensable for academical purposes, and these were of a miserable description.   It had little or no ground belonging to it, and
no endowments.   It had not the means of being an
Alma Mater to the young men who came thither for
education.   Some verses are quoted by Antony à Wood,
apropos of the poor scholar, which describe both his
enthusiastic love of study and the trial to which it was
put.   The following is a portion of them :—

> Parva domus, res ipsa minor, contraxit utrumque
> Immensus tractusque diu sub Pallade fervor,
> Et logices jucundus amor &c., &c.   .   .   .   .
> Pauperies est tota domus, desuevit ad illos
> Ubertas venisse lares ; nec visitat ægrum
> Copia Parnassum ; sublimior advolat aulas,
> His ignota casis.

  Accordingly, one of the earliest movements in the
University, almost as early as the entrance into it of the
monastic bodies, was that of providing maintenance for
poor scholars.   The authors of such charity hardly aimed
at giving more than the bare necessaries of life,—food,
lodging, and clothing,—so as to make a life of study
possible.   Comfort or animal satisfaction can hardly be

said to have entered into the scope of their benefactions ; and we shall gain a lively impression of the sufferings of the student, before the era of endowments, by considering his rude and hardy life even when a member of a College. From an account which has been preserved in one of the colleges of Cambridge, we are able to extract the following *horarium* of a student's day. He got up between four and five ; from five to six he assisted at Mass, and heard an exhortation. He then studied or attended the schools till ten, which was the dinner hour. The meal, which seems also to have been a breakfast, was not sumptuous ; it consisted of beef, in small messes for four persons, and a pottage made of its gravy and oatmeal. From dinner to five p.m., he either studied, or gave instruction to others, when he went to supper, which was the principal meal of the day, though scarcely more plentiful than dinner. Afterwards, problems were discussed and other studies pursued, till nine or ten ; and then half an hour was devoted to walking or running about, that they might not go to bed with cold feet ;— the expedient of hearth or stove for the purpose was out of the question.

However, poor as was the fare, the collegiate life was a blessing in many other ways far more important than meat and drink ; and it was the object of pious benefactions for centuries. Hence the munificence of Robert Capet, as early as 1050, even before the canons of St. Geneviève and the monks of St. Victor had commenced the University of Paris. His foundation was sufficient for as many as one hundred poor clerks. Another was St. Catherine in the Valley, founded by St. Louis, in consequence of a vow, which his grandfather, Philip Augustus, had died before executing. Another and later was the Collegium Bonorum Puerorum, which is assigned to the year 1245. Such too, in its original intention, was the Harcurianum, or Harcourt College, the famous College of Navarre, the more famous Sorbonne, and the Montague College.

These Colleges, as was natural, were often provincial or diocesan, being founded by benefactors of a particular district for their own people. Sometimes too they were connected with one or other of the Nations of the University ; I think the Harcurianum, just mentioned, was founded for the Normans ; such too was the Dacian, founded for the Danes ; and the Swedish ; to which may be added the Burses provided for the Italians, the Lombards, the Germans, and the Scotch. In Bologna there was the greater College of St. Clement for the Spaniards, and the Collegio Sondi for the Hungarians. As to Diocesan or Provincial Colleges, such was Laon College, for poor scholars of the diocese of Laon ; the College of Bayeux for scholars of the dioceses of Mons and Angers ; the Colleges of Narbonne, of Arras, of Lisieux, and various others. Such too in Oxford at present are Queen's College, founded in favour of north countrymen, and Jesus College for the Welsh. Such are the fellowships, founded in various Colleges, for natives of particular counties ; and such the fellowships or scholarships for founder's kin. In Paris, in like manner, Cardinal de Dormans founded a College for more than twenty students, with a preference in favour of his own family. A Society of a peculiar kind was founded in the very beginning of the thirteenth century. Baldwin, Count of Flanders, at that time Emperor of Constantinople, is said to have established a Greek College with a view to train up the youth of Constantinople in devotion to the Holy See.

When I said that there were graver reasons than

the need of maintenance, for establishing Colleges and
Burses for poor scholars, it may be easily understood
that I alluded to the moral evils, of which a University,
without homes and guardians for the young, would in-
fallibly be the occasion and the scene. These are so
intelligible, and so much a matter of history, and so often
illustrated, whether from the medieval or the modern
continental Universities, that they need not occupy
our attention here. Whatever licentiousness of conduct
there is at Oxford and Cambridge now, where the Collegiate system is in force, does but suggest to us how
fatal must be the strength of those impulses to disorder
and riot when unrestrained, which are so imperfectly
controlled even when submitted to an anxious discipline.
Leaving this head of the subject, I think it better to
turn to the consideration of an important innovation on
the character and drift of academical foundations, which
took place in the fifteenth century, when political changes
in the nations of Europe brought with them corresponding changes in their Universities.

I have lately alluded to these changes in introducing
the subject of the ancient University of Ireland. I said
that the multiplication of Universities, the growth of
nationalism, the increasing appreciation of peace and of
the conveniences of life, the separation of languages, the
Collegiate system itself, and similar and cognate causes,
tended to give these institutions a local, political, and, I
may now add, aristocratic character. At first Universities were almost democracies : Colleges tended to break
their anarchical spirit, introduced ranks and gave the
example of laws, and trained up a set of students, who,
as being morally and intellectually superior to other
members of the academical body, became the depositaries

of academical power and influence. Moreover, learning was no longer thought unworthy of a gentleman; and, while the nobles of an earlier period had not disdained to send their sons to Lanfranc or Vacarius, now it even became a matter of custom, that young men of rank should have a University education. Thus, in the charter of the 29th of Edward the Third, we even read that "to the University a multitude of nobles, gentry, strangers, and others continually flock;" and towards the end of the century, we find Henry of Monmouth, afterwards the Fifth, as a young man, a sojourner at Queen's College, Oxford. But it was in the next century, of which Henry has made the first years glorious, that Colleges were provided, not for the poor, but for the noble. Many Colleges too, which had been originally for the poor, opened their gates to the rich, not as fellows or foundation-students, but as simple lodgers, or what are now called independent members, such as monasteries might have received in a former age. This was especially the case with the College of Navarre at Paris; and the change has continued remarkably impressed upon Oxford and Cambridge even down to this day, with this additional peculiarity, that, while the influence of aristocracy upon those Universities is not less than it was, the influence of other political classes has been introduced into the academic cloisters also. Never has learned institution been more directly political and national than the University of Oxford. Some of its Colleges represent the talent of the nation, others its rank and fashion, others its wealth; others have been the organs of the government of the day; while others, and the majority, represent one or other division, chiefly local, of the country party. That all this has rather destroyed, than subserved, the University itself, which

Colleges originally were instituted to complete, I will not take upon myself to deny ; but good comes out of many things which are in the way to evil, and this antagonism of the Collegiate to the University principle was not worked out, till Colleges had first rendered signal service to the University, and that, not only by completing it in those points where the University was weak, but even corroborating it in those in which it was strong. The whole nation, brought into the University by means of the Colleges, gave the University itself a vigour and a stability which the abundant influx of foreigners had not been able to secure.

As in the twelfth and thirteenth centuries French, German, and Italian students had flocked to the University of Oxford, and made its name famous in distant lands, so in the fifteenth, all ranks and classes of the nation furnished it with pupils, and what was wanting in their number or variety, compared with the former era, was compensated by their splendour or political importance. At that time nobles moved only in state, and surrounded themselves with retainers and servants, with an ostentation which has now quite gone out of fashion. A writer, whom I have from time to time used, Huber, informs us, that, before the wars of the Roses, and when the aristocracy were more powerful than the king, each noble family sent up at least one son to Oxford with an ample retinue of followers. Nor were the towns in that age, less closely united to the University than the upper classes, by reason of the numerous members of it that belonged to the clerical order, the popular character of that institution, and its intimate connection, as now, with the seat of learning. Thus town and country, high and low, north and south, had a common stake in the academical institutions, and took a personal interest in the academical proceedings. The degree possessed a sort of indelible *character*, which all classes understood; and the people at large were more or less partakers of a cultivation which the aristocracy were beginning to appreciate. And, though railroad travelling certainly did not then exist, communication between the students and their homes occurred with a frequency which could not be when they came from abroad; and Oxford became in a peculiar way a national and political centre. Not only in vacations and term-time was there a stated ebbing and flowing of the academical youth, but messengers posted to and fro between Oxford and all parts of the country in all seasons of the year. So intimate was this connection, that Oxford became a sort of selected arena for the conflicts of the various interests of the nation, and a serious University strife was received far and wide as the presage of civil war.

> " Chronica si penses, cum pugnant Oxonienses,
> Post paucos menses, volat ira per Angligenenses."

But one may admire the position of a University, as a national centre, without any desire of renewing, in this day or in Ireland, the particular mode in which that position was in former times manifested in England. Such an united action of the Collegiate and of the National principle, far from being prejudicial, was simply favourable to the principle of a University. It was a later age which sacrificed the University to the College. We must look to the last two or three centuries, if we would witness the ascendency of the College idea in the English Universities, to the extreme prejudice, not indeed of its own peculiar usefulness (for that it has retained), but of the University itself. Huber, who gives us this account of Oxford, and who is neither Catholic on the one hand, nor innovator on the existing state of things on the other, warming yet saddening at his own picture, ends by observing : " Those days never can return ; for the plain reason that then men learned and taught by the living word, but now by the dead paper."

What has been here drawn out from the history of Oxford, admits of ample illustration from the parallel history of Paris. We find Chancellor Gerson on one occasion remonstrating in the name of his University with the French king. " Shall the University," he says, " being what she is, shut her eyes and be silent ? What would all France say, whose population she is ever exhorting, by means of her members, to patience and good obedience to the king and rulers ? Does not she represent the universal realm, nay, the whole world ? She is the vigorous seminary of the whole body politic, whence issue men of every kind of excellence. Therefore in behalf of the whole of France, of all states of men, of all her friends, who cannot be present here, she ought to expostulate and cry, ' Long live the king.' "

There is one other historical peculiarity attached to Colleges, to which I will briefly allude before concluding. If Colleges, with their endowments and local interests, provincial or county, are necessarily, when compared with Universities, of a national character, it follows that the education which they will administer, will also be national, and adapted to all ranks and classes of the community. And if so, then again it follows, that they will be far more given to the study of the Arts than to the learned professions, or to any special class of pursuits at all ; and such in matter of fact has ever been the case. They have inherited under changed circumstances the position of the monastic teaching founded by Charlemagne, and have continued its primitive tradition, through, and in spite of, the noble intellectual developments, to which Universities have given occasion. The historical link between the Monasteries and the Colleges have been the Nations, as some words of Antony à Wood about the latter suggest, and as the very name of "Nation" makes probable; and indeed the Colleges were hardly more than the Nations formally established and endowed, with Provosts and Wardens in the place of Proctors.

Bulæus has some remarks on the subject of Colleges, which illustrate the points I have last insisted on, and several others which have previously come before us. He says: "The College system had no slight influence in restoring Latin composition. Indeed Letters were publicly professed in Colleges, and that, not only by persons on the foundation, but by others also who lived within the walls, though external to the body, and who were admitted to the schools of the Masters and to the classes in a fixed order and by regulated steps. On the contrary, we find that all the ancient Colleges were established for the education and instruction of poor scholars, members of the foundation; but in the fifteenth century other ranks were gradually introduced also. By this means the lecturer was stimulated by the largeness of the classes, and the pupil by emulation, while the opportunities of a truant life were removed. Accordingly laws were frequently promulgated and statutes passed, with a view of bringing the Martinets and wandering scholars within the walls of the Colleges. We do not know exactly when this practice began; it is generally thought that the College of Navarre, which was reformed in the year 1464, was the first to open its gates to these public professors of letters. It is certain, that in former ages the teachers of grammar and rhetoric had schools of their own, or hired houses and hostels, where they received pupils ; but in this century teachers of grammar, or of rhetoric, or of philosophy, began to teach within the Colleges." He adds that in the time of Louis the eleventh, the Professors who lectured on literature, rhetoric, and philosophy in the town, were generally left by the students for those who had taken up their abodes in the Colleges.

This is rather an enumeration of some characteristics of Colleges, than a sufficient sketch of their relation to the University ; but it may suggest points of inquiry to those who would know more. I will but add, that at Paris there seem to have been as many as fifty Colleges ; at Oxford at present there are from twenty to twenty-four; as many, I believe, were at Salamanca ; at Cambridge not so many ; at Toulouse, eight. As to Louvain, I have been told that if a bird's-eye view be taken of the city, the larger and finer buildings which strike the beholder throughout it, will be found at one time to have belonged to the University.

CHAPTER XIX.

ABUSES OF THE COLLEGES.

OXFORD.

IF what has been said in former Chapters of this
volume upon the relation of a University to its
Colleges, be in the main correct, the difference between
the two institutions, and the use of each, is very clear.
A University embodies the principal of progress, and a
College that of stability ; the one is the sail, and the
other the ballast ; each is insufficient in itself for the
pursuit, extension, and inculcation of knowledge ; each
is useful to the other. A University is the scene of
enthusiasm, of pleasurable exertion, of brilliant display,
of winning influence, of diffusive and potent sympathy ;
and a College is the scene of order, of obedience, of
modest and persevering diligence, of conscientious fulfil-
ment of duty, of mutual private services, and deep and
lasting attachments. The University is for the world,
and the College is for the nation. The University is for
the Professor, and the College for the Tutor ; the University is for the philosophical discourse, the eloquent
sermon, or the well contested disputation ; and the
College for the catechetical lecture. The University is
for theology, law, and medicine, for natural history, for
physical science, and for the sciences generally and their
promulgation ; the College is for the formation of character, intellectual and moral, for the cultivation of the

mind, for the improvement of the individual, for the study of literature, for the classics, and those rudimental sciences which strengthen and sharpen the intellect. The University being the element of advance, will fail in making good its ground as it goes ; the College, from its Conservative tendencies, will be sure to go back, because it does not go forward. It would seem as if an University seated and living in Colleges, would be a perfect institution, as possessing excellences of opposite kinds.

But such a union, such salutary balance and mutual complement of opposite advantages, is of difficult and rare attainment. At least the present day rather gives us instances of the two antagonistic evils, of naked Universities and naked Colleges, than of their alliance and its benefits. The great seats of learning on the Continent, to say nothing of those in Scotland, show us the need of Colleges to complete the University ; the English, on the contrary, show us the need of a University to give life to an assemblage of Colleges. The evil of a University, standing by itself, as in Germany, is often insisted on and may readily be apprehended ; and therefore, leaving that part of the subject alone, I will say a few words on the state of things in England, where the action of the University is suspended, and the Colleges have supreme and sovereign authority.

At the Reformation, the State not only made itself the head of the Anglican Church, but resolved to suppress, or nearly so, its legal existence. It not only ignored the idea of a central authority in Christendom ; but it went very far towards ignoring the existence of a Church in England itself. I believe I am right in saying that the Church of England, as such, scarcely has a legal *status*. Its Bishops indeed are Peers of Parliament, its chapters have charters, its Rectors are corporations sole, its ministers are officers of the law, its fabrics have special rights, its courts have a civil position and functions, its Prayer-book is (as has been observed) an Act of Parliament ; but, as far as I know, there is no corporation of the United Church of England and Ireland, though that title itself be a legal one. The Protestant Church, as such, holds no property, and exercises no functions. It is an aggregate of many thousand corporations professing one object, and moulded on a common rule. The nearest approach to corporate power lay in its Convocations, which were at least three in number, not one,—those of Canterbury, of York, and of Dublin ; and these have been virtually long obsolete. The Protestant Church would be an *imperium in imperio*, considering the immense wealth, power, and influence of its constituent members, were it itself a corporation.

The same spirit which destroyed the legal incorporation of the religious principle, was the jealous enemy also of the incorporation of the intellectual ; and the civil power could as little bear a University as it bore a Church. Accordingly, Oxford and Cambridge shared the fate of the Hierarchy ; the component parts of those Universities were preserved, but they themselves were superseded ; and there would be almost as great difficulties now in Protestant England, in restoring its Universities to their proper place, as in restoring its Church. It is true, that the Colleges themselves are important political bodies, independent of the civil power ; but at the same time they are national bodies ; they represent not the human mind, but sections of the political community ; and the civil power is itself nothing else than an expression of national power in one or other of its aspects ; whereas a University is an intellectual power, as such, just as the Church is a religious power. Intellect, as well as Faith and Conscience, are authorities simply independent of State and Nation ; State and Nation are but different aspects of one and the same power : and thus the State and Nation will endure chapters and colleges, as they bear city companies and municipalities, but not a Church, not a University. On the other hand, considering the especially popular character of the English constitution, and how congenial to it is the existence of organs of public opinion and of representative bodies, it is not wonderful that the Collegiate system has not merely remained in these later centuries, but has been cherished and advanced.

I am not denying this political value of the Colleges as counterpoises to the government of the day. The greatest weight has actually been given to their acts and decisions in this point of view. Oxford has been made the stage on which political questions have been tried, and political parties have carried on their contests. This was particularly instanced at the time of that famous Session of Parliament, in which Catholic Emancipation was granted. It is well known that the king then on the throne was averse to the measure ; and it was felt that an adhesion to it on the part of the University would exert a material influence on his feelings ; and the question to be determined was what opinion had the University upon it. In the summer of 1828, Sir Robert Peel is said to have consulted* those who were most intimately in his confidence in Oxford, as to the effect which would be produced upon

* Since this was written, Sir. R. Peel's narrative has been given to the world, and seems to contain nothing inconsistent with it.

its members by a ministerial project in favour of Catholics. His friends belonged to a section of the University, who lived very much in their own circle ; and who, as resting both on academical distinction and connection with the great world, did not know, and did not represent, the sentiments of the Colleges. Accordingly, drifting with the current of London opinion themselves, which the necessities of the state and the convenience of the Government, and Parliamentary agitation, had for some time made more and more favourable to Emancipation, those considerable persons returned for answer, that the important act might be passed any day, and that men would go to bed and rise again, without being at all the wiser or more anxious for what had taken place. The Minister seems to have committed himself to this opinion ; and, in consequence, confident of a successful issue of the experiment, he took a bold, and as it turned out, an unlucky step. Member for the University as he was, and elected on the very ground of his opposition to the Catholic claims, he resolved on resigning his seat, and presenting himself for re-election, with an avowed change of opinions. He did this, or at least his friends for him, under the conviction that his triumphant appeal to the votes of the academical constituency, on which he reckoned, would be the best evidence to his Master that the feeling of the country had undergone that revolution which had already, openly or secretly, taken place among statesmen. And hence the extraordinary vehemence of the contest which followed ; the country party, which was represented by the Colleges, being confident of swaying the determination of the king and ejecting the Minister from office, if it managed to eject him from the representation.

Political importance is of course the protection of those who possess it. They who can do so much for or against a Minister, can do as much for themselves; and in consequence, the Colleges of Oxford and Cambridge are perhaps the best protected interests in the whole country. They have endured the most formidable attacks, without succumbing. It was against the wall of Magdalen College, as it has been expressed, that James the Second ran his head. That College received the brunt of the monarch's attack, and in the strength of the nation repelled it. Twenty years ago, when Reform was afloat, when boroughs were disfranchised, corporations created, sees united, dioceses rearranged, chapters remodelled, church property redistributed, and every parsonage perplexed with parliamentary papers of inquiry and tables of returns, the Colleges alone escaped. A determined attack was made upon them by the Ministry of the day, and great apprehensions were excited in the minds of their members. However, calm, perhaps selfish, calculators at Oxford said : " Nothing can touch us ; the Establishment will go, but not the Colleges :" and certainly after one or two sessions, after strong speeches in Parliament from Secretaries of State and experimentalists in Education, and after committees, gatherings, and manifestoes on the part of the members of Colleges, it was owned by friends of Government, that its attempt upon them was a mistake and a failure, and the sooner Government gave it up, the better for Government.

There is no political power in England like a College in the Universities ; it is not a mere local body, as a corporation or London company ; it has allies in every part of the country. When the mind is most impressible, when the affections are warmest, when associations are made for life, when the character is most ingenuous and the sentiment of reverence is most powerful, the future landowner, or statesman, or lawyer, or clergyman comes up to a College in the Universities. There he forms friendships, there he spends his happiest days ; and, whatever is his career there, brilliant or obscure, virtuous or vicious, in after years, when he looks back on the past, he finds himself bound by ties of gratitude and regret to the memories of his College life. He has received favours from the Fellows, he has dined with the Warden or Provost ; he has unconsciously imbibed to the full the beauty and the music of the place. The routine of duties and observances, the preachings and the examinations and the lectures, the dresses and the ceremonies, the officials whom he feared, the buildings or gardens that he admired, rest upon his mind and his heart, and the shade of the past becomes a sort of shrine to which he makes continual silent offerings of attachment and devotion. It is a second home, not so tender, but more noble and majestic and authoritative. Through his life he more or less keeps up a connection with it and its successive sojourners. He has a brother or intimate friend on the foundation, or he is training up his son to be a member of it. When then he hears that a blow is levelled at the Colleges, and that they are in commotion, —that his own College, Head and Fellows, have met together, and put forward a declaration calling on its members to come up and rally round it and defend it, a chord is struck within him, more thrilling than any other ; he burns with *esprit de corps* and generous indignation ; and he is driven up to the scene of his early education, under the keenness of his feelings, to vote, to sign, to protest, to do just what he is told to do, from confidence in the truth of the representations made to him, and from sympathy with the appeal. He appears

on the scene of action ready for battle on the appointed
day, and there he meets others like himself, brought up
by the same summons ; he gazes on old faces, revives old
friendships, awakens old reminiscences, and goes back
to the country with the renewed freshness of youth upon
him. Thus, wherever you look, to the North or South
of England, to the East or West, you find the interest of
the Colleges dominant ; they extend their roots all over
the country, and can scarcely be overturned, certainly
not suddenly overturned, without a revolution.

The consequences on the Colleges themselves are not
satisfactory. They are withdrawn in an especial way
from the action and the influence of public opinion, than
which there is no greater stimulant to right action, as
things are, nor a more effective security against derelic-
tion of duty. The Colleges, left to themselves, in the
course of last century became shamefully indolent and
inactive. They were in no sense any longer places of
education ; they were for the most part mere clubs, and
sinecures, and almshouses, where the inmates did little
but enjoy themselves. They did next to nothing for the
youth confided to them ; suffered them to follow their
own ways and enjoy their own liberty, and often in their
own persons set them a very bad example of using it.
Visitor they practically had, none ; and there was but
one power which could have exerted authority over them,
and most naturally and suitably too ; I mean the University ; but the University could do nothing. The University had no means of acting upon the Colleges ; it was
but a name or a privilege ; it was not a body or a power.
This seems to me the critical evil in the present state of
the English Universities, not that the Colleges are strong,
but that the University has no practical or real jurisdiction over them. Over the members of Colleges it has

jurisdiction, but even then, not as such, but because they are its own members also; over the Head of the College, over the Fellows, over the corporate body, over its property, over its officers, over its acts and regulations within its own precincts, the University has no practical jurisdiction at all. The Tutor indeed is a University office by the Statutes, but the College has made it its own.

In matter of fact the only mode of affecting the Colleges has been by the gradual stress of persevering efforts, by incessant agitation, and by improving the tone and enlightening the minds of their members,—by indirect means altogether. At the beginning of this century, when matters were at the worst at Oxford, some zealous persons attempted to bring the University to bear upon the Colleges. The degrees were at that time given upon no *bonâ fide* examination. The youth, who had passed his three or four years at the place, and wished to graduate, chose his examiners, and invited them to dinner, which the ceremony of examination preceded. Now a degree is a University, not a College distinction ; and the admirable persons, to whom I have alluded, made an effort to restore to the University the power and the practice of ascertaining by a *bona fide* examination the proficiency of every one of its members, who was a candidate for it. Could there be a case in which the right of the University was more clear ? It gave a privilege, and, one might surely think, had a right to lay down the conditions of giving it. Yet it found itself unable to exact of all its members, what was so imperatively its duty, and so natural. The Colleges had first to be persuaded to concede, what the University was so reasonable in requiring. What took place in detail, has never perhaps been published to the world : so much, however, is notorious, that for thirty years one College, by virtue of ancient rights, was able to stand out against the University, and demanded and obtained degrees for its junior members without examination. A generation passed, before its Fellows, acted on by the example and sympathizing in the sentiments of the academical society around them, consented to do for themselves what the University had in vain attempted to do for them.

The University has thus gradually progressed ever since that time; not indeed towards the recovery of that power of jurisdiction, which properly belongs to it, but in separate and particular measures of improvement. One measure was attempted nearly thirty years ago, by an eminent person, still alive, and well known in Dublin, and was thwarted by parties who are long dead; so that it may be spoken of without pain to any one. There are at Oxford several Societies or Houses, which have practically the rank and rights of Colleges, though they have not the legal *status*, or the property. Some of these at that date supported themselves by taking as members those, who, either would not be received, or had actually been sent away, by the Colleges. The existence then of these Societies mainly depended on the sufferance within the University of incompetent, idle, or riotous young men. As they had no endowments, they asked high terms for admission, which of course they could not fail in obtaining from those, who needed to be in some Society or other, with a view to academical advantages, and who could not secure a place in any other body. Evidently, nothing would have been more fatal to such establishments than any successful effort to purify the University of unworthy members. Now, in the gradual advance of reforms, it was attempted by the able person I speak of to introduce an examination of all members on their matriculation. But the independence and the interests of both endowed and not endowed Houses, were at once touched by such a proposition; and a vigorous opposition was set on foot, in particular by the Head of one Society, which abounded in gownsmen of the unsatisfactory character I have been describing. Of course he might as well have shut up his Hall at once, and taken lodgings in High Street, as consent to a measure which would have simply cut off the supply from which it was filled. The private interest prevailed over the public; had the question fairly come before the members of the Colleges generally, it might perhaps have been carried in the affirmative; but it had to be decided first in the board of Heads of Houses, and they were typical specimens of those very Collegiate vices of which I have been speaking. An oligarchy indeed of twenty-four men, perpetual, sovereign, absolutely sheltered from public opinion, and purely irresponsible in their proceedings; standing aloof from the Academical body itself, and intensely scornful towards its judgments, too well entrenched to be susceptible of fear and too majestic to be swayed by flattery or ridicule, they were a prodigy in the England of the nineteenth century.

> Omnis enim per se Divûm natura necesse 'st
> Immortali ævo summâ cum pace fruatur,
> Semota ab nostris rebus, sejunctaque longe :
> Nam privata dolore omni, privata periclis,
> Ipsa suis pollens opibus, nil indiga nostri,
> Nec bene promeritis capitur, nec tangitur irâ.

These authorities naturally were unwilling to handle a question, which concerned so nearly some of themselves; and to this day, though separate Colleges properly insist on the necessary qualifications, in the case of those who are to be admitted to their Lectures, the University itself is not allowed to exercise its reasonable right of examining its members before it matriculates them. It may here be added, that this time-honoured usurpation and abuse, the old Hebdomadal Board, which every thoughtful person felt could not much longer continue, has, amid the jubilations and thanksgivings of all parties, and with scarcely a sigh or murmur from any quarter whatever, expired ignominiously under the Act passed in the last Session of Parliament, 18 Vict.

As to that Act, however, its history is but a fresh illustration of the foregoing remarks. It did not dare to touch the real seat of existing evils, by restoring or giving jurisdiction to the University over the Colleges, much as it professed to effect in the way of radical reform. And in the passage of the Bill through the House of Commons, unless I am mistaken, Ministers found it impossible to get beyond that part of it which related to University alterations. As soon as it went on to legislate for the Colleges, the opposition was too strong for them, and the whole subject was postponed by Parliament, and made over for the consideration of a small Commission, with so many checks and limitations upon its proceedings, that there is reason for fearing that, whatever comes of them, the University will not be less enslaved by the Collegiate interest than it is at present.*

---

* Since this was written, there have been far larger changes in the polity and system of this University.

CHAPTER XX.

UNIVERSITIES AND SEMINARIES:
L'ECOLE DES HAUTES ETUDES.

NO two institutions are more distinct from each other in character, than Universities and Seminaries; and their very difference might seem a pledge that they would not come into collision with each other. Seminaries are for the education of the clergy; Universities for the education of laymen. They are for separate purposes, and they act in separate spheres; yet, such is human infirmity, perhaps they ever will be rivals in their actual working. So at least it has been in time past. Universities grew out of the Episcopal Schools; and then, as time went on, they returned evil for good, and gradually broke the strength, and drained away the life of the institution which had given them birth; an institution too, which was of far more importance to the Church than themselves. Universities are ornaments indeed and bulwarks to Religion; but Seminaries are essential to its purity and efficiency. It is plain then, if the action and interests of the two institutions have conflicted, which side the Church would take in the quarrel. She would side for the injured party, against the aggressor; for the party more important to her, against the party less so. Universities then for a long season have been sustaining the punishment of past ambition; and it seems hardly right to close this survey of them without saying a few words about them under this aspect.

As Seminaries are so necessary to the Church, they are one of her earliest appointments. Scarcely had the New Dispensation opened, when, following the example of the Schools of the Temple and of the Prophets under the Old, St. John is recorded, over and above the public assemblies of the faithful, to have had about him a number of students whom he familiarly instructed ; and, as time went, and power was given to the Church, this School for ecclesiastical learning was placed under the roof of the Bishop. In Rome especially, where we look for the pattern to which other churches are to be conformed, the clergy, not of the city only, but of the provinces, were brought under the immediate eye of the Pope. The Lateran Church, his first Cathedral, had a Seminary attached to it, which remained there till the pontificate of Leo the Tenth, when it was transferred into the heart of the city. The students entered within its walls from the earliest childhood ; but they were not raised from minor orders till the age of twenty, nor did they reach the priesthood till after the trial of many years. Strict as a monastic noviciate, it nevertheless included polite literature in its course ; and a library was attached to it for the use of the seminarists. Here was educated about the year 310, St. Eusebius, afterwards in Arian times the celebrated Bishop of Vercellæ ; and in the dark age which followed, it was the home from childhood of some of the greatest Popes, St. Gregory the Second, St. Paul the First, St. Leo the Third, St. Paschal, and St. Nicholas the First. This venerable Seminary, called anciently the School of the Pontifical Palace, has never failed. Even when the barbarians were wasting the face of Italy, and destroying its accumulations of literature, the great Council of Rome, under Pope Agatho, as I mentioned above, could testify, not indeed to the theological science of the school in that miserable age, but to its faithful preservation of the unbroken teaching of revealed truth and of the traditions of the Fathers. In the thirteenth century, we find it in a flourishing condition, and St. Thomas and Albertus Magnus lecturing in its halls.

Such a prerogative of perpetuity was not enjoyed elsewhere. Europe lay submerged under the waters of a deluge; and, when they receded, schools had to be refounded as well as churches. One of the principal results of Charlemagne's visit to Rome, was the reform or revival of education, both secular and ecclesiastical; and on his return to the north he addressed his well-known letter on the subject to the chapters and monastic bodies through his Empire. Henceforth the Pope made Seminaries obligatory in every Diocese: as to the laity, they attended the public Schools spoken of in a former Chapter.

Seminaries then were long in possession before Universities were imagined; and Universities rose out of them. And, when Universities were established, in order to preserve the *equilibrium* between clerical and lay education, it was decreed, by the authority of the Canons, that secular learning should be studied in the Seminaries, and that each Cathedral should maintain masters for its teaching. It was foreseen that, unless this was done, Universities would supply a higher and a wider education than the Episcopal Schools; and that the clergy would either become inferior to the monks and the laity, or would be drawn within the precincts and influence of Universities.

The latter of these inconveniences actually took place. The lectures in the Universities, after all, were necessarily superior to those which a Seminary could furnish. Accordingly, Colleges for ecclesiastical students were founded in their neighbourhood, and the Cathedral Schools fell in reputation, and were gradually deserted. The youths, who would have found their natural home there, sometimes entered the Colleges aforesaid, sometimes attended the schools of the Regulars, sometimes lived in lodgings as other students. It is sufficient to refer to the Lives of the Medieval Saints for instances of ordination taking place from or at the Universities without Seminary training; take, for example, St. Raymund, St. John of Matha, St. Thomas of Canterbury, St. Edmund, St. John Nepomucene, St. Caietan, St. Carlo, St. Ignatius and his companions, or St. Francis of Sales,—men, who lived in very various ages and countries, and some of whom had to repel the shameless assaults, to which their defenceless condition, in the midst of great cities, exposed them. And thus it was, that by the date of the Council of Trent, Seminaries had all but ceased to exist ; and the candidates for the Priesthood, who had any learning and any religious training, either gained it for themselves, as they could, amid the mixed concourse of a University, or as members of Colleges, which had themselves suffered materially in their discipline from University contact.

There would be danger to their faith and religious temper, as well as to their morals. In Universities, subjects of every sort were disputed publicly ; and boys, who ought to have been schooled at a Seminary in distrust of the intellect and modesty of speculation, were suffered to imbibe a critical, carping, curious spirit, most unbecoming in an ecclesiastic, on the interpretation of difficulties of Scripture, or on the deepest questions of theology. And the state of things became still more grave, when Protestantism arose, and its adherents found means of introducing themselves into the Professorial chairs.

It must be recollected, too, that none but the more able, or more wealthy, or more pushing, could succeed in paying their way at a University. But the majority of ecclesiastics would be poor, and without any great energy or enterprise. These, in the decay of Seminaries, were thrown for education upon the parish schools, which were obviously unequal to the task.

Such was the state of things, to which the Council of Trent put an end. Episcopal Seminaries were restored ; ecclesiastical Colleges in Universities suppressed ; the profounder studies were to be taught under the Bishop's eye : but, to make the observance of this rule easier, it was provided that poorer Dioceses might unite to establish a Provincial Seminary, where the students of each would be all educated together. Such, I suppose, in its ecclesiastical position is the College of Maynooth ; and it is able in consequence to present a staff of Professors, and it exhibits an amount and quality of learning and talent, which invest it almost with a University character.

A further step in the same direction has been taken by the present Pope. Without interfering with the constitution of the Seminaries of his States, he has founded at Rome, at considerable expense, the Seminario Pio, which is to be filled with young ecclesiastics, taken from all dioceses, selected from the whole number on the principle of merit. Their course lasts for nine years, and embraces philosophy, scholastic theology, Holy Scripture, the Fathers, canon law, rites, and ecclesiastical history. It has Professorial Chairs, and the power of granting degrees in Theology and Canon Law: it is in fact an ecclesiastical University.

It cannot be denied, that, while Seminaries have been

fostered and advanced during these last centuries, Universities have been out of favour. Two only were founded, as it would appear, in the sixteenth century, and these were expressly intended to counteract the spread of Protestantism. The last great Medieval University was the famous foundation, or foundations, at Alcala, due to the munificence of Cardinal Ximenes, in the year 1500. Since that date, it has been usual rather to bestow on Collegiate institutions the privileges of Universities, or in other words to erect a University in a College, than to adhere to the medieval type. Such appears to be the nature of the University, which, with the recognition of the British Government, has lately been founded at Quebec. To the same distinction another College seems tending, unless civil obstacles hinder it, which to us is of especial interest, for the sake of the prelate who founded it, from its progress hitherto, and because its Superior is an Irishman : I mean *L'Ecole des Hautes Etudes* at Paris. But, above all, it will have a definite place, if it proceeds, as it promises to do, in the history of Universities, and for that reason deserves some distinct mention here.

It was commenced by the immediate predecessor of the present Archbishop of Paris, a prelate of glorious memory ; whose blood, offered in behalf of his flock, seems already to have borne those fruits, which are the usual result of suffering in the cause of religion, and to have called down from Heaven upon his flock the blessings which he so ardently desired for them. As one of his scholars in the seat of learning which he has founded, expresses it,

> Audiit, et, miseratus oves per prælia promptus,
> Perque neces varias fertur, pia victima, pastor.
> Heu scelus infandum ! ruptæ dum fœdera pacis

Nectere, et insanos tentas cohibere furores,
Occidis, ac moriens extremâ voce " Beatos,
Si nostro," exclamas, " cessaret sanguine sanguis ! "

Nor has the Archbishop's been the only blood by
which his Institution has been sanctified, nor is that Institution the only school of devotion and science, which
has occupied the spot on which it is placed. That spot
was long ago, for centuries, the home of theologians,
and it has become in the generation before us the scene
and monument of Martyrs. It is no other than the
famous Carmes, where, on the terrible outburst of the
Revolution, in 1792, so many Bishops and Priests of
France were massacred.

This of course is not the occasion for enumerating
the noble foundations which of old time were brought
under the shadow of the great University of Paris, the
first school of the Church. I have touched upon the subject in a former Chapter. Nations, provinces, monastic
bodies, had their several houses there, and royal personages and wealthy ecclesiastics rejoiced to leave endowments there for the benefit of religion and learning.
The southern and more healthy bank of the river was
allotted to it, and its manifold establishments gathered
round the hill of St. Genevieve. The Carmelites were
originally at an inconvenient distance from the Saint,
till Philip the Fair, King of France, gave them ground
at the foot of her hill, sufficient for a Church and a
Monastery. This was about the year 1300; and for the
last two centuries before the dreadful events, to which I
have referred, it is described, in particular, as having
been one of the most peaceable asylums of science and
faith. When the Revolution came, and the clergy,
hindered, by their duty to the Church, from taking the
oaths which were presented for their acceptance, were

subjected to an imprisonment which was to end in death, the Carmelite Convent was one of the buildings selected for their confinement. Here, or rather in the small church attached to the Convent, in the month of August, 1792, were crowded, first 120, and at length as many as 175 or 200, according to various accounts, of all ranks and ages of the clergy.

The first prisoners seem to have been the secular clergy of the city ; to these were added a number of superannuated priests, who lived on pensions, and then a number of youthful seminarists. Besides these, were three Bishops, various Professors and Preachers, and the heads of certain religious congregations and collegiate bodies. The second of September was the day of their memorable conflict with the powers of evil, then for a brief season in the ascendant. On that day were imprisoned together in the house and garden of the Carmes (besides the Seculars), Benedictines, Capuchins, Cordeliers, Sulpicians, disbanded Jesuits, members of the Sorbonne, and of the College of Navarre. The revolutionary tribunal held its sitting in one of the rooms of the Convent, and pronounced them guilty of disloyalty to France ; and then the revolutionary soldiers impatiently burst in upon the prisoners to carry its sentence into execution. The massacre lasted for three hours ; eighty priests were slaughtered in the garden ; the walls of the orangery at its end, now a chapel, are still stained, or rather daubed over, with their blood. On about a hundred others the outward door of the Convent was opened for their passage into the street ; they were called forward one by one; the assassins stood in double file, and, as their victims ran the gauntlet between them, above sixty perished under their blows, thirty-six or thirty-eight escaping into the city. These noble soldiers of the Church waited for their turn, and went to death and died, with their office books in their hands, and its psalms and prayers upon their tongues.

To have lived in Paris then, and to have heard the report, and seen the tokens, of what was going on, was to have had some share in her agony, who of old time looked upon One uplifted on the Cross; yet, bitter as the sorrow must have been, surely it was lighter after all, than that which has oppressed the Catholic heart at other miserable seasons. It was surely lighter than that which overspread Christendom at the time when religion was overthrown in England, while, for a long course of years, for the greater part of a century, some fresh deed of sacrilege was perpetrated day by day, and a false-hearted clergy and a cowardly laity allowed the monarch and his nobles in their deeds of violence and avarice. For the death of traitors makes no sign, and whispers scarce a hope of a revival; but a martyrdom is a victory, and a Church which falls from an external blow, rises again by its inward vigour. This is fulfilled before our eyes in the instance of France, and of that memorable spot of which I have been speaking. Good reason why the late Archbishop should have placed his new institution in that sanctuary of martyrs, himself destined so soon afterwards to be gathered to their company.

Institutions, which are to thrive and last, generally have humble beginnings, sometimes a scope narrower than that which they eventually profess; as there has been enough to suggest, even in the sketches which have been set before the reader in these pages. So has it been, so is it still perhaps, in the case of the school now under consideration. Its first object, when it opened in 1845, was one indeed of high importance in itself, being no less than that of providing Professors for the *petits seminaires* of France. However, it is also described as "a noviciate of ecclesiastics intended for teachers of the young clergy," which is something of an advance in dignity and moment upon the object as originally conceived. When the title was given, by which the school is now designated, does not appear; but an "Ecole des Hautes Etudes," also promises, or presages, more than the first profession of its founder. It speaks of high studies, and studies for their own sake, which hardly is equivalent to a school for schoolmasters. Perhaps it was discovered, as soon as attention was directed to the subject, that, in order to teach well, more must be learned by the teacher than he has formally to impart to the pupil; that he must be above his work, and know, and know accurately and philosophically, what he does not actually profess. Accordingly, we find the students are instructed, not only in the languages, but in the literatures, of Greece, Rome, and France; in general history; and in philosophy, and in the bearings of religion upon it,—in which probably are included the study of the Evidences of Christianity, of the objections made to it and their refutation. Nor is the direct cultivation of their minds forgotten; the perfection of our intellectual nature seems to be judgment; and what judgment is in the conduct of life, such is taste in our social intercourse, in literature, and the fine arts. Now we are told that it is provided, with a largeness of view which does honour to the projectors of the Institution, that its students, though ecclesiastical, should be made acquainted with the ideas and sentiments, the tone of mind, and character of thought, and method of expression, which distinguish the great writers both of ancient and modern times; in order that, while they exercise themselves in composition, they may have a really good standard to work by, and may learn even unconsciously to imitate what has become familiar to them by frequent perusal.

Nor is this the limit of their studies; the present Archbishop has added mathematics, physics, and geology. Little is evidently now wanting to complete a University course ; and accordingly we find they have been led for some time to present themselves for the formal examinations which are the condition of an academical degree. Two years ago they numbered as many as thirty-two licentiates in arts; and the doctorate, which is preceded by the study of the Fathers and ecclesiastical history, had then been attained by three. Meanwhile the Synod of Paris has made the Institution the metropolitan school of the province. Moreover, an association has been formed for founding burses in favour of poorer students, to which the ladies of the higher classes and the curés of Paris are liberally contributing.

The Institution would have no pretension to the historical name of " University," while it was confined to ecclesiastics ; and the present Archbishop, pursuing the process of development, which had been so rapid in its movements before him, has opened it to the laity. The two descriptions of students are kept distinct, except at lecture, examinations, and literary meetings. The lay youths are received, as it would appear, after the age of eighteen, and are educated for the Professions, while they gain of course the benefit of being imbued with sound principles of religion. Literature and mathematics form their principal studies ; they are practised, moreover, as well as the ecclesiastics, in exercises of a logical character, in elocution and composition. Many of these youths pass on to the *Ecole Polytechnique,* or other government schools ; or even belong to them, while they attend lectures at the Carmes.

The cause of truth, never dominant in this world, has its ebbs and flows. It is pleasant to live in a day, when the tide is coming in. Such is our own day ; and, without forgetting that there are many rocks on the shore to throw us back and break our advance for the moment, and to task our patience before we cover them,—that physical force is now on the world's side, and that the world will be provoked to more active enmity against the Church in proportion to her success,—still we may surely encourage ourselves by a thousand tokens all around us now, that this is our hour, whatever be its duration, the hour for great hopes, great schemes, great efforts, great beginnings. We may live indeed to see but little built, but we shall see much founded. A new era seems to be at hand, and a bolder policy is showing itself. In particular, the Church feels herself strong enough in the provisions and safeguards which a painful experience has suggested against prospective dangers, to recommence the age of Universities. Louvain revived twenty years ago ; a new University of Paris seems to be in prospect, or at least in hope ; the report is current that a University is soon to be erected in Austria ; and the University of Ireland is proving its possibility by entering on its work, and presaging its future success by its triumph over the difficulties of its commencement.

II.

THE NORTHMEN AND · NORMANS IN ENGLAND AND IRELAND.

(From the *Rambler* of May and July, 1859.)

THE NORTHMEN AND NORMANS IN ENGLAND AND IRELAND.

§ I.

THE collection, under the author's revision, in one handsome volume, of the sermons, lectures, and speeches, delivered by the Cardinal Archbishop in the course of his late tour in Ireland, accompanied as it is with a connecting and illustrative narrative, is one of the most remarkable publications which has for some time issued from the press. It is the record of a visit which has a double claim upon our attention, both in its relation to the generous people who acted the part of hosts upon the occasion, and the distinguished personage who presented himself as their guest.

The facts of the case are these : the Cardinal, complying with the invitation of an Irish Prelate, who requested his presence at the opening of a new church, went at the appointed time, without expectation of any call upon him for more than such ordinary exertion of mind and body as the ostensible purpose involved ; but, to his great astonishment, he found that his coming had struck a chord in the heart of a Catholic people, whose ecclesiastical sentiments are the more keen and delicate, because they are seldom brought into play. A Cardinal of Holy Church was to them the representative of the Vicar of Christ, and nothing else ; his coming was all but the advent of the Holy Father ; and he suddenly found that he must respond most, out of his own extemporized resources, to the enthusiastic feelings and the acts of homage of the millions who were welcoming him. But he was equal to the occasion: meeting the run made upon him with a spirit and fertility of thought, which no other public man in England could have displayed. He was carried about, at the will of others, from one part of the island to another ; he found himself surrounded in turn by high and low, educated and illiterate ; by boys at school, or by the youth of towns ; by religious communities, or by official and dignified persons. He was called to address each class or description of men in matter and manner suitable to its own standard of taste and thought ; he had to appear in pulpits, in lecture-rooms, at dinner-tables, on railroad-stations, and always to say something new, apposite, and effective. How he met these unexpected and multifarious calls on him, the volume, to which we have referred, is, we repeat, the record ; and, though nothing else remained of Cardinal Wiseman for the admiration of posterity, of the many things which he has spoken and written, there is enough here to justify the estimation in which his contemporaries have held the talents and the attainments of the first Archbishop of Westminster.

Insufficient record it certainly would be, after all, of the actual resources of one who can speak with readiness and point in half-a-dozen languages, without being detected at once for a foreigner in any of them ; and who, at ten minutes' warning, can address a congregation from a French pulpit, or the select audience of an Italian Academy. Insufficient also for another reason, because it might be objected that the enthusiasm of a multitude is catching, and that, when a visitor is the stimulating cause of such transports and the object of such open-hearted greeting, on the part of a vast population, his whole heart responds to the call made upon its affections, and his intellect, as if spontaneously grateful, expands and revels in the enjoyment of those festive scenes and high celebrations by which it is successively solicited.

I.

It is not every guest who is invested with such pleasant associations, and elicits such joyous emotions in the Irish mind. It is not every stranger who is able to bask in the reverberation of those beams of light, which his own presence sheds over the Irish landscape. There is a visitor who rouses memories as dark, as the look and voice of a Cardinal are inspiring and consolatory. That visitor is the Saxon; and, if the Saxon happens to be a Catholic, he has in consequence a trial to sustain of his own, of which the continental tourist has no experience from Austrian police, or Russian douane, or Turkish quarantine. He has turned his eyes to a country bound to him by the ties of a common faith; and, when he lands at Cork or Kingstown, he breathes more freely from the thought that he has left a Protestant people behind him, and is among his co-religionists. He has but this one imagination before his mind, that he is in the midst of those who will not despise him for his faith's sake, who name the same sacred names, and utter the same prayers, and use the same devotions, as he does himself; whose churches are the houses of his God, and whose numerous clergy are the physicians of his soul. He penetrates into the heart of the country; and he recognises an innocence in the young face, and a piety

17

and patience in the aged voice, which strikingly and sadly contrast with the habits of his own rural population. Scattered over these masses of peasantry, and peasants themselves, he hears of a number of lay persons who have dedicated themselves to a religious celibate, and who, by their superior knowledge as well as sanctity, are the natural and ready guides of their humble brethren. He finds the population as munificent as it is pious, and doing greater works for God out of their poverty, than the rich and noble elsewhere accomplish in their abundance. He finds them characterised by a love of kindred so tender and faithful, as to lead them, on their compulsory expatriation, to send back from their first earnings in another hemisphere incredible sums, with the purpose of bringing over to it those dear ones whom they have left in the old country. And he finds himself received with that warmth of hospitality which ever has been Ireland's boast ; and, as far as he is personally concerned, his blood is forgotten in his baptism. How shall he not, under such circumstances, exult in his new friends, and feel words deficient to express both his deep reverence for their virtues, and his strong sympathy in their heavy trials ?

But, alas, feelings which are so just and so natural in themselves, which are so congruous in the breast of Frenchman or Italian, are impertinent in him. He does not at first recollect, as he ought to recollect, that he comes among the Irish people as the representative of persons, and actions, and catastrophes, which it is not pleasant to any one to think about ; that he is responsible for the deeds of his forefathers, and of his contemporary Parliaments and Executive ; that he is one of a strong, unscrupulous, tyrannous race, standing upon

the soil of the injured. He does not bear in mind that
it is as easy to forget injuring, as it is difficult to forget
being injured. He does not admit, even in his imagination, the judgment and the sentence which the past
history of Erin sternly pronounces upon him. He has
to be recalled to himself, and to be taught by what he
hears around him, that an Englishman has no right to
open his heart, and indulge his honest affection towards
the Irish race, as if nothing had happened between him
and them. The voices, so full of blessings for their
Maker and their own kindred, adopt a very different
strain and cadence when the name of England is mentioned ; and, even when he is most warmly and gene-
rously received by those whom he falls in with, he will
be repudiated by those who are at a distance. Natural
amiableness, religious principle, education, reading,
knowledge of the world, and the charities of civilization,
repress or eradicate these bitter feelings in the class in
which he finds his friends ; but, as to the population,
one sentiment of hatred against the oppressor "manet
altâ mente repôstum." The wrongs which England has
inflicted are faithfully remembered ; her services are
viewed with incredulity or resentment ; her name and
fellowship are abominated ; the news of her prosperity
heard with disgust ; the anticipation of her possible reverses nursed and cherished as the best of consolations.
The success of France and Russia over her armies, of
Yankee or Hindoo, is fervently desired, as the first in-
stalment of a debt accumulated through seven centuries;
and that, even though those armies are in so large a
proportion recruited from the Irish soil. If he ventures
at least to ask for prayers for England, he receives one
answer—a prayer that she may receive her due. It is
as if the air rang with the old Jewish words, " O

daughter of Babylon, blessed shall he be who shall repay thee as thou hast paid to us !"

And, sad to say, he feels that he is not the person to complain. What a writer in the *Atlantis* remarks of the behaviour of the English towards Joan of Arc, applies too truly to the case of others also who have resisted them and fallen into their hands. It was that *væ victis*, which they lately wreaked upon the natives of India ; it was that passionate indignation at insurgent feebleness, which has made them in past times so cruel and unjust to the Irish. "From the moment of her capture," says the writer in question, "the English set their hearts upon obtaining possession of her. That deep pride of character, which was, perhaps, a large element in their success, had its darker expressions. It rendered them intolerant of the slightest defeat or check, and engendered towards any enemy who might inflict it upon them, a hatred stopping short at no calumny and no cruelty. Their hatred of Joan was something wholly indescribable, and from the beginning they had spread the most abominable slanders concerning her. In their proceedings, two circumstances curiously characteristic of the nation appear : first their accomplishing their purpose under the colour and in form of strict law ; and secondly, their using as their instruments natives of the country whose subjugation they sought."[*]

2.

It is remarkable, that the Holy See, to whose initiative the union of the two countries is historically traceable, is in no respect made chargeable by the Irish people with the evils which have resulted to them

[*] Atlantis, vol. i. p. 272.

from it. And the fact itself is remarkable, that the Holy See really should be responsible for that initiative. There are other nations in the world illmatched, besides the English and Irish ; there are other instances of the rule of strangers, and of the compulsory submission of the governed ; but the Pope cannot be called to account for such political arrangements. The Pope did not give Greece to the Sublime Porte, or Warsaw to Russia, or Venice to Austria, or Belgium to Holland, or Norway to Sweden, or the cities of the Rhine to Prussia, or the Septinsular Republic to England ; but, even had he done so, still in some of these instances he would have but united together members of one race—German to German, Fleming to Fleming, Slave to Slave. But it is certainly most remarkable that a power so authoritative, even when not divine, so sagacious even when not supernatural ; whose acts are so literally the personal acts of the Pontiff who represents it for the time being, yet of such solemn force and such tremendous permanence ; which, by appealing to its present prerogatives, involves itself in its past decisions ; which " openeth, and no man shutteth ; and shutteth and no man openeth," —it does, we say, require some explanation, how an oracle so high and irrefragable should have given its religious sanction to a union apparently so unblest, and which at the end of seven centuries is as devoid of moral basis, or of effective accomplishment, as it was at the commencement. What time German and Italian, Turk and Greek, shall be contented with each other ; when " the lion and the sheep shall abide together ; " and "the calf and the bear shall feed,"—then, it may be argued, will there be a good understanding between two nations so contradictory the one of the other—the one an old immemorial race, the other the composite of a hundred

stocks ; the one possessed of an antique civilization, the
other civilized by Christianity ; the one glorying in its
schools and its philosophy, the other in its works and
institutions ; the one subtle, acute, speculative, the other
wise, patient, energetic ; the one admiring and requiring
the strong arm of despotic rule, the other spontaneously
developing itself in methods of self-government and of
individual competition.   And yet, not once or twice
only has the Holy See recognised in Ireland a territory
of the English Crown.   Adrian IV., indeed, the first
Pope who countenanced the invasion of Henry II., was
an Englishman ; but not on his bull did Henry rely for
the justification of his proceedings.   He did not publish
it in Ireland till he had received a confirmatory brief
from Alexander III.   Nor was Alexander the only Pope
who distinctly recognised it ;   John XXII., a hundred
and sixty years afterwards, refers to it in his brief addressed to Edward II.*

Such have been the dealings of the Holy See in times
past with Ireland ; yet it has not thereby roused against
itself any resentful feelings in the mind of its natives.
Doubtless their good sense understands well, that, whatever be decided about the expedience of the act of annexa-
tion itself, its serious evils did not begin till the English
monarchy was false to the Pope as well as to Ireland.
Up to that date the settlers in the conquered soil became so attached and united to it and to its people, that,
according to the proverb, they were *Hibernis hiberniores*.
It is Protestantism which has been the tyrannical oppressor of the Irish ; and we suppose that Protestantism
neither asked nor needed letters apostolic or consecrated
banner to encourage it in the war which it waged against
Irish Catholicism.   Neither Cromwell nor William of

* Lanigan, vol. pp. 165-6.

Nassau waited for the Pope's leave, or sought his blessing, in his military operations against Ireland, any more than Queen Victoria appeals to the Pope's grant for her title of Defender of the Faith, though from the Pope it was originally derived. The Tudor, not the Plantagenet, introduced the iron age of Ireland.

We are led, by the course of thought into which we have fallen, to attempt to investigate the policy of the Holy See in the twelfth century, in annexing Ireland to the English crown; and, in order to keep our eyes in the right direction in doing so, there are two points which it is necessary that we should steadily bear in mind :—the one is, that we ought to have at least some general notion of what really is the *object* of a spiritual power in political transactions of any kind ; and the other, that we ought to be careful to distinguish between the simple object, which in a given case such a power may set before itself, and the *circumstances* under which that object is actually carried out,—circumstances which, grievous though they be in themselves and contrary to its intention, it may, after all, think very light nevertheless in comparison of the importance and the solid advantages of the object itself. Thus, for instance, as regards England, the tyranny of the Conqueror might involve the English nation in terrible sufferings ; and yet the Holy See, in its calm wisdom, might deliberately take upon itself the responsibility, not of William's gratuitous tyranny, which it abhorred, but of his conquest notwithstanding, considering the vast spiritual benefits to the English which that conquest reasonably promised. Thus the object which the Holy See pursued in this case would be a *religious one*, and the circumstantial evils in which it had no real part were *temporal*.

The last sentence will suggest the point of view from which we mean to consider the question before us, and the sort of answer which we shall give to it. We say then, first, that the providential position and antecedents of England and Ireland respectively, whether ecclesiastical or civil, had been so parallel, as to constitute a sort of apology for the conduct of the Roman Pontiff, should he be found to have pursued the same line of policy towards the two islands : and secondly, that, in matter of fact, the policy which he pursued towards Ireland at the date in question, and which seems at first sight so unfair, is precisely that which he had adopted towards England a century earlier, except that its concomitants in the case of England were far more penal, in severity at least, if not in duration. In other words, looking at the course of events as a whole, we see that, in spite of the striking contrast in national characteristics which exists between the English and the Irish, in spite of their mutual jealousies and repulsions, in spite of the injuries which the one people has inflicted, and the other, according to its opportunities, has retaliated,—nevertheless their relation towards the rest of the world, and their circumstances, through the greater part of their Christian period, have been one and the same ; one and the same in their geographical, ecclesiastical, and political aspect, one and the same in their conversion, in their missionary labours, in their sufferings from northern pirates and Norman knights, in their religious molestation from the Welsh Tudors, and even now in their colonization of the whole earth external to the continent of Europe. They have seemed to the Pope as one, and as one he has treated them.

3

In entering upon this historical parallel, we have no

need to do more than refer to its earlier points ; they are
so well known, and have been so often enlarged on. We
are all familiar with the circumstances of the admission
of the two people into the Christian fold, their first fervour, and their opportune custody of sacred and secular
knowledge. Rome was the missionary centre, from
which each of them in turn received the revealed doctrine;
from Rome Patrick first, and then Augustine, received
both their mission and their tradition; and the grace and
merits of the two apostles so wrought in the countries
which they respectively converted, that those countries
became rivals of each other in sanctity, learning and
zealous works. The Irish saints are said to be more
than can be counted ; the English are remarkable for
being clustered into families, and those of royal lineage.
More than eighty princes are considered to have a place
in the glorious catalogue of England, and above thirty
rulers gave up their temporal power for pilgrimage or
the cloister. We should not give utterance to so familiar
a tale except for its bearing upon our main point,—that
countries which resembled each other in such great
points, were likely to be associated together by foreigners
as one in their ecclesiastical, nay in their secular and
political destinies. They were called " the Islands of the
Saints ; " and sanctity implies unity. The Pope could
wish for nothing better than that what was thus bound
together in heaven should be bound on earth also.

There were other striking points of a like character in
the two countries, which would forcibly affect the imagination of the Continent. They had been both the refuge of
Christianity, for a time almost exterminated in Christendom, and the centres of its propagation in countries still
heathen. Secluded from the rest of Europe by the
stormy waters in which they lay, they were converted

just in time to be put in charge with the sacred treasures of Revelation and of the learning of the old world, in that dreary time which intervened between Gregory and Charlemagne. They formed schools, collected libraries, and supplied the Continent with preachers and teachers. While the English Boniface and his followers formed churches in Germany and towards the north, under the immediate sanction of the Holy See, the Irish Columbanus, the representative of an earlier age, became the rival of St. Benedict in France and Lombardy.

All human matters tend to decay and dissolution : it was not to be supposed that what these two islands did for a season, they would do for ever. The time came when their special mission ended. In the first two centuries of English Christianity we may reckon up one hundred and fifty saints ; then they fall off. In the ninth century a superficial survey of history will furnish us with sixteen ; in the tenth with eight ; in the eleventh with ten. As to Ireland, a vision is said to have been granted to St. Patrick, in which he first saw the whole of Ireland brilliantly lit up ; then the mountains only; then only a few lamps twinkling in the valleys. The same decline of sanctity is intimated in the account of this vision given in Ussher's ancient catalogue. " The first order of saints is *sanctissimus*, the next *sanctior*, the third *sanctus*. The first flames as the sun, the second as the moon, the third as the stars."* A darkness was then to follow. Here we are led on to a further point in the historical parallel which the two Islands furnish. The darkness was not simply the inward decay of sanctity, which had already showed itself ; it was the in-rushing of troubles from without ;—or if a further decay, it was the decay which follows upon temporal tumult and dis-

---

* Usser. Eccl. Brit. Antiq. p. 474.

order. Most necessary and pertinent is the prayer, *Da pacem in diebus nostris;* for war is the destruction of religion,—first by cutting off the saints by the sword, secondly by hindering the opportunities of their reproduction, Such was the visitation coming on England and Ireland; it was the dark presence of the pirates of the North.

There was a fitness in the course of things, that the two people, who had rejoiced in one prosperity, should drink together the same cup of suffering : *Amabiles et decori in vitâ suâ, in morte non divisi.* They made what may be called their will at about the same date, and bequeathed their special schools, religious and secular, and professors to conduct them, to Charlemagne and the University of Paris. Hardly had they done so, when the countrymen of Ragnar Lodbrog appeared off their coasts. Alcuin went to Paris in A.D. 782 ; and the Northmen first landed in England in 787, and first landed in Ireland in 797.

4.

Hitherto the barbarian inroads had been but the migration of restless populations from the East to the West. Across the table-lands of Asia, or the vast plains of Europe, the mighty host moved on, with the speed of horsemen, or the slow pace of flocks and herds, or with temporary halts or long settlements here or there, as the case might be, according to their own pleasure, or the compulsion of an enemy in their rear. Before them the land was open and presented no obstacle, and they had only to move in order to go forward. The distant ocean was the only term of their wanderings and of their conquests. Thus the two islands of the West were safe from this invasion, which lasted for centuries. It was otherwise with the fierce northern tribes, who afterwards appear upon the scene of history. What the horse was to the Hun, such was the light bark to the Norwegian or Dane.* If the Hun was never on foot, the Northman never needed land. The sea, instead of being a barrier, was the very element and condition of his victories, and it carried him upon its bosom up and down with an ease and expedition which even in an open plain country was impracticable.

We must enlarge on these Northmen, from the course which their history takes in the sequel. Their chiefs, then, called the sea-kings, were the younger sons of the petty princes of Scandinavia, sent out to seek their fortunes and to win glory upon the wide ocean, with the outfit of a vessel and its equipments.† They ravaged far and wide at will, and no retaliation on them was possible ; for these pirates, unlike their more civilized brethren of Algiers or of Greece, had not a yard of territory, a town, or a fort, no property besides their vessels, no subjects but their crews. They were not allowed either to inherit or transmit the booty which these piratical expeditions collected. Such personal possessions, even to the gold and silver, were buried with the plunderer. Never to sleep under a smoke-burnished roof, never to fill the cup over the cheerful hearth, was their boast and their principle. If they drank, it was not for indulgence or for good company ; but, by a degrading extravagance, to rival the beasts of prey and blood in their wild brutality. Their berserkirs, half madmen, half magicians, studied to imitate dogs, or wolves, or bears, in their methods of attack, tearing off their clothes, howling, gnawing their armour, till they collapsed from the violence of their preternatural ferocity.

* Flanagan, English Church Hist. vol. i. p. 180.   † Turner, vol. i. p. 424.

Though the sea was their element, they were equally prepared to avail themselves of the land, and equally at home upon it. They seemed to have a ubiquitous presence. As the lightning, the hurricane, or the plague sweeps through its inevitable circuit, or hurries along its capricious zigzag path, so these marauders were at one time lurking in the deep creek, and darting out upon the unsuspecting voyager, at another hurrying along the coast, making their sudden descent and as suddenly re-embarking; and at another, landing, leaving their vessels, and running up the country. They had come and gone, and done their terrible work, before they could be encountered. Now they were on the German Sea, now in the Bay of Biscay, now in the Mediterranean. They were at Rouen, at Amiens, at Paris, on the Loire, in Burgundy.* They were in Brittany, in Aquitaine, at Bordeaux. They landed on the coast near Cadiz, and faced the Moorish monarch in three battles. Then, again, they were in Holland, on Walcheren, at Cambray, at Hainault, at Louvain, and other parts of Belgium. They set fire to the villages and to the crops; they massacred the peasantry; they crucified, they impaled; they spitted infants on their lances; cruelty was one of the glories of their warfare.

But England and Ireland, as first meeting them in their descent to the south, bore the brunt of their fury. The two islands could not escape the common lot; ruin had overtaken the Continent in the earlier centuries, and now their turn was come. It is scarcely necessary to trace out the particulars of that awful visitation, under which two nations, who had been rivals in saintly memories, became rivals also in the depth of a spiritual degradation; a degradation which made them reckless

* Vid. Palgrave's Normandy, vol. i. p. 418. etc. (1872.)

and desperate, and ungrateful to the record of God's past mercies and their fathers' noble deeds. England for two hundred and fifty years, and Ireland for an additional hundred, were the prey, the victims, the bond-slaves of these savage Northmen. What happened to one country, happened on the whole to the other; and what we have already said of their foe in his descent upon other countries, might enable us to compose a history of his dealings with these, though no chronicle remain to tell it. The Northman pillaged the great monastery of Banchor, and slaughtered or scattered its inmates; he burned Armagh and its Cathedral; he burned Ferns, and Kildare, with its famous church; he sacked Cork; he wasted the whole of Connaught. He cast his anchors in the Boyne and Liffey, and then spread his devastations inland over the plains through which those rivers flow, plundering churches, monastries, villages, and carrying off the flocks and herds as booty. In the long course of years no part of the island escaped; bishops were put to death, sacred vessels profaned and carried off, libraries destroyed. When at length the miserable population submitted from mere exhaustion, and when war seemed at an end, for resistance was impossible, and provisions were consumed, then the invading tribes quarrelled with each other, and a new course of conflicts and devastations followed.

As to England, who does not know the terrible epic, so it may be called, of the eighth and ninth centuries? How Ragnar Lodbrog, in opposition to his wife Aslauga's counsel, built two large ships in his pride, which were useless in the hour of defeat, when swiftness of flight was as necessary to him as vigour in attack; and how these clumsy vessels were wrecked on the Northumbrian

coast, and Ragnar taken prisoner ; and lastly, how the
barbarous Ella, the prince of the district, doomed his
fallen enemy to die in prison by the stings of venomous
snakes ? His *Quida*, or death-song, as he was supposed
to sing it in his dungeon, is preserved,* and traces out
the history of those savage exploits which were his sole
comfort when he was giving up his soul to his Maker.
Fifty-one times, as he recounts, had he rallied his people
around his uplifted lance ; and he died in the joyful
thought that his sons would avenge him. He was not
wrong in that belief. Alfred was a youth of nineteen in
his brother's court, when the news came that eight kings
and twenty earls, all relations or friends of Ragnar,
headed by three of his sons, of whom the cruel Ingwar
and Hubba were two, had landed on the east coast.
They moved to York, gained possession of Ella, split
him into the form of a spread eagle, and rubbed salt
into his wounds. Next they got possession of Notting-
ham. Then they were back again into Lincolnshire,
desolating and destroying the whole face of the country.
They burned the famous abbeys Bardeney and Croyland, and tortured and murdered the monks. Then they
went to Peterborough and to Ely, where the nuns, according to the well-known history, mutilated their faces
to preserve their honour. Then they fought, defeated,
captured, tortured, and martyred St. Edmund. Next
they got possession of Reading. We mention these
familiar facts not for their own sake, but to illustrate
that fearful celerity and almost caprice of locomotion,
with which they rushed to and fro about the country.
At Reading they were met by Alfred, who shortly after
succeeded to the throne of Wessex, and who in the first
year of his royal power fought eight pitched battles with

* Turner, Anglo-Saxons, vol. i. p. 464.

them.   Such is our introduction to the romantic history of that celebrated king.

5.

Let not the reader suppose that we are referring to this history for its own sake, forgetful of the argument which we are pursuing.   We have now arrived at a fresh point in the parallelism which exists in the fortunes of the two islands ; for, strange to say, Ireland had its Alfred also,—that is, its champion of its own people against the Northmen, as brave and as wise, as successful in his own time, as unsuccessful in the ultimate result. This was the great king of Munster, Brian Boroimhe.

Alfred crowded the exploits of his life in the short space of fifty-one years.   He is known in history from his boyhood, when he was sent to Rome ; and he succeeded to his brother's throne and to the conduct of the Northman war at the age of twenty-two.   Brian too succeeded to his brother in the government of Munster ; but he was not elevated to the royal prerogatives of king of Ireland till he was in his seventy-sixth year. Maelseachlainn, or Malachi, in whose line the royal power was hereditary, had in the former time of his life defeated the Northmen in three great battles, in one of which he had taken from their chief's neck the famous collar of gold, which is said still to be preserved in Dublin ; but the time came when he seemed to have lost the energy which he once displayed, and to be unequal to the emergency.   At length he was forced to surrender his sovereignty to Brian, and Brian was installed in his place at Tara ; and now, at the advanced age which we have mentioned, Brian's historical existence begins.

Brian was the choice of the great men of the country, but he got possession of the royal power by his own act ;

and his mode of substituting himself for Malachi was characterized by a picturesque chivalrousness which reminds us of the era of the Crusades. He came up against the king with a large force, to compel his resignation. Nothing was left to the weaker but to submit, and Malachi came to his rival's camp for the purpose. Brian received him with all courtesy, condoled with him on the fickleness of his friends, declined to accept his resignation at once, and gave him a year to recover his broken fortunes. He accompanied this respite with the present of two hundred and forty fine horses, though not in that spirit of mockery which accompanied a like offer made of old by an Assyrian monarch to a Jewish king, and with other presents of great value to the king's attendants. At the end of the year Malachi quietly gave in.

Brian was not possessed of the literary attainments and general cultivation of mind which were so conspicuous in Alfred ; but he equalled him in his patriotism, in his patronage of letters, and in his devotion. As soon as he was king, he confirmed the chieftains in their ancient privileges, and attached them to him by presents. He revised the genealogies of families and distributed them into houses, and regulated the precedence of the nobility. He reformed the laws, and enforced their observance ; and we have the pleasing and well known legend, in illustration of the peaceful condition of the country, that in his days a young and beautiful lady, arrayed in the most costly apparel, with all her jewels on, and a wand in her hand surmounted by a precious ring, traversed the island from sea to sea without attendant and without mischance. As to the pirates of the North, he took the best means of preventing their inroads by building a fleet. He erected forts in various parts of the country.

18

He repaired the high roads, and cast bridges over the rivers. Nor was religion a secondary concern with him. He addressed himself to the rebuilding of churches and monasteries, which had been destroyed ; he restored the public schools, and multiplied them ; he did his best to collect new libraries. Such was the energy of this wonderful old man.

These were the great works of twelve years ; and at length the time came, though long delayed, when he was to end a glorious reign with a more glorious death, as a sort of victim for the people he had so largely benefited. In the great battle of Clontarf, fought in 1014, he engaged the united forces of Scandinavians and Scots, Britons from Wales and Cornwall, Danes settled in the country, and insurgents of Leinster. The day of battle was Good Friday, which in that year fell as late as St. George's Day, April 23rd. With the crucifix in his left hand, and the sword in his right, he rode with his son and heir Morogh through the ranks of his army, exhorting them gladly to shed their blood for the Church, as the Lord of the Church had shed His precious blood for them. He gained the victory with the slaughter of 16,000 of the enemy ; but it was at the price of his own and of his son's life. He was slain in his eighty-eighth year, and his son in his sixty-third. An historian of the day says, he received his death-blow *"manibus et mente ad Deum intentus."** Morogh had time to make confession and receive the Viaticum.† This was a hundred years and more after Alfred's death.

In spite of these two great monarchs, it is not to be supposed that centuries of civil disorder should not have had the most grievous results in the spiritual condition of both countries ; nor need we feel any surprise,

---

* Marianus Scotus.   † Lanigan, vol. iii. p. 424.

considering the difficulty with which religion is built up, and the ease with which it is pulled down, if the Northmen could demolish, but the zeal of pious monarchs and the labours of saints could not restore. As to England, Englishmen freely confess it. The passage of Alfred is well known: "Very few are the clergy on this side the Humber who could understand their daily prayers in English, or translate any thing from the Latin. I think there were not many beyond the Humber. They were so few, that I cannot recollect one single instance on the south of the Thames, when I took the kingdom." In his reign, and the century which followed it, the absence of invaders, his own exertions, and the reforms of St. Dunstan, availed in a great measure to reverse this lamentable condition of things; but the evil had struck too deeply into the heart of the social fabric to admit of eradication. The last state of the nation became worse than the first. The tradition of piety seemed almost extinct; peace, instead of inspiring thankfulness and devotion, caused a reaction into open licence and neglect of religion. Then the Northmen came again; and the people was again consigned to the sensuality, the intellectual sloth, and the national impotence, from which Alfred had laboured to rescue it: "Many years before the Conquest," says William of Malmesbury, "both sacred and secular studies had come to an end. The clergy, content with a slovenly knowledge, scarcely managed to pronounce the formal words of the sacraments, and thought it a thing prodigious and miraculous if one of themselves knew grammar. The monks, by their delicate clothing, and their free use of whatever food came to them, made their rule a mockery. The nobles, given to gluttony and debauchery, instead of coming to Church of a morning, as Christians should, heard a hasty mass and matins, if it could be called hearing, they and their wives, ere they had risen from their beds. The common people were the defenceless prey of the powerful. Unnatural as was such conduct, it was often the fact, that heads of families, after seducing the women of their house, either sold them to other men, or to houses of bad repute. Drinking was a common vice, and was continued day and night."*

They are said to have learned drinking from the Danes.† The most startling evidence of depravity was their selling their own children. They were exported to Ireland. Bristol seems to have been the slave-market ; for it is one of the good deeds of St. Wolstan, shortly before the Conquest, that he was able, as the lesson for his Feast tells us, to "bring the citizens of Bristol to a better mind, who, in spite of king and Pope, had persisted in their nefarious practice of selling their own people into slavery."

It is remarkable that the Synod of Armagh, after Henry's invasion, touchingly confesses this sin of slave-dealing as having brought upon the Irish the yoke of foreigners, and decrees that all the English slaves throughout the country should be emancipated.‡ That they were the purchasers, and the Anglo-Saxons the purchased, shows us that in the eleventh and twelfth centuries there were classes of society in Ireland higher in the grade of civilization than the whole English nation ; for it is inconceivable that such a merchandise could be possible, unless all ranks were degraded, and the ruling power utterly feeble. Indeed, the purchase and possession of English slaves was eventually Henry's pretext for his expedition against the Irish. Nor, indeed, are we without proofs to convince us that, in spite

* Reg. Angl. p. 57. † Turner, vol. ii. p. 270 n. ‡ Lanigan, vol. iv. p. 196.

of the Northmen, Ireland had much of its ancient force of character, nay of learning and virtue, left among its people. The very aberrations of such men as Erigena are a proof at least of mental culture ; for heresies do not commonly break out among the ignorant, and are often even united with strictness or severity of life. Still, after all due allowances on his head, we cannot follow M'Geoghegan and others in considering that Brian restored the state of things to what it had been before the North-men came. He did not, could not do in Ireland, what Alfred failed to do in England:—this we shall now show.

6.

The authors, then, in question point to the Saints who flourished between Brian and Henry II., to the learned Irishmen in foreign countries, to the Bishops who at-tended foreign synods, and to the monarchs who gave up the world for the cloister. Lanigan observes[*] that "there were excellent Bishops in the country, such as Ge-lasius of Armagh, and Christian of Lismore ; and that the Irish Church was not then in so degenerate a state as to require any foreign intervention." M'Geoghegan speaks at greater length, and observes that "it must be allowed that for nearly two centuries the Northern pirates had never ceased committing devastations on the island, pillaging and burning her churches and religious houses. The public schools were interrupted ; ignorance spread its influence widely, and religion suffered much in its practice ; without, however, becom-ing entirely extinct. After the complete overthrow of those barbarians, in 1014, in the battle of Clontarf, the inhabitants began to rebuild their churches and public schools, and to restore religion to its primitive splendour."[†]

* Vol. iv. p. 159.　　　† O'Kelly's Translation, p. 243.

He adds, " From the battle of Clontarf to the reign of Henry II., about a century and a half elapsed, during which time all ranks were emulous in their endeavours to re-establish good order in the government and discipline in the churches."

Accordingly he refers to saintly prelates, such as St. Celsus, St. Malachi, St. Lawrence, St. Imar, Gilbert, Malchus, and others. Such, moreover, were Ernulph and Buo, who preached the gospel in Iceland. Doubtless these are names in which any country might reasonably glory ; but are they sufficient to prove his point ? for we have to go back to the previous question, Is a Christian country in a satisfactory religious condition simply because there are saints in it ? The state of things at the same period on this side the Channel shall be our answer. We have been giving evidence above of the degraded state of the English population, from the coming of the Northmen down to the Conquest ; yet it is quite notorious that no mean saints were found among them both before and after Alfred. Such are the glorious martyrs whom the Danes sent to heaven, Edmund, Humbert, and Elphege ; such are the Bishops Ethelwold, Elphege, and Brinstan of Winchester, Odo and Dunstan of Canterbury, Oswald of York, and Wolstan of Worcester. Some of them too were missionaries, and that to the very tribes who were laying England waste,—a lesson to the ill-treated to return good for evil;—as St. Sigfrid, the apostle of Sweden. Then, again, there was the royal saint, St. Edward ; and, on the other hand, St. Walstan,* a layman, who, without embracing the monastic state, gave away his patrimony at the age of twelve, and made himself a mere farm-servant in an obscure village for the love of God, fasting, praying, and working miracles, as

* Vid. Dr. Husenbeth's Life of him, and Alban Butler, May 30.

peaceful and serenely as if trouble and sin were not in the country. William of Malmesbury adds, at the end of the very passage which we have quoted above, in disparagement of the Anglo-Saxons, " I know many clerks at that time were walking in simplicity the path of sanctity ; I know that many of the laity, of every kind and condition in that nation, were in God's favour ; but, as in a time of peace His clemency doth cherish the bad with the good, so in the time of captivity His severity sometimes involves the good with the bad."* Such was the case with England ; it had saints in the midst of its degeneracy : and in like manner Ireland, though it had its saints, might still be degenerate in the very presence of its sanctity.

Still less is the flourishing state of the schools of Ireland an index of the intelligence, education, order, or religion, then existing in the mass of her people. The country indeed was still a great centre of learning ; and under all circumstances this fact is very remarkable. Loss and suffering, disappointment and hopelessness, could not quench that activity of intellect and zeal for knowledge which had been the characteristic of her children from the earliest times. We read of schools at Kells, Kildare Killaloe, and other places, especially at Armagh, which, even down to the time of the Conqueror, was frequented by British youths. Sulger, afterwards Bishop of St. David's, spent from ten to thirteen years in Ireland in the study of Holy Scripture, and a portion of Armagh even went by the name of the Saxon quarter. It is not the least striking circumstance in those dreary times, that, in an age when even kings and great men often could not read, professors in the Irish colleges were sometimes men of noble birth. St. Malachi's father,

* Page 58.

though a member of a family of distinction, as St.
Bernard tells us, was a celebrated professor at Armagh.
History records the names of others similarly eminent,
both by their descent and by their learning.   It is impossible not to admire and venerate a race which displayed
such inextinguishable love of science and letters ; but at
the same time, not even numerous instances of this noble
trait of character in individuals are sufficient to prove
any thing as to the point immediately before us, viz.
the actual condition of the people in general, contemporaneous with them.   There is in most countries a strongly
marked line dividing the educated and illiterate classes,
which not even the closest proximity tends to obliterate.
Science is a sort of *disciplina arcani*, whether we will or
no ; and the presence of a learned man has no tendency
whatever to make others learned with whom he is in
habits of familiarity.

It is otherwise with sanctity ; a saint will influence by
his conversation, and preaches by his life : and yet even
saints, as we have been showing, are no necessary guarantee of the sanctity of their people.   Much less has a
school, or college, or seminary, any power to communicate its own attainments or refinement to the neighbourhood in which it is placed.   There is a story of a
practical joke executed by a famous wit of Oxford some
fifty years ago, on occasion of the visit of some foreign
potentate to the University, which it may be allowed us
perhaps to introduce here.   When the great person
changed horses at Benson, the stage before coming to
Oxford, he found the landlord, waiters, ostlers, stable-
boys, and postillions arrayed in the black gowns and
cassocks, and red hoods and large bands, proper to doctors
of divinity, and shouting one to another as they brought
out the fresh horses and harnessed them to the travel-

ling carriages in classical Latin, in the style of the *Heus Rogere, fer caballos*, of the Wykehamist song. On his asking the meaning of this, he was gravely informed by one of the masquerading undergraduates, that the influence of the University penetrated the peasantry for ten miles on every side, and that no farm-labourer or hodman was to be found in that circuit who had not taken his degrees, and could not support a thesis against Bellarmine or Socinus. It was a ponderous pleasantry to act, but it is an apposite illustration to adduce in our present argument. A University does great things; but this is just one of the things it does not do; it does not intellectualize its neighbourhood. No Oxford scout, by serving a score of undergraduate masters, ever caught the trick of construing Horace, or reducing a *Bramantip*. And, in like manner, while we do not doubt that there were far more Irish than English scholars in the eleventh century, we cannot fairly deduce from that superiority that the country priests or peasants of Meath or Leinster had more knowledge of the canons or of the Decalogue than had the clergy and laity of Wessex.

And, in fact, there seems to have been little sympathy between the two classes in question. How came it to pass else, that during those centuries of confusion, so many Irish scholars, *greges philosophorum*, as they are called in the trite passage in Eric, crossed over to the Continent? Their convents and colleges, indeed, were in flames or in ruins; but their country remained. Why did they not betake themselves to the bosom, and share the hospitality and privations, of either rich or poor within the four seas of Ireland? Is it not the true solution of this phenomenon, that, as soon as they set foot beyond their own homestead, they came at once upon almost a foreign soil? We cannot refer it to any want of patriotism or Christian charity in their own breasts, that St. Donatus or St. Andrew found a domicile in Italy in the ninth century, Mark and Marcellus in Switzerland, others who might be named in the West of England, and others in the calm monastic dwellings of Cologne or Ratisbon; but if these holy men were not, and could not be, indifferent to their countrymen, was not the state of the case really this, that their countrymen were indifferent to them?

And St. Bernard seems to answer our question in the affirmative. We are far indeed from taking to the letter all that he says of the Irish. We believe that, as in other passages of his history, his ardent temper carried him beyond the truth. We believe that the statements contained in his well-known Life of St. Malachi are exaggerations; still, it must not be forgotten that he was a personal friend of St. Malachi, who had visited him at Clairvaux on his way to and from Rome, whither he repaired expressly on the ecclesiastical affairs of Ireland. Now St. Bernard, who thus had his information at first hand, and from the most venerable authority, says, in his Life of him, "Our Malachi, born in Ireland, *of a barbarous people*, was there brought up, was there taught letters. However, from the barbarousness of his birthplace he contracted nothing, no more than the fish of the sea taste of their maternal salt. He who brought honey out of the rock, and oil out of the hard stone, it was He who did this."[*] It must be recollected, that we are saying nothing of the Irish people which we do not in another respect impute to our own. Both nations had

---

[*] Vit. c. i. Vid. also what he says on Malachi being made his bishop's vicar : "Seminare semen sanctum *in gente non sanctâ*, et dare *rudi populo et sine lege viventi* legem vitæ et disciplinæ," c. iii.

lost their first fervour ; they had not fallen away in the same direction, but neither of them was fitted any longer for the high mission which they had fulfilled in earlier and happier times. The declension was deplorable, and what was to be the end of it ?

7.

In one respect England had been the more favourably circumstanced of the two ; but the ultimate result was the same. Alfred has been able to do for his country, what, from the circumstances of the case, was impossible to Brian. Brian was not in the line of the old kings of Ireland. He was but the representative of a Munster dynasty which had been successfully insurgent against them ; and he was unable to secure the throne for his descendants. One thing he could do, and did : he so effectually destroyed the prestige and power of the old monarchy, that though Malachi regained his former dignity, still, on his death, for many years there was no king of all Ireland at all. It follows, that though Brian delivered his country from her external foe, he actually threw her back as regards the prospect of internal consolidation. This great misfortune Lanigan remarks upon. "The anciently established system of succession to the throne of the whole kingdom," he says, "was overturned ; and there remained no paramount power authorized to control the provincial kings or minor chieftains. The Irish," he continues, "were during a great part of the eleventh century engaged here and there in wars among themselves ; and we find now and then one or other party of them assisted by the Danes settled in Dublin or elsewhere." *

* Vol. iii. p. 427.

As to England, on the contrary, both Alfred and the Danes, in different ways, had tended to her political progress. They played as it were into each other's hands; and, while the Danes broke up the Heptarchy, Alfred developed the monarchical power. England was not illegally seized, but fell into his hands. Before the resistless energy of Ingwar and Hubba, down went Northumbria, East Anglia, and Mercia, almost at a blow, till Alfred was left the sole representative of Anglo-Saxon royalty in the island. Brian had to conquer for himself; but the Danes conquered for Alfred. If ever there was a king who attained to wide sovereignty by the force of events, and without any violent acts of his own, his was that unusual blessing; and he had another still more unusual, that of being supremely happy in his immediate descendants. Charlemagne, a century before, had done his own work on a larger scale; but it came to naught for want of those who could carry it on. But Edward and Ethelfleda, the children of Alfred, and Athelstan his grandson, were, in their place and day, as great as he had been in his. Alfred had been the first king of the English, and Athelstan was the first king of England.* He brought under the Danes, and extended his sovereignty to the furthest point of the north, and became nominal lord even of Wales and Scotland. Thus *suaviter et fortiter*, with the vigour yet the deliberateness of some natural growth, was the English monarchy brought into existence. What has been so gradually and carefully accomplished, has never broken into parts again.

It was not the will of Heaven that such a blessing should be accorded to the sister island. That state in which the Northmen found England, is the state in

* Turner, Anglo-Saxons, ii. p. 187.

which they left Ireland. Moore reminds us of this in the
words with which he introduces to us their incursions.
" In the one small kingdom of Northumbria," he says,
" we find represented upon a smaller scale almost a
counterpart of those scenes of discord and misrule
which form the main action of Irish history in those
times ; the same rapid succession and violent deaths of
most of the reigning chieftains, and the same recklessness of the public weal, which in general mark their
career."* So it had been before the time of Brian, and
so it was after him. They even joined the Northmen
in their quarrels, whether with Irish or Northmen, and
they imitated them in their reckless and sacrilegious
deeds. " Several of the Irish princes and chieftains,"
says Lanigan, " had imbibed the spirit of the Danes,
sparing neither churches, nor monasteries, nor ecclesiastics, according as it suited their views ; a system
which was held in abhorrence by their ancestors, and
which often excited them to unite in defence of their
altars against the Scandinavian robbers,"† In the
previous sentences he had given some instances of their
devastations ; such as their burning and pillaging the
church of Ardbraccan with a number of people in it in
1109 ; of their plundering and destroying the monastery
of Clonmacnois in 1111 ; of their killing the Abbot of
Kells on a Sunday in 1117 ; of their burning Cashel
and Lismore in 1121 ; of their plundering Emly in
1123 ; and of their burning the steeple of Trim, with
the people in it, in 1127. He expressly tells us that
these outrages arose in consequence of the want of a
central and sovereign authority in the country. It was
" one of the sad effects," he says, " of the contests
between various powerful families aspiring to the

* Vol. ii. p. 6.   † Vol. iv. p. 55.

sovereignty of Ireland, and again between diverse members of said families quarrelling among themselves for precedency."

Brian, then, was raised up to accomplish for his country great works of a material kind. His arms broke the power of the Northmen; he rebuilt the fabrics of religion; but, as to moral and social matters, he left behind him the bad and the good which were before him. He did not reverse the national degradation. There had been literature among the Irish all along, and civil war all along: he found both, and he left both. Schools had still endured when the Northmen were victorious; slaughter and sacrilege were still rife when they had been chastised. So too was it with the ecclesiastics: the well known disorders in the church of Armagh, which continued up to the time of St. Malachi, are a clear evidence of it.

8.

Here we must pause in our subject, ere we turn from the contemplation of the religious declension of the two islands, to a review of the means which the Holy See adopted to meet the evil. It was surely incumbent on that power, which had coverted them, to interfere when they were lapsing back to barbarism. Every one has a love and a care for his own work; and if children are not always fond of their parents, at least the parents, as the great philosopher says, commonly yearn in affection over the children. Rome had had a great success in English and Irish zeal; it had no wish that that success should be reversed. But at this time the people of England were sunk in sloth, luxury, and depravity; and Ireland was convulsed with feuds and conflicts, their scholars having as little power to restore order, ecclesiastical or civil, as faith is able to ensure charity, or knowledge is the guarantee of virtue.

What should the Pope do? He took time to deliberate on the course to be pursued, and then he acted boldly. He applied one and the same remedy to both. He gave commission to a foreign power to take possession of both islands. He did not set one island to convert the other; he did not send the debased English to heal the quarrels of the Irish; he did not send those who sold their own children to the Irish, to lord it over the Irish who bought them. He sent against each of them in its turn the soldiers of a young and ambitious people, first to reform them, secondly to unite them together;—and strange to say, the warlike host he sent was an offshoot of the very race which had brought them both to ruin. The Northmen had been their bane; and, in the intention of the Pope, the Normans were to be the antidote.

II.

IT would be an interesting work, to trace out the causes and the course of civilization, in the case of particular nations compared one with another. Some nations have been civilized by conquering, others by being conquered. The moral and social advancement of Spain, Gaul, and South Britain under the Roman yoke is an instance of the latter process; but more commonly the victorious people has been the pupil, not the teacher, and has voluntarily placed itself at the feet of those, whom it began by treading under its own. This appears from the nature of the case: the more favoured countries of the earth are the natural seats of civilization; and these are the very objects of the cupidity of northern or eastern races, who are at once more warlike and less refined. Accordingly, the rude warrior quits his icebound crags, his desolate steppes, or his burning sands, for the sunny hills or the well-watered meadows of the temperate zone; and when he has made good his footing in his new abode, what was the incentive of his conquest becomes the instrument of his education. Thus it was that Goths and Lombards put off their national fierceness; thus it was that the fanatic Arab was transmuted into the polished knight of Seville of Granada; and thus the Northman also softened both his name and his nature, and over his characteristic qualities,—the cruelty, the cunning, and romantic ambition of his barbarism,—threw the fantastic garb of Christian chivalry.

The ordinary course of barbarian invasion is such as this:—Certain tribes are in the advance of the rest,

being the van-guard of a large host or the fugitives of
unsuccessful war; they come down upon the country
which is to be their prey in successive expeditions; like
billows tumbling one over the other, they sweep
through it; then, like waves, they retire, and then
again, after an interval, they return. Next, they exact
contributions, and are again and again bought off.
Next, either by violence or by treaty, they gain possession and occupation of some territory, and take their
place as landed proprietors amid the old tenants and
institutions of the soil. This turns out to be a more
politic bribe than gold; it is a gift once for all; it puts
them under teaching, and imposes on them responsibili-
ties. In a while they are found to be happily influenced
by the civilization, be it greater or less, into which they
have thrust themselves. They imitate the customs and
manners of their new country; they acquire a moral
perception and a standard of judgment to which before
they were utter strangers; they give up their old idolatry. They trade and make money; they grow conservative; they learn to be ashamed of the savage
habits of their forefathers; they make common cause
with the old inhabitants in repelling the fresh invasions
of their own kindred. Perhaps they even act a charitable part towards the latter, sending them missionaries,
or returning the captives or hostages whom they have
taken, to teach them a purer faith and the arts of life.

These successive steps in the course of civilization took
a character of their own in the remarkable race whose
history has so intimate a bearing on the two islands of
the North; and as we have enlarged above upon the
terrible and revolting features of the Scandinavian
character, so it is to our purpose now to speak of the
singular alleviations with which its enormities were, as

time went on, accompanied, till it changed into the chivalrous Norman. Though of the same stock as the Saxons, the Northmen were gifted with a more heroic cast of soul. Perhaps it was the peculiar scenery and climate of their native homes which suggested to them such lofty aspirations, and such enthusiastic love of danger and hardship. The stillness of the desert may fill the fierce Arab with a rapturous enjoyment,* and the interminable forests of Britain or Germany might breathe profound mystery; but the icy mountains and the hoarse resounding waves of the North nurtured warriors of a princely stature, both in mind and body, befitting the future occupants of European thrones. Cradled in the surge and storm, they were spared the temptation of indolence and luxury : they neither worshipped the vivifying powers of nature with the Greek, nor with the Sabean did they kiss the hand to the bright stars of heaven; but, while they gave a personal presence and volition to the fearful or the beautiful spirits which haunted the mountains or lay in ambush in the mist, they understood by daily experience that good could not be had by the mere wishing, and they made it a first article in their creed that their reward was future, and that their present must be toil.

2.

The light and gloom, the nobleness, the sternness, and the fancifulness, of the Northman character are admirably portrayed in the romantic tales of Fouqué. At one time he brings before us the honour-loving Froda, the friend of the Skalds, who had been taught in the book of

* "A young French renegade confessed to Chateaubriand that he never found himself alone galloping in the desert without a sensation approaching to rapture, which was indescribable." Notes to the *Bride of Abydos*.

a learned Icelander how the Lady Aslauga, a hundred years and more before, had in her golden veil of flowing hair won the love of King Ragnar Lodbrog, and who, smit with devotion to her, saw from time to time the sudden apparition of his bright queen in the cloudy autumn sky, animating him to great and warlike deeds. At another time, it is the Lady Minnetrost, the good Druda, far up upon the shores of the Baltic, on her high moonlit tower, with her long white finger lifted up and pointing to the starry sky. Then, again, we have the tall slim form of the beautiful Sigrid, with her large blue eyes, singing her charm, gathering witch-herbs, and brewing her witch-draught, which makes heroes invincible in fight, and works in the banquet a black mysterious woe. Then we have the gigantic form of men on the islands of the lake, with massive breastplates, and huge brazen bucklers, and halberts so high that they seemed like the masts of vessels. And then the vessel comes in sight, ready for the use of the sea-knights in their pirate expeditions; and off they go over the bounding waves, on their terrible errands of blood and fire, to gain immortal glory by inflicting untold pain. And suddenly appears one of them at a marriage feast in Normandy, the sea-king Arinbiorn; one of those warriors in the high-coast country who own little or nothing on the mainland, but who sail round the earth in their light barks in the company of brave and devoted followers, passing from one side of the North Cape, nay, even from distant Iceland, down to imperial Constantinople, or along the coast of blooming Asia or of burning Africa, where almost all other seamen are at fault. And at another time we are shown the spectres of remorse and death and judgment, and the living forms of pride, passion, and temptation, in the history of the troubled child of the fierce warrior of

Drontheim ; and, on the other hand, the pattern knight and his lady bright coming back to their old country from the plains of Frank-land, and presenting to the savage northern race the very ideal which they vaguely sought after, but could not adumbrate ; and the pale dark-haired Sintram, calmed and vanquished by the voice and lute of the fair Gabrielle.

This of course is romance ; but if it may be taken as an anticipation of what the Northmen became in the Normans, their descendants, it will suggest to us that there certainly existed between the latter people and the Church of the middle age a ground of sympathy and mutual respect which is not found, at least to the same extent, between her great Pontiffs and either Anglo-Saxons or Scots. The ministers of peace and the messengers of war, though as contrary as life and death, nevertheless had a bond of attachment and union in the thorough-going simplicity of purpose with which they fearlessly worked out their respective objects. The Norman knight recognized no earthly standard, no earthly recompense ; his end might be fanciful and eccentric, but it was ideal ; it might be honour, glory, the noble, the sublime, but at least it was unselfish ; and so far it resembled Christianity. The first transaction between this strange people and the Pope was a significant introduction to the relations in which they stood towards each other in the times which followed. St. Leo IX. had led out a force against them ; they fought him, gained the battle, took him prisoner, and then, prostrating themselves at his feet, asked his forgiveness and his blessing.* He consented, and made them his allies. Not many years after, they were the protection of the great Hildebrand against the Emperor. That magna-

* Bowden's Hildebrand, vol. i. p. 165.

nimous Pope, and his contemporary, William the Conqueror, may be taken as types respectively of their opposite
missions ; and they were apparently shy of each other.
It is the greatest compliment that the secular historian
can pay to William, that Hildebrand kept at a distance from him ; it is the greatest compliment that the
historian can pay to Hilbebrand, to say that William
wished to gain his approbation.

3.

So different, however, at first sight, is this Norman of
the eleventh century from the savage pirate who ravaged
England and Ireland in the ninth and tenth, that it is of
importance in the history of civilization to be able to
trace some points of connection between their respective
national characteristics. This we can succeed in doing
to a certain extent ; and we think there is no extravagance in professing to be able to detect the germs of
the knight of chivalry, and noting down the dates of
their gradually taking form and development, in the
chronicles of the wild Scandinavian. For instance, as
we have already suggested, the distinctive trait of the
barbarian of the North, as contrasted with other barbarians, was his perception and pursuit of the *pulchrum*, his
belief in some excellence more than ordinary, his worship of some recondite incommunicable perfection, which
excited in him an enthusiastic passion, and required for
its attainment a superhuman effort. This great quality
of mind showed itself in the rude Northman as well as
in the Norman, and as regards lesser matters, became
that affectation of the rare and uncommon which we
afterwards find in history as a familiar attribute of the
latter people. As an instance, we may specify the value
he set on proficiency in bodily exercises. Feats of

strength, indeed, are held in esteem by all nations, barbarous or not ; but the Scandinavian aimed not at mere
muscular energy, but at a proficiency which has something of an intellectual character,—a strength united to
dexterity, versatile in its exhibition and ready for the
emergence.   Olaf, son of Triggva, was a genuine sea-
king in the lawlessness of his deeds and the romance of
his fortunes.   Born fatherless, on a small island, whither
his mother had fled for her life, captured and sold into
Russia, escaping and turning pirate, sweeping round the
coasts of Scotland, Ireland, Wales, France, Flanders,
and Friesland, converted to Christianity in the Scilly
islands, marrying, or rather married by a princess of
Dublin, and at length made king of Norway,—he seems
to have his character sufficiently described in this mere
outline of his history, and to promise nothing at best
beyond the resolve, daring, and fortitude of a piratical
adventurer.   But he had accomplishments too.* That
he should have been able to climb precipices and run
down them again heavily laden with spoil,—this, indeed,
was a talent suitable and needful to the plunderer ; but
we should hardly have expected in so rude a personage
that he was practised in certain gymnastic arts, that he
could run along upon the oars while the rowers were
pulling, that he could throw at once two darts to their
respective marks, or that he could play at flinging up
swords and catching them alternately, after the manner
of an Indian juggler.   Perfect command of the limbs,
skill, neatness and grace in their exercise, were as much
in honour with the Northman as with the knights of a
tournament.   He could govern his vessel as readily as a
horse ; he could wrestle, swim, skate, row, and, though
a sea-king, he could ride.

* Turner, Middle Ages, vol. i. p. 65 ; Thierry, Normans, book ii.

Character, we have said, is shown in little things : it is for this reason that in this connection we remark, by the way, that the precision and exquisiteness of the Scandinavian appeared also in his choice of food and apparel. The Anglo-Saxons wore beards ; the Normans shaved ; now in doing so they did but follow the custom of the old country which they had left. Thus Harold, who waged war against the pirates, let his hair grow, as a sort of penance, till he had been successful in his enterprise ; when he became king of Norway, he submitted to his father's cutting it off. The ancestors of the fastidious Normans trimmed and combed their hair even up in Scandinavia ; they bathed frequently, dressed handsomely, and ornamented their war-vessels. They were nice in their eating ; and, as we observed in a former page, disdaining wine as a mere incentive to conviviality, were temperate in the use of it.

These, however, are lesser matters ; the most obvious and prominent point of character, common to the Northman and Norman, is the peculiarity of their warlike heroism. War was their life ; it was almost their *summum bonum ;* good in itself, though nothing came of it. The impetuosity of the Norman relieved itself in extravagances, and raises a smile from its very intensity ; at one time becoming a religious fanaticism, at another a fantastic knight-errantry. His very worship was to do battle ; his rite of sacrifice was a passage of arms. He couched his lance to prove the matter of fact that his lady was the beautifullest of all conceivable women ; he drew his sword on the blasphemer to convince him of the sanctity of the Gospel ; and he passed abruptly from demolishing churches and burning towns to the rescue of the Holy Sepulchre from the unclean infidel. In the Northmen, too, this pride of demolition had been

their life-revel. They destroyed for destroying-sake, because it was good to destroy ; it was a display of power,
and power made them gods. They seemed as though
they were possessed by some inward torment, which
needed outlet, and which degraded them to the mad-
ness of their own Berserkirs in the absence of some
nobler satisfaction. Their fearful activity was their
mode of searching out something great, they knew not
what, the idea of which haunted them. It impelled
them to those sudden descents and rapid careerings
about a country, of which we have already spoken ;
and which, even in modern times, has broken out in
the characteristic energy of Gustavus and Charles XII.
of Sweden. Hence, too, when they had advanced
some steps in the path of civilization, from this nature
or habit of restlessness they could not bear neutrality ;
they interfered actively in the cause of right, in proportion as they gave up the practice of wrong. When
they began to find out that piracy was criminal, instead
of having recourse to peaceful occupations, they found
an occupation cognate to piracy itself in putting piracy
down. Kings, indeed, would naturally undertake such
a mission, for piracy interfered with their sovereign
power, and would not die of itself ; it was not wonderful
that Harold, Haco the Good, and St. Olaf should hang
the pirates and destroy their vessels ; but the point of
our remark is this, that they pursued the transgressors
with the same furious zeal with which they had heretofore committed the same transgression themselves. It
is sometimes said that a reformed profligate is the stern-
est of moralists ; and these northern rovers, on their
conversion, did penance for their own piracy by a relent-
less persecution of pirates. They became knight-errants
on water, devoting themselves to hardship and peril in

the protection of the peaceful merchant. Under Canute of Denmark a confraternity was formed with this object.* Its members characteristically began by seizing on vessels not their own for its prosecution, and imposing compulsory loans on the wealthy trader for their outfit, though they professed to indemnify their owners out of the booty ultimately secured. Before they went on board, they communicated ; they lived soberly and severely, restricting themselves to as few followers as was possible. When they found Christians in the captured ships, they set them at liberty, clothed them, and sent them home. In this way as many as eight hundred pirate vessels were destroyed.

Sometimes, in spite of their reformation, they still pursued a pirate's trade ; but it was a modified piracy. They put themselves under laws in the exercise of it, and waged war against those who did not observe them. These objects of their hostility were what Turner calls "indiscriminate" pirates. "Their peculiar and self-chosen task," he says, "was to protect the defenceless navigator, and to seek and assail the *indiscriminate* plunderer. The pirate gradually became hunted down as the general enemy of the human race." He goes on to mention some of the laws imposed by Hialmar upon himself and other discriminating pirates, to the effect that they would protect trade and agriculture, that they would not force women into their ships against their will, and that they would not eat raw flesh.

Now, in what we have been drawing out, there is enough to show both the elementary resemblance of character, and yet the vast actual dissimilitude, between the Scandinavian and the Norman. There is likeness enough to show that the dissimilitude is a *change :* when

* Lappenberg's England.

there is no resemblance at all between a former state and a latter, we do not consider it a change but that one thing has been substituted for another. Here, however, is a change, and a vast change ; and then the question follows, how was it brought about ? There is enough in the picture to show that the knight of chivalry may have been made out of the barbarian sea-king ; but not enough to suggest, on the other hand, how the barbarian sea-king came ever to be made into the knight of chivalry. It was of course, to answer in general terms, the triumph of Christianity. Hrolfr, or Rollo, left the North a lawless marauder, being driven out by the reforming energy of King Harold of the fair hair ; and when he came to France, it was in order to inflict upon it the wars which his kinsmen had inflicted upon England and Ireland. Nor was he remiss in his dreadful mission : for, after devastating England in company with his countrymen, he landed on the French province which has since been called Normandy, plundered Cambrai, menaced Rouen, besieged Paris, took Bayeux, ravaged the neighbourhood of Sens, and levelled St. Lo to the ground. These are specimens of the successful outrages which Rollo committed on an unoffending country ; but somehow they ended in his being baptized, receiving a large grant of territory, and at length taking his place among the landholders and nobility of France. He was not the first of his savage countrymen who in that same France had submitted to the Church, and had been naturalized, on condition of defending the soil against fresh invasions from the north. And the policy and the compact were perfectly successful. In the course of one hundred and fifty years the race made such advances in the arts of life, as to stand foremost in the civilization of the day, to be specimens of a particular kind of refinement, and to be in a condition to present religion and to teach manners even to Christian populations of historic name and ancient faith.

4.

And now we come to the question, for the sake of which we have introduced this lengthened notice of the Northmen and their French colony. Why was it that a like process, with a like issue, did not take place in England and Ireland, when barbarians settled among them ? Why did not the Danes in both islands succumb to influences which were so potent and so successful on the opposite continent ? One and the same fierce foe comes from the North, and extends his devastations on both sides of the British and St. George's Channels ; he is so identically one as to have the same leaders, who sometimes carry on their raids in one country, sometimes in another. Ragnar not only ravaged England and Ireland, but he penetrated with his bands to the walls of Paris. Hasting, the formidable opponent of Alfred, plundered on the Seine. Rollo, as we have said, made a descent on England before he came to France. It needs explanation, then, how it came to pass that the same race, being settled, during a contemporaneous period, in two countries, made such very unequal advances in civilization in the one and in the other.

We conceive the facts to be as we have stated them ; the period of settlement is certainly contemporaneous, and the advance in civilization is as certainly unequal. The country above the Humber was in the possession of Danish princes from A.D. 870 down to the Norman Conquest ; East Anglia was colonized by Danes from A.D. 878. The Danes founded or rebuilt Dublin,

Wexford, Waterford, Cork, and Limerick, about the
year 850; and held them still in 1171, at the date of
what we should call the "Norman Conquest" of
Ireland.* Rollo, on the other hand, gained Normandy
about 912. If, then, long and intimate intercourse is
a necessary condition of influencing, improving, and
changing a barbarous race, both Anglo-Saxons and
Irish had the opportunity of such intercourse with the
Danes more fully than the Franks with the Normans.
And yet the Danes did not gain any such benefits from
their settlement in England and Ireland, as the Normans
reaped from their French inheritance. This is the second
point to which we ask the reader's attention.

It may be replied, that English and Irish converted
them to Christianity, and that to a higher blessing and
greater change they could not have been instrumental.
It is true : this conversion was the work of holy men
and zealous priests ; and that there were such is
certain, and that their efforts were prospered is certain,
as might have been expected from their zeal and
their holiness. But we speak here not of mere submission to the Church and faith in her word, which is
commonly all that a preacher would effect in the case of
ignorant barbarians ; but of that formation and elevation
of character, that unity and community of thought, that
hold and application of religious principles, that self-
command, that social progress, which is what we
commonly mean by the word "civilization." Civilization, like barbarism, is a social, not simply an ethical
term ; it is the attribute of a people. Individuals are
not called civilized, as such, but as members of a body
politic, and a body politic is not civilized by the mere
action of the evangelist or missionary. What is needed

* Lyttelton, Henry II. vol. v. p. 35 ; Lanigan, vol. iii. p. 326, &c.

for that purpose is the influence of pastors, rulers, and schoolmasters, or the presence or neighbourhood of races civilized already. This is the benefit which France bestowed on the Normans,—not that their civilization was perfect, but it was substantially such. The Normans learned to live in peace with their neighbours; when they warred, it was according to rule; they reverenced law; they could govern and be governed: they could adopt a course of policy; and they had refined manners. "A steady justice in his own conduct," says Turner, speaking of Rollo, "an inflexible rigour towards all offenders, and the beneficial results which every one experienced from these provisions, gradually produced a love of equity and subordination to law among his own people. Under his administration Normandy is declared to have had neither thieves, plunderers, nor private seditions." And after quoting a passage from Glaber Rodulphus, which bears witness to the Norman people living "like one great family of relations," to their care of the poor and distressed and strangers, and to their religious liberality, Turner goes on to speak of their love of glory, their incipient love of literature, their general decorum, and lasting steadiness of moral character. That this was the effect of contact with French civilization, and not from any natural internal force in the Norman colony itself, seems undeniable, not only from that identity, on which we have already dwelt, of the Normans of Frank-land with the Danes of England, and from the fact that fresh and fresh Northmen were continually joining and disturbing, if that had been possible, the Norman body politic, but, on the other hand, from what history tells us of the rapid and complete assimilation of the Norman people to the French, even to the adoption of the French

language, and of their utter alienation from their
mother country. "The Northmen who settled in
Neustria," says Lappenberg, "gradually became lost
among the French. French and foreigners have visited
Normandy in search of some traces of the old Scandinavian colonies; but vainly have they sought for the
original Northmen in the original inhabitants; with
the exception of some faint resemblances, they have
met with nothing Norsk." "All remembrance of their
national poetry," he says presently, "was as completely
obliterated from the posterity of the Northmen as if,
in traversing the ocean, they had drunk of the water of
Lethe."* By the end of the tenth century, "the difference of language," says Thierry, "which had at first
marked the line of separation betwixt the nobles and
the people of Normandy had almost ceased to exist;
and it was by his genealogy that the Norman of Scandinavian descent was distinguished from the Gallo-
Franks."† And, "when the use of the *lingua romana*
became general throughout Normandy, the Scandinavians ceased to look upon the Normans as their natural
allies by kindred; they even ceased to call them by
the name of Normans, but called them French, Romans,
and Velskes or Welches, their names for the entire
population of Gaul." Lappenberg says the same:
"If the inhabitants of Normandy cared little about their
northern native country, the inhabitants of the north,
on their part, almost forgot their fugitive kinsmen, who
had gained for themselves another home."

5.

Such is the surprising and speedy change which took

---

* England, pp. 66, 84, transl. Vid. also Palgrave, vol. i. p. 700; vol. ii.
p. 257, and elsewhere. (1872.)   † Norman Conquest, p. 39, transl.

place in the Northmen when domiciled in France; not that the Norman character became French, but it ceased to be barbarian, and became Christian; it was a great change. Now let us contrast with it the state of the Danes, or Northmen, or Ostmen, as they are variously called, in England and Ireland. The author last quoted is a most unexceptionable witness, because his leaning is against the Normans and the Holy See; as if the Anglo-Saxons would have recovered their former state and have managed their own matters better, if they had been let alone. Now he says, speaking of the "colonies of the Vikings," "on the coast of Ireland they possessed Dublin, Waterford, Limerick, and Cork. At Dublin resided the principal king of the Northmen; Waterford had also its kings. These colonies, which sometimes made war on each other, and at others combined together against the Irish or the English, preserved their warlike spirit, by which, although possessing only a few ports and a small portion of the interior, they were able to maintain themselves for some centuries. Christianity encompassed them on every side; and in the eleventh century they adopted it themselves."* Here, then, is a Scandinavian colony far smaller, or at least more dispersed, than that in Normandy, actually surrounded by Christian populations, and populations of a far earlier Christianity than the Franks, and acted on by them at length so far as to embrace their religion, yet so little subdued by Christian influences, that there is nothing more to be recorded of them than that they warred on each other and on their Irish neighbours. And it is observable, that, considering there was one king over all their Irish settlements, at least till the beginning of the eleventh century, these wars of the Danes among them-

* Page 64.

selves must have been of the nature of civil wars. Lanigan speaks to the same effect. After saying that the Danes of Dublin were the first of their nation in Ireland who became Christians, he adds, "which, however, did not prevent them from afterwards practising ravages in the same manner that their predecessors had done."* Let it be observed, he does not speak merely of their going to war, which, alas, the most civilized and Christian nations can do, but of continuing the savage raids of their forefathers.

It must be added, that whereas the Normans were converted as early as the date of their coming, the Danes, even of Dublin, were not converted till at the end of a hundred years from their settling there, and those of other Irish cities much later. In the beginning of the eleventh century, near two centuries after their arrival, though "a certain progress," the same writer says, "was made by the Danes in piety and religious practices, yet we find them now and then, even during this period, committing depredations in religious places."† How great a contrast to the notorious devotion of the Normans! In spite of all the shortcomings of the latter people, their cruelty and their dissoluteness, they were exemplary in their maintenance of religious worship. "They caused," says Lappenberg,‡ "an incredible number of churches and chapels to be built." They became so greatly changed in this particular, that is, from their pagan practices, which led them to destroy churches, and in which the Christian Danes of Ireland still indulged, "that there were none in France who so zealously built churches and cloisters as they. They even established conveyance-fraternities for the erection of churches. People took the Sacrament, reconciled themselves with

* Vol. iii. p. 376.   † Page. 433.   ‡ Page. 69.

their enemies, and united for this object, choosing a chief or king, under whose direction they drew carts loaded with all kinds of building materials. Probably there were also fraternities of masons." In Ireland, on the contrary, so far from the old Christian inhabitants leading their Danish neophytes to build churches, the Danes taught the Irish to plunder and destroy them, as appears from a passage of Lanigan, which we quoted in the former part of this discussion. Nay, it is remarkable that the Scandinavian countries themselves received Christianity at as early a date as the bulk of those emigrants from them, who for two centuries had been in a Christian country ; and, again, the Norwegian and Danish Christians on their own soil were much more changed by their conversion than their kinsmen on Irish. "These people," says a contemporary, speaking of the Norwegians, "have learnt to love peace and gentler manners." And another says of the Danes, "They have made progress in the liberal arts ; the nobles send their sons to Paris for education, not only for the ecclesiastical offices, but also for secular employments."[*] It is abundantly confirmed by results such as these, which history accidentally records, that Paris had a gift of civilization at that time which the Irish schools had not.

Let it be observed, too, that the Irish Church had accidentally a collateral assistance in her work, which seemed to make the civilization of these settlers comparatively an easy task. In consequence of their position, by race Northmen, by birth Irish, by dwelling maritime, they were the natural medium of intercourse between their own and their adopted country, and, in consequence, they took to mercantile occupations. Now,

* Adam of Bremen and Arnold of Lubeck, in Lappenberg, pp. 61, 62. Vide also Neander, Hist. vol. v. p. 403, Bohn.

the pursuit of wealth is at least antagonistic to barbaric turbulence, even if not directly congenial to Christianity; but in this instance it did not even thus negatively assist the communication of Christian manners from the old Christians to the new. Lyttelton has this apposite remark : " About this time (1095) a civil war divided the Ostmen (Danes of Ireland). From henceforward this people, addicting themselves wholly to commerce, lost much of their valour and military spirit, without making any great improvements in politeness or the civil arts of life."[*]

It does not seem, indeed, as if there were any tendency whatever in the Danes of Ireland, we will not say to amalgamation, but to intimacy with the people among whom they were settled. On the contrary, they drew off from the Irish, and when the Normans had got possession of England, they fell back upon the Normans. Here they are in remarkable contrast to the Normans themselves, who loved their new country so well as to forget "their people and their father's house." So far from such a feeling, the Ostmen would not even allow the ecclesiastical jurisdiction of those who converted them. When Sitric, Danish king of Dublin, endowed a see there for his countrymen, A.D. 1040, its first bishop was necessarily an Irishman,[†] but no sooner had the Normans come to England, than the Dublin Danes put themselves under the metropolitan see of Canterbury ; the reason being, as Lanigan states, not only the great reputation of Lanfranc the Archbishop (though it is not easy to see what the Danes would care about a great logician and controversialist), but "because William and his Normans, being masters of England from the year 1066, were considered by the Irish Danes as their countrymen." That is, the outlandish Franco-Normans

[*] Vol. v. p. 42.　　　　　　　　　[†] Lanigan, vol. iii. p. 433, etc.

had an influence with them which centuries of neighbourhood and intercourse had not given to the Irish.
Nor was this the act of the Danes of Dublin only; the
Danish Bishops of Waterford and Limerick were consecrated from Canterbury also.[*] Elsewhere Lanigan says,
"A very great antipathy existed between the two
nations, even after the conversion of the Danes; and the
Danish clergy of Dublin and the Irish clergy of Armagh
were constantly at variance." [†]

Once more; till the Normans came to Ireland, the
Danes (or Ostmen, as they were called) continued to be
distinct communities from the Irish: when the Normans
had come, the Normans too remained distinct from the
Irish; but the Danes simply disappear from the page of
history. "English," says Lappenberg, explaining that
by English he means Anglo-Normans, "English, Irish,
and Northmen formed three distinct races," in the beginning of the thirteenth century, that is, upon the Norman
conquest of Ireland; but at a later period mention
occurs of two nations only, Irish and English; the
Ostmen, or Northmen, having disappeared."[‡] What
is clearer than that the Northmen, who had resisted all
assimilation with the Irish for above three centuries,
had at once felt the attraction of their kindred, and had
been absorbed by the conquerors,—absorbed as promptly
and spontaneously, as the Normans, on their part, had
been united, not to any of their own compatriots, but to
the Franks around them?

If, then, the Ostmen, or Danes, of Ireland needed
civilizing, and the Irish could not civilize them, and
the Normans could, then, for the sake both of the Danes
who needed a great benefit, and of the Irish who could
not supply it, it was surely not unreasonable in the

[*] Ibid. p. 464.   [†] Vol. i. p. 75.   [‡] Ibid.

Pope, nor unsuitable to his high mission, to sanction the expedition of the Normans to Ireland with the object of converting the one and reforming the other. We do not deny that there was something of a grave rebuke in sending to that old Catholic population specimens of barbarians whom others had civilized, in order to the civilization of kinsmen of those barbarians, whom, though living among them, they have been unable to civilize themselves. At the same time, this measure was no disparagement of the Irish schools, or of the learning and sanctity of their members ; for, as we have already had occasion to observe, it is not of the nature of colleges or cloisters to radiate knowledge and manners through a population.

6.

Now to pass on to the case of England. What the schools were to Ireland, such was the monarchy to our own country ; each institution was the seat of national life and the hope of national reformation. There were certainly weak and unworthy Anglo-Saxon monarchs ; and there was both rash speculation and ecclesiastical disorder in the Irish schools, as is clear from the instance of Erigena and others on the one hand, and from the strange and lasting scandals of Armagh on the other. Still the schools were the salt of Ireland, and acted on the population, Christian and pagan, at least indirectly, by means of the holy preachers who went out from them ; and in like manner there were among the English kings so many able, successful, and, we will add, religious rulers, that they may fairly be taken to represent the monarchy. Such are Egbert, Alfred, Edward, Athelstan, Edgar, and Edmund. They were the instruments of the conversion of vast numbers of the Northmen to the Christian faith. It was Alfred who adopted the policy, which had succeeded so well across the Channel, of settling the Danes in the east of England, on condition of their baptism. Athelstan, in like manner, when he subjected the Northumbrian Danes to his sway, made them Christians. The same prince was entrusted with the education of Haco the Good of Norway, who, though he did not succeed in bringing his subjects to the faith he had himself embraced, contributed much towards their national civilization. St. Olaf, king of the same country, who sent for Bishops and priests from England, did but avail himself of what Haco had begun. Yet, though a royal court could exert more influence both at home and abroad than a number of scattered convents and colleges, it could neither do a people's work, nor educate a people into doing it. What was wanted in England was a Christianity so living, as to leaven and transform the pagan neophytes. The monarchy might effect the conversion of the Danish settlers, but it could not effect their civilization. If the Anglo-Saxon population was in a state of disorder, despondency, and misery, it would only be further de-graded by the contact of barbarians, instead of having any power to raise them even to its own unsatisfactory level. And this, we know, was the case. The savage invaders had demoralized the English : can there be a more pregnant fact than that of which we have already spoken, that from the reign of Ethelred (A.D. 1013) to that of Henry II. (1171), for at least one hundred and fifty years, the Anglo-saxons sold their relatives, and even their children, into foreign slavery, as if they had been a tribe of unreclaimed Africans ? *

* Turner, Anglo-Saxons, vol. ii. p. 322 ; Lingard, Hist. vol. i. p. 244 ; Lyttelton, v. p. 91.

Moreover, though England had an advantage over Ireland in the unity of its governing power, on the other hand it had this counterbalancing disadvantage, that the foreign settlers were far more numerous, and the territory they covered far more extensive. If Ireland was broken up into small principalities, its Danish inmates, too, were divided from each other, and surrounded by the Christian population. But as to England, at one memorable date the whole of it was in the power of the Danes except Somersetshire and the far west. At Alfred's death all the country was theirs to the north of the Humber and the East of the Thames and Ouse. Later, a line drawn from Chester to the mouth of the Thames through Bedfordshire, serves to describe their frontier. Even when they were subjects of the Anglo-Saxon monarchs, they had their own laws. At length a Dane became monarch of the whole country ; and did more for its welfare than the Anglo-Saxon kings who preceded him. The choice seemed to lie between Dane or Norman, if the nation was to be raised from its abject condition ; and the Norman, not more cruel than the Dane, was far more advanced in civilization.

It must be recollected too, that, whatever might be the advantage of a monarchy, one bad king could undo the work of three or four vigorous ones : and bad or worthless there were. One act reversed all the efforts of the great princes whom we mentioned above. The Anglo-Saxons could not hope to convert the Danes after the crime of St. Brice's day, 1002, which is the St. Bartholomew's Eve of our history. On the eve of that festival, " every city," says Turner, " received secret letters from the king, commanding the people, at an appointed hour, to destroy the Danes there suddenly, by the sword, or to

surround and consume them with fire."* Though at
that time they were living in peace with the English,
the royal mandate was obeyed. All through England,
Christians as they were for the most part, the Danes,
their wives, their families, their infants, were mercilessly
butchered. "The horror of the murder," says Lingard,
"was in many places aggravated by every insult and
barbarity which national hatred could suggest. At
London they fled for security to the churches, and were
massacred in crowds round the altars."† The number
of victims and extent of the massacre are unknown. It
could hardly, indeed, include the old settlers, now half
English, in the north and east. Some authors have
maintained that the savage command was only directed
against the Danish soldiers in English pay ; Thierry,
apparently disbelieving that it was the act of the Anglo-
Saxon king, would make us believe that the only victims were the Danes, who had just before made a truce
with Ethelred, and who after receiving, according to the
bargain, their price for leaving the kingdom, had broken
their engagement by a renewal of their excesses. But
in that case women and children would not have suffered. Gunhilda, the sister of the Danish Sweyn, the
father of Canute, had embraced Christianity, and had
married Palig, a naturalised Dane. Her children and
husband were slaughtered before her eyes ; then she was
put to death herself. She predicted the vengeance that
would follow.

Her prediction was in no long time fulfilled. The
shrieks of the victims of that day were the knell of the
Anglo-Saxon power, The savage Sweyn wreaked his
vengence in fresh devastations and slaughters, which
terminated in the subjugation of England and the

* Vol. ii. p. 312. † Hist. vol. i. p. 240.

successful usurpation of Canute. St. Edward who followed was the morning star of a heavy day, saintly and beautiful himself, but the forerunner of the foreigners in his acts, and the harbinger of woe in his last words.

7.

Our immediate question, however, here, as in the case of Ireland, is, how were the Danes to be civilized ? Anticipating the future by the best lights of prudence and experience, we should have said at that time, that with these Danes lay the prospects of good or evil for that England, of which they had so long been the scourge and the ruin. They were a young, energetic, enterprising, ambitious people. They could fight, they could trade ; but they had to learn the lessons of the gospel and the arts of life. Could England be their teacher, after the massacre of St. Brice ? If a Christian nation slaughtered its unsuspecting converts, who would be converted by it henceforth ? The poor Anglo-Saxons had only strength for a treacherous and impotent revenge ; they had fallen from that state of ethical and social advancement, which the Danes had not yet attained.

Neither island then could either expel the Northmen nor civilize them. Men of their own race, already converted and civilized, were equal to the enterprise, and these the Pope sent first to England, then to Ireland, to undertake it.*

---

* This paper is but a fragment, in consequence of the author's suddenly retiring from the Editorship of the *Rambler* Magazine.

III.

MEDIEVAL OXFORD.

(From the *British Critic* of July, 1838.)

MEDIEVAL OXFORD.

MOST persons who fall in with Dr. Ingram's "Memorials of Oxford," will only consider it as a collection of beautiful prints in illustration of a beautiful city. In consequence they will be likely to place it on their drawing-room table, and to consider that, having done this, they have sufficiently recognized its claims upon their notice. And it is really a most interesting publication, viewed merely as a work of art; but those who have been led to cast their eyes upon its letter-press, will find there matter of a very different complexion from the dull running accompaniment, large in type and small in sense, which is commonly introduced into such artistic publications, by way of increasing their bulk without changing their character.

The President of Trinity, in truth, the learned writer of this letter-press, is evidently not a man to figure as a mere *chevalier aux dames*, or to serve up to proper style some elegant offering to the fashion of the hour. Never was a man less like the writers of the prose of an annual or an album. He is, to all appearance, one of a race of men, now almost extinct, who lived all their days in and for the University. A place like Oxford, it need scarcely be said, alters very much year by year in the outward characteristics of its society; and more so, in a time like this, when alterations and developments of a serious nature are taking place in the structure of society in general. The movements which have had so successful a course in the metropolis and great towns of England, cannot be altogether unknown and unheeded in the groves and halls of academic repose ; newspapers, magazines, and reviews cannot possibly be made contraband ; the fact cannot be concealed from Oxford residents that they are the objects of dislike to a considerable portion of the community, and of assault in certain august assemblies ; and, in consequence, there has been, more or less, a revival in the members of the University of that energetic spirit, that resolve to take part and have a voice in the world's matters, which is one of its distinguishing marks in history. They have long determined that Church and State shall neither do nor suffer, without their own doing and suffering too. The circumstances of the times seem to force such a course upon an ancient institution, which has never been a mere abode of the Muses, but has ever twined the myrtle round the sword ; yet, at the same time, granting this, so much is clear, that the Muses suffer by it, and do not thank the times for its necessity.

They have to mourn over the gradual disappearance of classical taste, antiquarian research, and local knowledge. Oxford was a place of leisurely thought, of multifarious, though undigested erudition, of wayward irregular exertion, of enthusiastic College feeling, of chronic indulgence illuminated by the graceful or brilliant sallies of wit. It was a place impartially the *Alma Mater* both of genius and of abuses. No examinations or class-lists directed the mind either of tutor or of pupil to definite studies and honourable toil, or raised his eyes from his College garden to the University schools, and from the schools to the busy walks of life. Oxford was his home, and with the advantages of home, it had the disadvantages ; it was a very dear place, but a very idle one ; it was one

Long Vacation. It was not a place of passage, not a lodging house for a term of years, not a means to an end,—as it is commonly now. Such a state of things, indeed, if its capabilities had been rightly understood, might have been productive of most beneficial results; the fault was, not that inducements for exertion were not sought for from without, but that there were no active principles spontaneously stirring within. One good effect, however, actually followed; very few Fellows of Colleges, we suspect, could now be found, who are well acquainted with the history or antiquities of their own Society, how it grew up into its present state, and by whose munificence it has been gradually enriched. On the other hand, talk with an old incumbent visiting the place for a few days, and, if a resident yourself, you will be surprised, if you have not cause to be ashamed, at his accurate knowledge of the minute circumstances of the domicile, where your outward man has lived perhaps for years, but whence your mind has been away. While you, rightly or wrongly, have been absorbed in ecclesiastical proceedings or scientific associations, he knows all about the College, from the curious show-books or the manuscripts of the library, and the number in full of old silver tankards in the buttery, down to the excellence of the pump-water, or the history of the common-room chairs. Such is the difference between the past age and the present;—between this busy anxious day and a time when Oxford was loved for its own sake, and was enjoyed with scarce a thought of what was outside of it.

The learned work, to which we referred in our first sentences, is an instance in point, to what good account a resident there may turn his devotion towards a place, which is beautiful as youth, and venerable as age; and since the antiquarian lore which is its characteristic is uncommon just now, we think it may be interesting to put together here some leading facts about the early history of the University, which are scattered through its pages, before and apart from the history of its Colleges. Facts we call them in an antiquarian sense, not as ignorant that every single statement which we shall make has been, and will be controverted, (for what are the annals of the world in the judgment of this day but one large story book ?) but in order to intimate that it is not our intention to dispute or to prove, but that we mean to surrender ourselves to the pleasing illusion, that there is such a thing as certainty attainable by the human mind, as regards matters which we can neither see nor touch.

I.

Little can be narrated in any connected way con-cerning the University previously to the Norman con-quest. The ravages of the Danes, civil troubles, and the debased state of religion, interrupted and dispersed, at least the records, if not the schools and studies them-selves, of the peaceful place ; and the scanty glimpses, which are left to us, are like the broken remembrances with which we retrace that first mysterious portion of our childhood, ere memory has yet become continuous, and we begin to live in the thought of our own identity. However, amid the dim notions of almost fabulous ages, on which the institutions existing in later times force us back, we are naturally drawn to one passage of Saxon history, both from its interesting character, and the satisfactory evidence adducible for its main outline,— the history of St. Frideswide. It seems, that, about the year 727, a certain governor, provost, or vice-roy, " sub-regulus," he is called, of the name of Didan, ruled over a large portion of the city of Oxford with dignity and honour. His wife's name was Saffrida, and their daughter was called Frideswide. Having received a religious education from a female of eminent sanctity, this young lady, not only embraced the monastic life herself, but induced certain others among her equals, of respectable families, to do the like. Her mother dying, her father, sought consolation, according to the fashion peculiar to those times, in a work of piety, and employed himself in the construction of a convent, with its church, within the precincts of the city ; and, having dedicated it to St. Mary and all Saints, he made over his foundation to his daughter. This Church, which was known by the name of St. Mary of Oxford "prope Tamesin," or "on the Thames," was the rudiments of the present cathedral, as the priory attached to it was of the present Christ Church.

Frideswide's priory was, even from the first, something beyond a simple religious foundation. She died on October 19, 740, and was buried in her own church ; but, even before her death, or shortly after, the king of Mercia, in whose territory Oxford lay (Ethelbald), constructed certain inns for the advancement of learning in connection with the sacred edifice. Alfred, 150 years later, after wresting the city from the Danes, restored them. Nothing is known of her foundation for another hundred years, that is, till A.D. 1000, by which date the priory of St. Frideswide has been richly endowed, its lands increased, and its church enlarged. Oxford was, at that time, the metropolis of Mercia, and had been a favourite seat of both Saxon and Danish monarchs. King Ethelred (1004) built the church tower, which, with the addition of a Norman story and spire, is still standing. So great was the king's satisfaction at his own work, that he calls it, in the half-modernized spelling of an extant MS. "myn owne mynster in Oxenford." Another hundred years brought with it a fresh series of changes; the nuns were gone, never to return; secular canons had succeeded, had fallen into disorder, and in turn been dispossessed; and in their place an austere Norman, chaplain to Henry I., was made the prior of an establishment of regulars. Under this form the foundation stood till the time of Wolsey, when those further changes were made which brought it into its present shape. Meanwhile, the prior of St. Frideswide and his community were among the most learned and scientific persons of their times, and their sainted patroness was proportionally honoured. Her relics, as it seems to be ascertained, were in 1180 translated, in Wood's words, "from an obscure to a more noted place in the church," being deposited in a reliquary, which Dr. Ingram supposes to remain to this day; miracles are said to have followed; rich offerings were made at her shrine, and ample endowments were added to her foundation. A more splendid shrine received her relics in 1289, and one still more splendid about 1480. Sermons were preached at her cross, the University authorities went in annual procession to her altar, and as late as 1434 she is called in a public instrument "the special advocate of the flourishing University of Oxford."

2.

Such is the history of the earliest endowment for learning, in a place which was destined to be so fruitful in similar noble institutions. The next that has to be noticed takes us back to the important era, which, while it forms a sort of commencement of our civil history, brought the University also up on to a new stage of its existence. Only ten years had passed after the troubles attendant on the conquest, in which Oxford largely partook, when we find signs of returning peace, religion and learning in that city. The Castle Tower, which still is seen on the left hand of the road by travellers leaving for Bath or Cheltenham, belonged to the collegiate Church of St. George, and was founded at that date by Robert d'Oiley for secular canons of the order of St. Augustine, being such, (observes Wood) as were "most fit for a University, and not bound to keep their cloister, as regulars are." Here they continued till their translation to Oseney in 1149, "at which time," says the same writer, "this their said habitation became a nursery for secular students, subject to the chancellor's jurisdiction." Brumman le Riche endowed this same Church of St. George, on its first foundation, with land in the northern suburbs of Oxford ; whence, as Dr. Ingram supposes, came the tradition that the University was anciently on that side of the town. Thus established as a scholastic institution, St. George's continued, as a dependency of Oseney Abbey, till the dissolution of the latter, being governed by statutes similar in some respects to those of more recent colleges, and consisting of a warden, fellows, and scholars. The warden was always to be chosen from the canons of Oseney ; the fellows and scholars were sworn to the performance of divine service, and to obedience to the warden and to a life of charity and purity. There were five secular priests, and the scholars were in number twelve, for the most part Welshmen. Such was the record of the earliest scholastic foundations of Oxford, being situated on a spot originally a palace, and now a gaol.

Since Oseney has been mentioned, it may be allowed us to bestow a few words of notice on this celebrated

21

foundation, though it lies somewhat off the line of University history. It was founded, as we have said, in the early part of the 12th century, where the castle now stands, as a priory of Augustinian canons; and, when it had removed to the adjacent isle of Oseney, so many benefactions poured in, that the priory became an abbey, and ultimately one of the largest and most magnificent in the kingdom. From the great extent and splendour of its buildings, Wood says, "it was one of the first ornaments and wonders of this place and nation." The island, on which it was placed, was one of those formed by the winding branches of the Ouse or Isis, whence it derived its name of Oseney. The church, dedicated, as St. Frideswide's, to St. Mary the Virgin, was lofty, and was adorned with two towers; its bells were celebrated as the best in England in those times, and are those known in Dean Aldrich's time and in our own, as "the merry Christ Church bells." The famous Tom of Oxford, which tolls nightly at nine o'clock, was the bell in the clock-tower. The edifice was enriched with a variety of chapels, having not less than twenty-four distinct altars. The abbot's house was also celebrated for its splendour, and was frequently honoured by the company of kings, high prelates, and nobles of the first rank; having a hall, as a writer describes it, "more befitting a common society than a private man." The cloisters, the kitchen, the great hall, and the infirmary, were on a corresponding scale of magnificence. King Henry III., after he had raised the siege of Kenilworth, passed his Christmas here, celebrating the season for seven days' space, "with great revelling and mirth." Of all these gorgeous buildings scarcely a vestige now remains; and, had not a knowledge of the site been preserved by tradition and the diligence of antiquarians, it could not from the face of the land have been conjectured. Some unevenness in a broad and fertile meadow marks the site of the great quadrangle; and a wall, gate, and window, belonging to its outbuildings, are still standing, near a mill which inherits its name. Its church bells its sole extant memorial, were transferred, as we have said, together with its endowments, to Christ Church at the date of the Reformation.

3.

The schools of which we have already spoken, were situated on the banks of the Thames : but now, receding from the river, we must proceed up the rising ground to the north, to the spot occupied by the present Worcester College, where lay the land with which le Riche endowed the Church of St. George. Here was the great Benedictine College, founded by John Giffard, Baron of Brimesfield, in 1283, for the reception of the novices sent from the Benedictine Abbey at Gloucester. In the original documents connected with this place, its site is much extolled for its suitableness to an abode for study : a consideration which seems to have induced Giffard to enlarge his establishment, in order to be a "studium generale" for all the Benedictine youths in the province of Canterbury ; three-fourths of such novices being, it is said, at that time sent to Oxford, and the remainder to Cambridge. The Benedictines were then, as in later times, a learned body of men, as their founder designed ; and, a tax being imposed at a general chapter of the order on their greater abbeys, buildings adequate to the occasion quickly rose. Those belonging to each community were distinct from each other, and distinguished each by appropriate escutcheons and rebusses over the doors, some of which remain to this day. The students were governed by a superior called "Prior Studentium," chosen by themselves, by a rule similar to that which is still nominally observed in the University, as regards the election of the Principals of Halls. About the year 1343 we find two chairs of theology established for their instruction, one in this establishment, and the other at Durham College.

Thus we are introduced to a sister foundation. Durham College was the seminary of the Benedictine priory at Durham. It was founded about 1286, under a grant of land made "to God, and to our Lady, and to St. Cuthbert, and to the prior and convent of Durham," and it was placed, not far from Gloucester College, on about the present site of Trinity. Several bishops of Durham became the benefactors of the foundation, among whom Richard Angervyle, or de Bury, in the beginning of the fourteenth century, left them his great collection of books, which was to be open for the use of all students. The building erected to receive this collection by his immediate successor, still remains ; and there are those among the living generation of Trinity men, who, though not Benedictine novices, were gainers in their undergraduate days by a like liberality on the part of the College, and associate a summer vacation, long past, with the calm recesses of its library. At the end of the thirteenth century the foundation consisted of eight fellows, who were to be priests or monks, one being warden or prior, and eight secular scholars ; at the time of the great religious revolution of the sixteenth, it was, with other regular houses, suppressed, and its revenues transferred to the new dean and chapter of Durham.

4

The institutions, and the schools connected with them,

which we have hitherto described, were of a monastic character, richly endowed, and situated in the suburbs of the town, as beseemed places of retirement and of dignity. But meanwhile inside the town, and without the advantages resulting from the power and wealth of Augustinians or Benedictines, was growing up a distinct family, as it may be called, of schools,—secular schools as the former were claustral, which were the germ out of which the collegiate system was afterwards formed. There is a spot in the centre of the city, where Alfred is said to have lived, and which may be called the birth-place or fountain-head of three societies still existing, University College, Oriel, and Brasenose. Brasenose claims to preserve the memory of his palace, Oriel of his church, and University of his school or academy.

(1.) Of these Brasenose is still called in its formal style "the king's hall," which is the name by which Alfred himself in his laws calls his palace ; and it has its present singular title from a corruption of *brasinium* or *brasin-huse*, as originally occupying that part of the royal man-sion which was devoted to the purposes of brewing.

(2.) The history of the adjacent church, which has belonged to Oriel College for the more than 500 years which have elapsed since its foundation, is a sort of repetition of what had already taken place in the in-stance of Frideswide's. A convent of women had been the beginning of the first schools, and of a church of St Mary, on the banks of the Thames ; and a convent, though a little way out of Oxford, was closely associated with the later schools, out of which came the present Colleges, and with a second St. Mary's in the heart of the place. The liberty of Littlemore lies on an elevated plain, two or three miles from Oxford. Of old it was covered with woods, and is bounded by a brook which joins the

Thames. Situated upon this brook, even in Saxon times, was a Benedictine nunnery, which was rebuilt after the conquest, and the remains of which still bear the Saxon name of Mynchery. What was its original connexion with Oxford does not appear; but for some reason or other, the church which Alfred is said to have built on the site of the present University Church, and which is spoken of as "St. Mary's," in the Doomsday survey, is known to have been dedicated to "our Lady of Littlemore." This Church, it is supposed, Alfred made the nucleus, or at least it was in fact the starting point, of a large collection of schools, both claustral and especially secular. They ran from the west end of the Church, at right angles to it, and towards the north, flanking "the king's Hall of Brasinhuse," as we have described it, in a long street, called School Street, which reached the northern wall of the city, that is, up to the present Broad Street. These schools were large rooms, which either were integral portions of the several halls or inns for students, situated in the street, or were first-floors over tradesmen's shops, and were dependencies on monastic bodies in the neighbourhood. Among the latter the convent of Littlemore had a place; besides possessing the ancient hall, now called St. Alban's, and then Nun Hall, to the south of the Church, it had schools in the street just mentioned, which were called after the name of St. Mary of Littlemore.

Moreover, as time went on, the Church of St. Mary became almost the domicile of the students, who had from the first lived under its shadow. In School Street there were, even as late as the fifteenth century, as many as thirty-two schools; at an earlier date the want of room for lectures and exercises, especially in the case of Lent Bachelors, led to encroachments upon St. Mary's.

By permission of the Crown, to whom, till the foundation of Oriel, the Church belonged, as many as six of its chapels or chantries were used as schools for public acts and degrees, being assigned to separate Faculties. The public library, erected over a chapel of Henry I., still remains, and is the present law school. The foundation of Oriel seems to have the beginning of a change. A new church was projected to the south of the old building. Adam de Brom, rector of the Church, and first founder of Oriel, began, or at least completed, its tower; the chancel was built by a Provost of Oriel in the middle of the fifteenth century; and the nave and aisle by the University at the end of it.

The same causes which led to the erection of the Church, led also to the contemplation of Schools, worthy of a great University. They were withdrawn from the chapels of St. Mary's, and from the halls of School Street, and gradually brought together at its upper end, on their present site. Of the existing buildings the beautiful Divinity School was not finished, till towards the end of the fifteenth century, nor the quadrangle before the time of James I. In the interval between these dates a remarkable instance occurred of the vicissitudes to which the abodes of learning are exposed. The ordinary exercises and scholastic acts in the University being suspended during the religious troubles of Edward VI.'s reign, the present ante-chapel, as it may be called, of the Divinity School was converted into a garden and a pig-market; and the schools themselves, being abandoned by the masters and scholars, were occupied by glovers and laundresses. In Wood's words, " There where Minerva sat as regent for several ages, was nothing remaining all the reign of King Edward VI. but wretched solitariness, and nothing but a dead silence appeared."

(3). We have seen Alfred's residence develop itself, if I may so speak, into St. Mary's Church and the University Schools, as representations of the two great elements of education, religion and learning; but to complete the account, notice must be taken of the much-debated point, whether that celebrated king gave to any of his schools a principle of continuity, or, in more intelligible language, whether he founded or established any particular society or college. This, as is well known, is maintained in the affirmative by University College, which claims to be the identical school, hall, or inn, which Alfred instituted; and Dr. Ingram considers that its pretensions to this high antiquity and glorious parentage are not so shadowy as is commonly supposed. Such a claim is recognized in an order of Parliament as early as 1384, and in licenses of mortmain and other grants from the Crown in the reigns of Henry IV. and VI., Elizabeth and James I.; moreover, it is indirectly but distinctly confirmed in a judgment of the Court of King's Bench in 1726. As far, however, as the question is an historical one, this only can be said for it,—that the bequest of the founder of the College in the thirteenth century was laid out in getting possession of the Brasenose or Brasin-huse with its schools, which has already been described as Alfred's palace; near which the members of the College resided for about eighty years, when they seem to have removed to their present site.

5.

Whatever becomes of this question, we may at least recognize in the foundation of University College the commencement of that collegiate system, which is the form into which the present University is almost or altogether cast. Colleges seem to have arisen, in consequence of the irregularities and disorders of University life, when it had lost the checks which a religious rule originally provided. When literature, no longer confined within the precincts and discipline of a monastery, wandered forth into the halls and chambers of School Street, and dispersed itself among a hundred separate circles, what was to be expected as its lot but confusion and trouble ? During the first part of the thirteenth century the disorders, consequent upon such free trade in letters, reached their height, and what aggravated their seriousness was the almost incredible number of students, whom the reputation of the place attracted thither. In the last years of Henry III., they are said to have amounted to thirty thousand ; while in the beginning of that monarch's reign there had been no more than three thousand. Just before he came to the throne, all three thousand on one occasion seceded from the university, as Matthew Paris tells us, leaving not one behind. Serious quarrels and tumults between hostile parties were also frequent, of which loss of life was no uncommon issue. Moreover, the buildings themselves, in which the students were lodged, were of a wretched and unsafe character. Fires were frequent ; this led to the citizens building with stone and slate, instead of timber and thatch ; and when they could not afford this expense, they raised a high stone wall between every fourth or sixth house, remains of which are still to be seen. But the institutions, which came in with the middle of the thirteenth century, brought a remedy for both the physical and moral evils of the place. To Walter de Merton, the founder of Merton College (A.D. 1264), is commonly attributed the introduction of the collegiate system ; and to William of Wykeham, the founder of New, in the latter part of the following century, the praise of establishing it in buildings of suitable splendour and solidity.

The history, however, of the Colleges has been too often gone over, and is too familiar to the world, to call for any notice here. We have preferred to confine our remarks to the original shape in which an academical system showed itself, when as yet it was cherished in the bosom of sacred institutions, which, as not existing at this day, are in consequence almost forgotten. The monastic bodies of the middle age, have not even left their names to the flourishing establishments, which are erected on their site, and, more or less, endowed with their property. Yet that they should have risen again in any shape in these latter days, is remarkable enough, and most en- couraging to those whom the turbulence and the dan- gers of the present hour might else induce to despond as to the future. St. Frideswide's Priory, St. George's Church, the Abbey of Oseney, the establishments for the Gloucester and Durham Benedictines have gone their way ; but Christ Church is a magnificent monument to the memory of the abbots and canons regular whom it has succeeded ; Trinity College occupies the place of Durham, and Worcester the buildings of Gloucester ; St. John's is a revival of a Cistercian establishment, founded on its site in the fifteenth century, and Wadham has risen amid the ruins of a foundation of Augustines in the thirteenth, whose disputative powers were kept in memory in the exercises of the University schools down to 1800.*

* The practice of holding disputations apud Augustinenses, colloquially called "doing Austins," continued down to the introduction of the new examination statute. They were held in the school of Natural Philosophy, every Saturday in full term ; and every B.A., after his Lent determination, was bound to dispute there once every year, either as opponent or respon- dent, before he could proceed to his Master's degree.

6.

Such is the vitality, such the reproductive powers, of this celebrated University. If any of her children, who have no special claim to speak, may presume to offer her counsel, ours would be that she should never forget that her present life is but the continuation of the life of past ages, and that her constituent members are, after all, in a new form and with new names, the Benedictines and Augustinians of a former day. The monastic principle, a most important element in the social character of the Church, lingers among them, while it has been absorbed elsewhere in the frivolous or selfish tempers and opinions of an advanced period of civilization. To the Universities is committed the duty of cherishing and exemplifying Christian simplicity, nobleness, self-devotion, munificence, strictness, and zeal, which have well-nigh vanished in other places. To them only it is allotted, especially if chapters are to be swept away, to show that the Christian can be deeply read in the philosophy of ancient truth, and serenely prescient of the future from his comprehension of the past. To them only it falls, as being out of the world, to measure and expose the world, and, as being in the heart of the Church, to strengthen the Church to resist it. It is their very place to be oldfashioned; let them have but the moral and intellectual strength not to forget or to be ashamed of being so, but to carry out the doctrines, which are their inheritance, boldly, without haggling at the price they must pay in order to act consistently with their mission. We say this the rather, because it is impossible not to see a disposition in certain questions to shrink from that line of conduct which alone has saved them heretofore, or can maintain for them their historical position in time to

come. Institutions come to nothing which are untrue
to the principle which they embody ; Oxford has failed
in all respects, has compromised its dignity, and has
done injury to its inward health and stability, as often
as it has forgotten that it was a creation of the middle
ages, and has affected new fashions, or yielded to external pressure. It conceded nothing at the time of the
Rebellion, but waited to be robbed, and it gained all
back in the course of a few years ; it submitted, by its
own act, to William of Orange, and years of disgrace
followed. A few years ago, a passing humour seized it to
open its gates to the Association for Science; Dissenters
of all hues were brought to gaze upon its buildings, "its
precious things, the silver and the gold, and the spices
and the precious ointments,"—there was nothing among
its treasures that it showed them not. Four of the most
eminent among them, each of a separate persuasion, were
honoured with degrees; and it was condescendently predicted by not the least eminent of his body (Unitarian, I
believe) that by such a policy Oxford had added a hundred years to its existence. Scarcely had a twelvemonth
passed, when the fruits of that policy appeared : those
who had been admitted to covet, felt disposed to steal ;
they felt a greater pang that its gates were closed against
them, than pleasure in the memory of the short week,
during which they had been opened to them ; and the
visit of the *savans* to Alma Mater was the precursor of
the Bill, introduced into the Commons, for the permanent
admission of Dissenters to its lecture-rooms. Such is
the inevitable consequence of aping or of trembling at
the external world.

7.

And while Oxford never shows so well as when resisting innovation and rallying round an ancient principle which is imperilled, it never shows so cowardly as when, professing to be doing this, it nevertheless thinks it right to protest against and dissociate itself from those, who did the same in their own day centuries ago. Yet this is an inconsistency, into which its members, in common with our whole Church, have been again and again betrayed ever since the Reformation, when political changes and the growth of liberal notions have rendered the principles cherished in the University unpopular in the nation. Men cannot bear to be associated in the present day with those of former times whom the present day contemns; and, instead of denying that those old worthies are really contemptible, they set about proving that they themselves do not resemble them,—though they do. Hence the common practice, in other places especially, of men's purchasing for themselves a toleration of what the world calls intolerance, by their own declarations against the alleged intolerance in their forefathers, and of managing to hide their own modicum of so-called formality and superstition, by loud denunciations of those who in time past had just a little more of both than themselves. And hence they try to escape the odium of being anti-Reformers in the nineteenth century, by professing to be true sons of the Reformation made in the sixteenth; and to wash themselves clean of the imputation of Popery by laying it on thick as regards historical characters who are incapable now either of selfdefence or of retort.

How much better and more honest would it be, when

asked whether their zeal against innovation now would not have been zeal against reformation three centuries back, to avow that it is our duty to stand by what is established till it is proved to be wrong, and to maintain customs which we have inherited, though it would be a duty to resist them before they had been actually received! Who considers it an inconsistency in Sir Robert Peel to stand by the Reform Act, now that it has become law, which, before it passed, he strenuously resisted? How would it be wise in him to oppose what has been carried, yet how would it not be absurd in him to defend it on its intrinsic merits? This way of viewing the position of the University is intelligible; but it really is losing time and toil to deny, what is as plain as day, that Oxford has, and ever has had, what men of the world will call a Popish character, that in opinion and tone of thought its members are successors of the old monks, or that those who now speak against Wesleyans and Independents, would also have opposed the Foxes and Knoxes of the Reformation. Surely it is our wisdom, as we follow, so to profess we follow, ancient times. Let us not fear to connect ourselves with our predecessors; let us discern in our beautiful homes the awful traces of the past, and the past will stand by us. Let us stand upon the vestiges of the old city, and, with the hero in the poet's romance, we shall find a talisman amid the ruins. "The talisman is Faith." Or in the words of another poet, who speaks with the affection of a son of Oxford,

But thou, my mother, green as erst and pure,
   Thy willows wave, thy meeting waters glide :
Untarnished on thy matron breast endure
   The treasured gems, thy youth's delight and pride ;

Firm Loyalty, serene and fond,
Wearing untired her lofty bond ;
Awful Reverence bending low
Where'er the heavens their radiance throw :
And Wisdom's mate, Simplicity,
That in the gloom dares trust the guiding arm on high ;
These of old, thy Guardians tried,
Daily kneeling at thy side,
And wont by night to fan our vigil fires,
We feel them hovering now around the aërial spires.

IV.

THE CONVOCATION OF THE PROVINCE OF CANTERBURY.

(From the *British Magazine* of 1834-5.)

CONVOCATION.

I. ITS CONSTITUTION AND RIGHTS.

II. ITS LOWER HOUSE IN A.D. 1700, IN RELATION TO ITS UPPER.

III. VIEWS OF THE LOWER HOUSE IN OPPOSING THE UPPER.

IV. ITS RELATION TO THE ECCLESIASTICAL ESTABLISHMENT.

V. ITS RELATION TO THE CROWN.

I.

THE CONVOCATION OF THE PROVINCE OF CANTERBURY.

I.

Its Constitution and Rights.

THE Convocation of the Province of Canterbury, called, *par excellence*, the Convocation, is generally known to us as the State meeting of the clergy, convened, as the representatives of the Church, at the commencement of every new Parliament, and as consisting of two Houses, the bishops in the Upper, and, in the Lower, the deans, archdeacons, and proctors (that is, representatives) of the chapters, one for each, and of the parochial clergy two for each diocese. The whole number of the members of the Lower House is between a hundred and forty and a hundred and fifty, of which about one-third is parochial clergy. It is generally known, moreover, that the Convocation is called, under king's writ, by mandate of the Archbishop; that it is opened with divine service and a sermon; that an address follows from the Archbishop, its president, to all its members; that, at the direction of the Archbishop, the Lower House withdraws and chooses a Prolocutor, or Speaker,

from among its members ; that, though the Convocation
thus assembled may address the King or Parliament on
behalf of religion, or the redress of Church grievances,
it is not at liberty to confer to constitute canons, that
is, to act as a Council, without the king's license, nor even
with it to execute any which are against the king's prerogative, the common or statute law, or any custom of
the realm ; lastly, that, in matter of fact, after the introductory solemnities, it is always prorogued, and has been
in this dormant state for about a hundred and twenty
years.   This is as much as is generally known about the
Convocation.   Now it is a question which often rises in
a churchman's mind, " Is it not an anomaly that we have
no ecclesiastical synod ? "   And times may be coming
of so grave an aspect as to turn this anomaly into a
great practical evil and misfortune.   Then the questions
follow, " Are we still to account this long-suspended
Convocation the synodal representative of our Church ?
If so, what if the king altogether refuse his writ to assemble, or license to debate and enact canons ? or what
if, on the other hand, the Convocation is made use of
by the civil power, to force upon the Church measures
destructive of her purity or constitution ? "   Questions
such as these become more urgent year by year ; and
the first step towards answering them is to be put into
possession of the facts of the case, that is, the history of
the Convocation.

    This history was fully discussed and brought to light
in the beginning of the eighteenth century, in the course
of those dissensions which ended, A.D. 1717, in its suspension.   I propose to give some account of this quarrel, and
such information concerning the constitution and history
of the Convocation as may be necessary to illustrate the
points debated in it.

I.

When King William was called from Holland to the throne from which James had retired, he promised the nation such a comprehension as should heal the chief differences which distressed the Protestant world. With the circumstances which encouraged him thus to pledge himself, we are not concerned here,—his own feelings on the subject are obvious. Being external to the Church himself, he naturally thought it a matter of little consequence whether a man were without or within it ; Protestants might be considered as all of one religion, inasmuch as they were not Papists, the enemies of intellectual and political freedom ; and, coming, as he professed and was acknowledged, as the Great *Liberator* of the Church of England "from Popish tyranny," he reasonably expected churchmen to sacrifice somewhat of their prejudices and peculiarities for the blessing of his patronage. Accordingly he promised a comprehension ; but, when it came to the point, unexpected difficulties encountered him. First, as many as nine bishops refused to acknowledge the obligation under which he had laid the Church, in taking the place of James, and declined the oath of allegiance. Four hundred clergy followed their example ; and there seemed a danger (which in the event was realized) lest he should be obliged to have recourse to measures against the Church even more arbitrary than those which had disgraced the dethroned monarch. Under these circumstances, to have altered the liturgy or discipline of the Church at his own royal will would have been a gratuitous insult, as impolitic as it was unprecedented in the history of the English monarchy since the reign of the tyrannical Henry.

There were persons however, at the time, even among

the dissenters, the especial champions of liberty of conscience, who were desirous of such a measure, pointed
to the precedent of Henry, and maintained with truth,
that the Church would never be reformed to their satisfaction without some such summary process on the part of
the civil power. Calamy takes this line in his account
of his own life and times. " I am well assured," he says,
observing on the failure of William's attempt, "that it is
the wish of many . . that, when the next *fit opportunity*
arrives for such an healing attempt, . . . it may be taken
with more vigour and less formality. The Reformation
had never been brought about had it been left to a Convocation ; nor will our breaches be ever healed but *by a
true English Parliament.*" And he speaks of the proceeding actually advised by Tillotson, as the "*unhappy* step
of this great and good man."

Such a mode of acting, however, was so contrary to
the principles and sentiments which the dissenters had
ever expressed, that it is no unpardonable blunder in
Tillotson to have supposed that the opposite procedure
would be more pleasing to them. He and his friends
felt that one popular objection to the Church of England,
on the part of Papists as well as Puritans, had ever been
its being what was called parliamentary—as created by
human law, and living by the breath of princes ; and
they considered that a concession was made to the prejudices of all its opponents, as well as a deference shown
to its own members, by advising the new monarch to
call a Convocation for the settlement of the proposed
comprehension. For these various reasons, then, William
resolved on committing religious matters to the clergy;
and, accordingly, appointed a commission of bishops and
presbyters to determine the proposed changes, which
were then presented for the sanction of the Convocation.

The Convocation, however, did not answer his expectations. He had, indeed, so revolutionized the Upper House that its members were incapacitated from acting or were already in his interest. But the Lower House consisted of men over whom he had no power, full of jealousy and suspicion of his intentions, who had unwillingly taken the oaths, and thought they had conceded enough in allowing the overthrow of episcopacy in Scotland and the suspension of their own bishops. Accordingly a determined stand was made against the project of comprehension, till the king, despairing of success, fearful of increasing the party of the nonjurors if he converted a political into a religious question, and embarrassed by the absence of the metropolitan, gave over his attempt, and closed the Convocation.

He had, however, an easy mode of retaliation in his power, for which he was indebted to Henry VIII. By the Act of Submission, passed in Convocation in the 25th of Henry's reign, that assembly could not meet, much less frame canons, without his permission. He availed himself of this power ; and, though in the coronation oath he had sworn to "preserve unto the bishops and clergy of this realm, and to the churches committed to their charge, all such *rights and privileges* as by law do or shall appertain unto them, or any of them," he suspended these meetings of the clergy till close upon the end of his reign. Mr. Hallam makes the following defence for this procedure : " The Church had, by prescription, a right to be *summoned* in Convocation, but no prescriptive right could be set up for its longer continuance than the Crown thought expedient ;" and, admitting the analogy between Convocation and Parliament, for which the clergy contended, he says, that "the king may, legally speaking, prorogue the latter at his pleasure," and that, "if neither money were required to be granted, nor laws to be enacted, a Session would be very short." This is true, but the nation would not be satisfied if the king took on him to decide of himself, whether laws were required or not. However, this was the view of the subject maintained by the State party at the time.

So matters rested the better part of ten years ; Convocations being called, and then prorogued. Towards the end of William's reign, dissatisfaction began to be openly expressed by the friends of the Church, who were apprehensive of these continual adjournments being drawn into a precedent for a perpetual suspension of Convocation, a catastrophe which the State party, on the other hand, professed to deprecate. In 1695, the controversy between Sherlock and South, on the doctrine of the Holy Trinity, giving an advantage to the Socinians, had occasioned the king's Injunction forbidding all such explications of it as were not commonly received in the Church. This proceeding, though strictly according to the precedent of the reigns of James and Charles, turned the minds of men more strongly, by way of contrast, to the suspension of Convocation, and seems to have opened the controversy.

In 1696 was published an anonymous pamphlet, entitled "A Letter to a Convocation Man, concerning the Rights, Powers, and Privileges" of that body, supposed to be written by Dr. Binckes, in which it was maintained, that, though the king's writ is the formal instrument of summoning the Convocation, it has, by our ecclesiastical constitution, *a right to be* summoned, and to be let sit and act, and that its meeting is determined by law and custom to coincide with the Session of Parliament ;

further, that the king's license of its sitting as a Council, and enacting canons, is contained in the writ of summoning; lastly, that the canons enacted do not need the confirmation of Parliament in addition to that of the king, provided they are consistent with common law, statutes, customs, or prerogative. Letting alone the last position, which is of inferior importance in the controversy, we may observe that the two former impugn the received interpretation of the famous Act of 25 Henry VIII., already referred to. They maintain that the king's license is unnecessary, and that his writ somewhat resembles, for instance, a marriage license, which may not, under certain circumstances, be refused by the functionary who has the office of granting it.

In 1697, a few months after the publication of this pamphlet, an answer to it appeared by Dr. Wake, afterwards Archbishop of Canterbury, maintaining the received opinion of the king's absolute control over the Convocation. It elicited a reply the same year, written on a very different basis, by Hill of Kilmington, entitled, " Municipium Ecclesiasticum ; or, the Rights, Liberties, and Authorities of the Christian Church asserted, against all Oppressive Doctrines and Constitutions." Waving the legal and constitutional question, the author asserts the divine right of synods in general, a right inherent in the Church, and prior to civil institutions ; and, accordingly, condemns the Act of Submission as inconsistent with the first principles of ecclesiastical polity.

Wake defended himself (1698) by " An Appeal " "in behalf of the King's Supremacy " as established by the law, and sanctioned both by Convocations and by our most eminent bishops and clergymen, among whom he enumerates Jewel, Whitgift, Bancroft, Bilson, Nowell, Hooker, Andrewes, Laud, Heylin, Taylor, and Barrow.

This Tract was supported, in 1699, by an anonymous "Brief Inquiry into the Ground, Authority, and Rights of Ecclesiastical Synods, upon the Principles of Scripture and right Reason," in which the author of the "Municipium" was met on his own ground, the abstract constitution of the Church, Wake having argued from history and authority.

Lastly, in 1700, appeared Atterbury's work, the first edition of which was without his name, in which "The Rights, Powers, and Privileges of an English Convocation" were "stated and vindicated, in answer to a late book of Dr. Wake's, entitled 'The Authority,' etc." It is written on the legal and constitutional ground, contending that the statute of Henry is not inconsistent with ecclesiastical liberty; that the Convocation had the legal right of meeting with every new Parliament, and might frame and present canons to the king, and do anything short of enacting them without his license.

2.

So far the controversy had proceeded at the meeting of the new Parliament of 1700, which was attended by an accession of some of the Church party to the ministry. This occurrence was, of course, favourable to those who desired the restoration of the Convocation to its ordinary powers ; and the ground which had been openly taken by Wake's party, almost rendered its meeting necessary in order to allay that suspicion of the Government, which the friends of civil liberty might entertain from its continued suspension.

There was just so much *prima facie* similarity between Parliament and Convocation, in the relation of each to the king—in their times of meeting, and their twofold internal structure—that to assert the king's absolute power over the latter seemed a preparation for a similar claim in civil matters. Politicians, of all classes and opinions, looked upon Ecclesiastical Councils as mere creations of the State,—such is Burnet's professed opinion ; but the more entirely the religious character of the Convocation was merged in its civil establishment, for that very reason the more ominous was the arbitrary conduct of the Crown. As for the bishops, they, it might be said, were but the tools of the government,— fifteen had been made in the two first years of William's reign ; it was only by the clergy in the Lower House of Convocation that the Church was truly represented, and they were not allowed liberty of speech. If such was the fortune of that high-spirited order, which had stood foremost, whether in the person of their prelates, in their Universities, or in their churches, in resisting the encroachments of James, what was to be expected by the people at large ?

And, farther, the ecclesiastical principles laid down broadly by Wake, were such as would have justified King James, had he proceeded of his own will to alter the Liturgy and Articles, and to exact the submission of the clergy, who would have been bound, not, indeed, legally, till Parliament had confirmed the alterations, but, *in foro conscientiæ,* to accept them. In debating the question, "Whether the prince should be allowed a power to *alter* or *improve* what a Synod has defined, to *add* to, or *take from* it," Wake remarks, "Sure I am that this princes have done, and *so I think they have authority to do.* For, since the legislative power is lodged in their hands, so that they may make what laws or constitutions they think fit for the Church, as well as for the State ; since a Synod, in matters relating to discipline, is *but a kind of Council* to them in ecclesiastical affairs, whose advice having taken, *they may still act as they think fit;* seeing, lastly, a canon, drawn up by a Synod, *is but, as it were, matter prepared for the royal stamp,* the last forming of which, as well as enforcing whereof, must be left to the prince's judgment, I cannot see why the supreme magistrate, who confessedly has a power to confirm or reject their decrees, may not also make such other use of them as he pleases; and *correct, improve,* or otherwise *alter,* their resolutions, *according to his own liking,* before he gives his authority to them." This is spoken of the power of princes generally; yet, as Atterbury observes, he afterwards says that, "by our own constitution, the King of England has *all* that power over our Convocation that *ever any* Christian prince had over his Synods." In another place he asserts that this power exists, "not only in matters of discipline, but *in matters of faith too;* " and he cites the example of Henry VIII. in his modelling the Articles, which, he says, "relate to doctrines of faith, and that in the most necessary points of it; and yet, see what liberty the king took in judging, as well as correcting, of what they [the Synod] had done." If this be the constitutional power of the king over the Church, it is plain that the clergy, who risked so much against James, are the only body of men who have not gained legal rights and liberties by his expulsion; and it curiously fulfils the words of the incensed monarch to the seven protesting bishops, that "they were raising a devil, which they would never be able to lay, and were the unconscious tools of men who aimed at the ruin of the Church as well as of the throne." Ken and Sancroft might have the simplicity of the dove in slipping between James and William; but the Comptons and Atterburys, who had not this grace, should, at least, have had enough of the serpent's wisdom to have bargained for ecclesiastical liberties as the price of their changing their king. But to return.

The mode in which Wake attempted to anticipate the objection which the jealousy of the friends of liberty made against his statements, was to maintain that, in "an extreme case," resistance to the royal authority would be justifiable. "Whenever," he says, "the civil magistrate shall so far abuse his authority, as to render it necessary for the clergy, by some extraordinary methods, to provide for the Church's welfare, that necessity will warrant their taking of them." Further, both he and Dr. Kennett, who wrote against Atterbury in 1701, candidly lament the tyrannical character of the Act of Submission, and are manly enough to protest against what, at some future day, though not under their then gracious sovereign, might be an instrument of deplorable mischief to the highest interest of the Church. Dr. Wake, says Kennett, "does not dwell so much upon the *equity* of the Act ; but he proves the *obligation*, and there in law leaves it : because, perhaps, he might think this submission was a little hardly obtained by a prince of excessive power, and in a time of some ill designs ; and, however safe and expedient for us, under princes of our own faith and communion, yet, *under the government of heretics and heathens*, it may lay too hard a yoke upon the Church, when the archbishop shall have no power to assemble the bishops and clergy of his province, nor they any liberty to attend him, (without a *præmunire*,) let the necessities of the Church be never so urgent, and Christianity itself in utmost danger. Dr. Wake, who pleads for *present* submission, *seems aware of ill consequences that might arise in future times of trial.*"

The odiousness, then, of that constitutional right in

the Crown, by which alone the suspension of the Convocation could be defended when assailed, seems to have forced the State bishops to give way; and the two Houses were accordingly opened, in due form, in February, 1700.

The clergy, having now gained one victory (so to call it) over the Crown, proceeded, in the next place, to attack the authority of the archbishop. They maintained that the Lower House had the independent right of debating whenever they would, (as fully as the House of Commons,) without reference to the meetings of the House of bishops; or, (as it was worded,) they contended for the right of "adjournments," which now became the great question in dispute. The mode of reasoning adopted was, as before, the asserted analogy between the Parliament and Convocation; and they contended that—if even the king had no constitutional power to hinder their meetings, much less had the archbishop, the president of the Convocation, whose rights, at least, were certainly destroyed by the Act of Submission in the reign of Henry VIII. And thus we have three main inquiries before us,—the relation of the Convocation to the Church; the power of the king over Convocation and other synods; and the power of the Lower House to transact business independently of the Upper.

3.

These shall be discussed in due order. Before proceeding, however, there is a call on us seriously to reflect upon the anomalous state of the opposing parties in the dispute, and to ask ourselves the question, whether the Church had not, somehow or other, got into some wrong position, which put all its functions out of order, and made them work in perverse and fantastic ways? On the one hand, the Tory and (so called) high-church party were in opposition to authority, resting on law rather than on ecclesiastical principles, attacking the conduct of Laud and his sovereign towards the Church, and rising up against the rulers of their own day, while aiming thereby at a blow at the low theology of the school of Burnet;—a position which they never can again occupy, considering the dependence of the Lower House, as regards the appointment of its members, on the Crown and the Bishops. On the other hand, the superior clergy were the advocates of episcopal rights, and conducted themselves with the temper which became their station, though they had confined, unchurchmanlike views, and were more or less the creatures of the court. Some of them, as Burnet, were open Erastians, and willing to admit presbyterian Ordination. Others, with Wake, made the historical precedents of the country, of whatever nature, the law of the Church, so that it was sufficient that only one tyrannical act of the Civil Power in former ages should be producible, in order to its being assumed and used as an ecclesiastical principle. And others, with Hody, while seeming to allow that the Revolution was attended with encroachments on ecclesiastical liberty, maintained nevertheless that the Church must ever submit to an irresistible necessity, as if sanctioning a cowardly surrender of the trusts which had been committed to her.

Meanwhile, Ken and his company stood by on dry land, far removed from the scene of confusion into which the politics of the time had precipitated their hapless brethren. Whether they were right or wrong in declining the oaths of allegiance to William, still they, at least, had a compensation for their worldly losses. They had no need to reconcile their duty to the faith with their duty to their Church; to obey the authority of its rulers while they resisted their doctrines,—a more grievous conflict than that which they themselves had encountered once, between loyalty and conscience. At length, they dropped off, one and one, from this troublesome stage, and their race is long extinct; but the English Church, my mother, is still encompassed with the waters into which she then was plunged.

2.

Its Lower House in relation to its Upper.

I LEFT off, in my first paper, with the meeting of the Convocation in the last year of William, the immediate subject of dispute between the two Houses being as to the power of the Lower to adjourn itself independently of the Upper. It may seem surprising, at first sight, that there should be room for dispute, where an appeal to usage might settle the matter at once. But the genius of the union of Church and State had been opposed to frequent meetings of the clergy, who had been called together for business only on especial occasions; and a good part of the records of Convocation had been lost in the fire of London. On the other hand, there had been so many alterations in the constitution of the country in the foregoing two hundred years, that it seemed hardly safe or fair to rest upon precedents of a very remote date. And there was certainly a close analogy between the actual origin and formation of the Parliament, and the assumed history and state of the Convocation on Atterbury's theory, which seemed to render recent precedents scarcely necessary. In truth, the ecclesiastical system which the Reformation undertook was never completed; and, much as Laud did for the Church, there was no call upon him in his day, with such a king as Charles, to place its synods on an intelligible and consistent footing.

However, there was, after all, sufficient information to be had as regarded the general relation of the Lower

House to the Upper, which nothing but the impetuosity of faction could obscure; especially a memorandum of Archbishop Parker's, which seems entirely to bear out the bishops in their resistance to what were dangerous innovations on the part of the inferior clergy. Indeed, that, on the whole, the Upper House was in the right, and the Lower in the wrong, is sufficiently clear to my mind, first, from Bull and others, who were members of the Lower House, taking the side of the bishops; next, from the indecency of the Lower House deciding by themselves in favour of their pretended rights, and, acting on their own decision, considering that the existing usage was on the side of the bishops.

I.

The Convocation took its rise in the course of the fourteenth century, between three and four hundred years before the controversy which I am employed in relating, under circumstances which shall be mentioned at another time. At present, I will but describe its internal structure, by way of throwing light upon the question of "Adjournments," which was immediately in dispute. Originally, it consisted, as the Parliament itself, only of one House, the inferior clergy being rather assistants to the bishops than possessed of co-ordinate authority, and being allowed a place in it principally on account of those money-questions which interested lower as well as superior ecclesiastics. It was called by the Archbishop's mandate, directed to the Bishop of London as Dean of the Province; to the Archbishop the returns of members were made, and before him, as President of Convocation, the members appeared on the day fixed for assembling. The members thus convened representing different interests, it was natural that, from time to time, they should, for dispatch of business, be divided into several committees, that the whole meeting might be enabled the better to ascertain and to forward the views of each section of their constituents. Hence, it is said, there were sometimes as many as four separate assemblies transacting business in the Convocation ; the Bishops, the regulars, the deans and chapters, and the parochial clergy. In process of time, however, these settled into the two main divisions of the bishops and the inferior clergy, at present called, as in Parker's "Descriptio," the two Houses of Convocation. Thus, the Lower House, in its origin, had no independent existence, being a mere appendage to the Upper, separated off from it for convenience, sent out from it to debate on this or that question specially submitted to it, and recalled at the President's pleasure to report the opinions and advice of its members. Accordingly, at first it had no separate place of meeting, but merely retired to a distant part of the room where the Bishops assembled. Though, however, originally merely a committee of the Convocation, in process of time it gained powers by the force of custom, which, in consequence, it was very difficult to distinguish from legal rights. Usage is a sufficient sanction, whether in civil or ecclesiastical matters, where antecedent principles, moral or religious, do not stand in the way. In the quarrel before us, there was the twofold controversy—first, what the usage was ? next, whether, granting it to emancipate the Lower House as fully as the clergy of the day maintained, such usage was not counter to the principles of the episcopal regimen, and therefore invalid as an authority? It had long been the custom for the inferior clergy to hold their meetings in a separate room, though in the same place with the Bishops. They had long received and reported business through one of their number, called the Prolocutor, Referendary, or, "organum vocis Domus Inferioris," who also presided at their debates. Such was the received usage ; but, owing to the infrequency of the meetings of Convocation, and to the absence of a jealous accuracy in the proceedings of an assembly of men who were in the mutual relation of fathers and sons in the ministerial office, it was scarcely possible to decide exactly the limit of the power possessed by the Lower House, especially considering there was the parallel and complete history of the two Houses of Parliament, (which also originally formed but one House,) to supply and comment upon the deficient precedents of the Convocation. Accordingly, to this parallel the champions of the Lower House had recourse, in order to establish their independence ; while the Bishops appealed first to the original state of the Convocation, next to the principles of episcopacy and the precedents of primitive Synods.

In the meanwhile, thus much was granted on all hands to the Lower House, which implied a very considerable power in presbyters, had it nothing more—the right of presenting their grievances to the Upper, of offering petitions for making canons, revising old ones, etc., of being assessors of the Upper in judicial matters, and, lastly, of having a veto on synodical acts. But the main object coveted by the Lower House was the power of originating measures, and, in 1689, they had ventured to exercise it, when they made a representation to the Bishops about some of the latitudinarian and scandalous books of the day. On the other hand, the Upper House maintained, in opposition to such spontaneous movements on the part of the Lower, that the power, not only of origination, but also of jurisdiction, lay solely with the

Bishops, who were to prescribe to them their subjects and times of debate, the choice and number of their committees, to determine the question of elections, to censure for absence, and especially to prorogue their meetings, the claim which of course most effectually interfered with that independence which the Lower House affected. On this last point, the power of Adjournments, the controversy turned, in the proceedings of 1700—1 : the Lower House asserted they might remain sitting after the adjournment of the Upper, and that they might adjourn themselves to any time or times before, and need not meet upon, the day fixed for its re-assembling.

In the language of Convocation, as of other Church Synods, a *Session* has not the meaning given to it in Parliament, but stands for every separate meeting devoted to discussion ; and to *prorogue* or *continue* the Convocation is to end the Session, or to adjourn. This was customarily done by schedule from the Archbishop, (unless he declared it by word of mouth to the members of the Lower House present,) sent down to the clergy, and conveyed to them through the Prolocutor ; and as the dispute turned, in the first instance, upon its wording, I will here transcribe it, as used by Tenison, in 1700 :

"In Dei Nomine, Amen. Nos Thomas, Providentiâ Divinâ Cantuariensis Archiepiscopus, totius Angliæ Primas et Metropolitanus, rite et legitimè procedentes, præsentem sacram Synodum sive Convocationem Prælatorum et Cleri nostræ Cantuariensis Provinciæ, usque ad et in hunc diem, horas et locum continuatam et prorogatam, necnon omnia et singula certificatoria, hactenus introducta, et introducenda et non introducta, in eodem statu quo nunc sunt, ad et in diem Veneris, 28vum diem instantis mensis Februarii, inter horas 8vum et 11mam ante meridiem ejusdem diei in hunc locum, una cum ulteriori continuatione et prorogatione dierum extunc sequentium, et locorum, si oporteat, in eâ parte fiendis, continuamus et prorogamus in his scriptis.

" THO. CANTUAR."

The form of prorogation in the Lower House, consequent upon this, as used by the Prolocutor, was as follows: "Intimamus hanc convocationem esse continuatam usque ad et in diem . . . . in hunc locum ; e monemus omnes ad tunc et ibidem interessendum." From the former of these two forms, the Bishops argued that the Lower House, being included in "*præsentem sacram synodum sive convocationem,*" was adjourned by the Metropolitan ; the other party replied that, in like manner, the phrase *præsens parliamentum* was used in the adjournments of the House of Lords, yet at that day it referred to the proceedings of that House alone. Upon this, the advocates for the Upper House observed that "Prælatorum et *cleri*" was added in the schedule ; that its actual effect had ever been to prorogue the Lower House, as was confirmed by the oldest convocation-men then living ; and, further, that it was also declared in it that the matters in debate must remain in *statu quo*, sealed and secured, till the next Session,—a provision quite inconsistent with the claim of the Lower House, to open and discuss them in the interval. They added that the schedule could not be altered except by Act of Parliament. Moreover they referred to the word *intimamus*, in the Prolocutor's form, as corroborating their position concerning the dependent character of the Lower House.

The opposite party maintained a different interpretation of the word *intimamus*, which in the ecclesiastical courts and in Councils (they said), was a word of authority, being even used by the Pope in the Council of Constance. Then they went on to destroy the evidence derivable from the form of the schedule, which, they said, was unknown till the reign of Henry VIII., introduced by Archbishop Warham, who was bred up in the canon law, after the pattern of the Lateran council, but accompanied on its introduction into England by a new clause, inserted in the Archbishop's mandate of summons, calling on the clergy, to send up proctors "habentes authoritatem *continuationi et prorogationi consentiendi,*" as if to avoid encroachment on the rights then enjoyed by the Lower House, of voting on the question of adjournment. Further, they maintained, that not even the wording of the schedule was against them, that is as interpreted by the practice of the Upper House ; for the schedule seemed to place the adjournment in the Archbishop's hands absolutely, whereas the Bishops certainly had a voice in it ; if, then, he did but declare the adjournment, the question whether any other than the Bishops had a share in it was left undecided.

On the other hand, the advocates of the Bishops further appealed, in support of their claim of jurisdiction over the Lower House,—first, to the circumstance that the catalogue of the Lower House was prefixed to their own register ; next, that the names of proxies for its absent members were lodged with their registrar; thirdly, that, according to Archbishop Whitgift's tables, his registrar had the sole right of fees for exhibiting these proxies ; fourthly, that, in these matters, the actuary of the Lower House was accustomed to act only as the registrar's deputy.

The members of the Lower House, in reply, brought together, from their own journals, what they considered to be precedents for their exercising the independent right of Adjournments. The alleged precedents were as follows : that in 1586, Sessions 3, 4, 5, 6, 9, 11, it is recorded that the *prolocutor*, (and in the 10th, that a member of the Lower House, "*nomine* prolocutoris,") "*continuavit* hujusmodi convocationem *quoad hanc domum."* In 1640, sess. 7, *"Domini continuarunt et prorogarunt* ulteriorem sessionem," etc. In 1677, March 21st, *"Prolocutor continuavit,"* he being Stillingfleet, and, in 1678, "Dominus *prolocutor continuavit,* hanc synodum."

The Bishops answered, that these expressions " prolocutor continuavit," etc., were undeniably *exceptions* to the ordinary style, and were most naturally accounted for as familiar and inaccurate modes of speaking, hastily adopted by the actuary ; that, in these very instances (except those of 1640), the Upper House (as its registers showed) was adjourned by the Archbishop from and to the very same day and hour as the Lower House, showing clearly that the Lower House followed herein the movements of the Upper ; and that, with the exception of 1586, the instances were adduced, not from registers, but from short, confused, and ill-written minutes—a mere scribble, taken down at the time, and attested by no one—a circumstance especially to be kept in view in considering the very different precedents of 1640, which they confessed were, at first sight, deserving of attention.

2.

These important precedents were as follows :—on May 5th, 1640, both Houses sat ; the register of the Upper says, that the Archbishop's commissioner prorogued the whole Convocation to May 9th, and from thence again to May 13th ; whereas by the minutes of the Lower House the clergy adjourned from May 5th to May 8th, and so to May 13th. However, this was explained, as the Bishops argued, from the history of that troubled time. On May 5th, Charles dissolved his Parliament ; but, desirous to have the grant of the subsidies which he expected from the clergy, he consulted the Lord Keeper whether the Convocation might still sit, though Parliament was dissolved. Finding that it was possible, he directed the Archbishop to go on with the business they had begun ; but he, hearing that some of of its members had doubts about the point of law, advised a further reference to his Majesty's Council, who determined as the Lord Keeper had done before them. Accordingly a new commission was issued, the former having limited the Session of the Convocation to the Session of Parliament, and they set to business again on May 13th. The interval, then, was a time of confusion, there being continual informal meetings through it ; some of which, mentioned by Fuller and Heylin, are are not even noticed either in the register or minutes. After the 13th, all is regular and correspondent again, in the times of adjournment, as recorded in the journals of the two Houses.

The other instance brought forward by the clergy was from the end of the same year. According to the register of the Upper House, the Convocation was prorogued from December 19th, 1640, to January 13th, 1641 ; but the minutes of the Lower mentioned an adjournment from December 19th to December 23rd, and from thence to January 13. Now it so happens that on December 18th the Archbishop was accused of high treason, and committed to the custody of the usher of the black rod; and it also happens, that, in the preceding May, after an assault upon his palace, the rabble who made it turned their fury on the Convocation, who were forthwith protected by the train bands. All this was enough to put its members into confusion on the present occasion ; and December 23rd, two days before Christmas, is not a probable time for an ordinary meeting, as is implied by the adjournment of the Upper House from the 19th to January 13th. Further, there is no proof the Upper House did not in the event meet on the 23rd, since its register breaks off abruptly upon the Archbishop's arrest. The only difficulty on the face of the documents was the actual *intention* of the Lower House on the 19th, to meet on the 23rd, whereas the Upper did not so intend ; to which it was answered, that there were the strongest reasons for thinking this entry in the register of the Lower House was not made till afterwards. In the five Sessions, from December 9th to January 17th, (of which December 19th and 23rd were two,) no business was done; and the minute of them seems, from the ink, which is different from what comes before and after, to have been made at one and the same time. Further, there is great inaccuracy and irregularity in the minutes at other times : such as the joining together in the same paragraph the acts of several Sessions, and a confusion of dates. Such was the explanation offered by the Upper House. To which it was added, that, in 1689, a committee had been appointed to inspect the registers, and adjust the privileges of both Houses, and at that time the lower clergy did not allege the quotations now produced in behalf of their claims of independence.

But the advocates of the Lower House did not rest their case on the result of an inquiry into one or two mere precedents ; they appealed, as their chief argument, to their resemblance to the House of Commons ; and they contended that, in spite of forms and precedents, the Act of Submission, in 25 Henry VIII., had, in matter of fact, destroyed the power of the Metropolitan altogether, and placed the king in his stead; so that the clergy being now under the king, and the king having allowed them to meet, the Archbishop could not interfere with them. This famous Act will come under our notice by-and-by ; here it is enough to observe, in opposition to this theory, that it does not hint at any change in the relation between Archbishop and clergy in synodal matters ; only subjecting the whole Church to the king. In spite of every attempt to assimilate the Convocation to the Parliament, both in its internal structure and its relation towards the sovereign (and undoubtedly there is a resemblance), these distinctions between them are undeniable : viz., that the king summons the Parliament in his own name, under the great seal, through the Lord Chancellor ; receives the returns, receives the Commons on the first day of meeting, directs them to choose and confirms their Speaker : whereas it is the Archbishop, empowered indeed by king's writ, but by his own mandate, addressed to the Bishop of London, who convenes the Convocation, in his own name, under his own archiepiscopal seal ; receiving the returns, receiving the Lower House on their first meeting, and directing them to choose, and confirming when chosen, their prolocutor. Accordingly, Parker's "Descriptio," which, in other respects also, substantiates the claims of the Upper House, so far from countenancing Atterbury's Erastian notion, that the Archbishop became, by the Act of 25th Henry, a mere officer of the king, as regards the Convocation, professes, in the Introduction, to be the " forma convocationis celebrandæ *prout ab antiquo* observari *consuevit,*" and presently introduces the phrases, "*ex more,*" "*ex laudabili et antiquâ ordinatione,*" and "*solet observari.*"

But the Lower House considered they had another ground of civil right, which might avail them in their contest. It had been usual, since Edward the First's reign, to introduce into the writ, summoning the bishops to Parliament, a clause (called, from the first word, the

" Præmunientes,") in which each Bishop was required to
bring with him certain of his clergy.   This clause was
very distasteful and insulting to the Church, when first
inserted, and had scarcely been obeyed from Edward's
time.   It was now almost obsolete, though formally
continued in the parliamentary writ ; but it now was
turned to account by the lower clergy in their contest
against their rulers.   The latter answered, with justice,
that this supposed right of the clergy had nothing to do
with the *Convocation ;* that the writ came from the king,
and the return was made to him ; that those select
clergymen might proceed with their respective Bishops
to the king in Parliament, if they would, and take the
place he chose to give them.   Meanwhile, the Archbishop surely might be allowed to preside over his own
provincial Council, according to custom.   However, this
alleged claim, though thus successfully disposed of,
seems to have had some influence in inducing the court
to allow the meeting of the Convocation.   Some of the
Bishops, urged by the clamour, had summoned their
clergy to Parliament by virtue of it ; and a source of
embarrassment and annoyance was thus opened upon
the government.

  Lastly, the Lower House argued that, from the nature
of the case, it was absurd to allow them to sit separate
from the Bishops, if they were not allowed to sit at
pleasure—the very notion of a *House* implying a right
of separate debate, a right of separate judgment, and
a right of sitting at discretion ; to which the Upper answered, that points of privilege and jurisdiction were determined by usage, not by the nature of things ; and,
moreover, that there was much more of incongruity in
the idea that the lower clergy had a power which, in its
full exercise, was contrary to all episcopal government

and the Metropolitan's rights, and tended to overthrow the Church.

3.

This is an account of the main points in dispute and main arguments employed. If, however, we inspect the history of the Session of 1700 itself, we shall find the above to be a very inadequate representation of the actual course of the controversy. So many are the little annoyances offered by the Lower to the Upper House, so marvellous their encroachments on precedent and breaches of order, that we can only account for their conduct by supposing the body of the clergy at that period thoroughly dissatisfied ; dissatisfied with their condition, with their prospects, and, above all, with themselves ; suspicious not only of their new king and his Bishops, but of their own straightforwardness in the course of late events ; feeling that somehow things had got wrong, and not seeing how they could be righted, yet without the consciousness that they were altogether free from blame themselves.

For instance, on the 25th of February, they prejudged the question in dispute, by continuing to sit after the receipt of the Archbishop's schedule, and then adjourning to a place different from that specified in it. When called to account for this irregularity, they did not answer in that respectful and obedient manner which superiors had a right to expect from them. The Archbishop had put to the Prolocutor these two questions : " Whether the Lower House of Convocation did sit, after they were prorogued by his grace, on February 25th ? " —And " Whether they did meet that present morning (February 28th) without attending on their lordships in the place to which they were prorogued ? " An answer as to the matter of fact was required, first by common decency, next because their exercise of a right actually under dispute was itself an important measure, and called for the attention of the Upper House, whatever became the question of right itself. However, instead of answering, they merely sent in a paper of precedents, in defence of their side of the argument. Nor was this all ; for they entitled it, the "Report of the *committee* of the Lower House ; " thus ruling in their own favour, and in the very presence of the Bishops, another point in controversy : the Upper House maintaining that the Lower House itself was but a committee of the Convocation, and that all power of separating off portions of its members lay with them.

Again, they renewed the attempt which they had made, against all precedent, in 1689, to communicate with the Upper House through other members besides the Prolocutor ; the only defence they were able to offer for this conduct being, the inconvenience resulting to them by the frequent absence of their chairman in his attendance on their lordships ; whereas the very inconvenience was itself a token, if they would take it rightly, that such continued and independent discussion was not part of their rights or business. Their own mode of stating their complaint (which they published) provokes a smile in the reader of after times. The then Warden of All Souls was sent up to the Upper House, instead of the Prolocutor, on which "his grace was pleased to return this answer, ' Dr. Finch, since the Prolocutor is not with you, I say nothing.' " "Admit," they argue, " the Prolocutor, as the *os et organum vocis* of the House, to be in most cases the properest person to report their sense, this does not hinder but a message *in scriptis,* such as this was, *especially when brought up by a person of the honourable Dr. Finch's quality,* might be fit to be received."

Further, they maintained they might take the first step in censuring irreligious publications of the day, such as Toland's "Christianity not Mysterious," and proceeded to submit certain resolutions, drawn up by a committee of themselves, to the Upper House; though it was as yet undecided, first, whether they themselves had such a right of origination, whether they might appoint a committee, and receive its report, and further, whether the Convocation might, as the Law then stood, enter upon judicial proceedings at all.

Further still, the Bishops had given to their paper of precedents a distinct and careful answer in writing, which I do not know where to find, though I am pretty sure I have seen it among the pamphlets of the day. "A Narrative of the proceedings of the Lower House, in 1700-1, *drawn up by the order of the House,*" (supposed to be written by the Prolocutor Hooper, afterwards Bishop of Bath and Wells,) instead of furnishing this paper, says, "It cannot be expected we should here insert a copy of their lordships' papers, which make up many sheets, ... but possibly the reader may be curious to know, at least, the substance, etc.," and then it proceeds to give its *own version* of it. This is surely unfair and disrespectful to the Upper House. But the conduct in Convocation of the same party, on receipt of the Bishops' paper, was actually offensive. Without prosecuting the argument which they themselves had begun, they *voted,* first in committee, then in the House, that they had a right to adjourn themselves; then they sent the Prolocutor with a message to the Bishops, signifying that they considered their lordships' reply unsatisfactory, and praying for a free conference on the matter in debate.

24

Here was a fresh assumption of a privilege enjoyed by the Lower House of Parliament; for, in Convocation, such conferences had ever been held at the invitation of the Bishops, not to mention their general claim to direct the proceedings of the Lower House in all matters. This was urged by the advocates of the Upper House; —also, that written statements, specific quotations, etc., were more to the purpose in such a matter than speeches, and, besides, that the dispute had hitherto been conducted on paper.

Lastly, when the Bishops, with the hope of smoothing matters, appointed a committee of five of their number to meet ten of the clergy to inspect the acts of both Houses during the then Convocation, and report judgment upon them, the Lower House, by a new and unprecedented disobedience, declined to act with them for such a purpose.

The reader may be curious to know whether such factious conduct was supported by a large majority of the Lower House. The resolution that it had power to adjourn itself, was carried by 66 against 24, proxies included; the neuter members (taking the whole number to be 145) being 55. Of this minority of 24, only 13 were present, and these seem to have offered a determined opposition to the course pursued by their brethren. Two months afterwards, a protest was presented to the Archbishop, from 13 members of the Lower House, against its proceedings, who probably were about the same who voted in the minority on this occasion. I will here insert it, as it contains fresh argument against the candour of their brethren:

"To his Grace, etc. We, whose names are underwritten, do humbly beg leave to represent to your Grace, that, whereas we did move in the Lower House of Convocation that we might enter our protestation against all intermediate Sessions of the Lower House betwixt your Grace's ordinary prorogations, the question being put upon the said motion, it passed against us in the negative ; and a further motion being made, and the question put, whether the said vote should be registered, it likewise passed against us, that it should not be registered at [as] yet. Wherefore we humbly beg leave that we may be admitted to enter our protestations against all such intermediate Sessions. (Signed.) Wm. Sherlock, Dean St. Paul's ; G. Verney, Proct. Linc. ; J. Wichart, Dean Winton ; S. Freeman, Dean Peterbor. ; G. Bull, Archd. Landaff; W. Stanley, Archd. London ; J. Jeffery, Archd. Norwich ; C. Trimnell, Archd. Norfolk ; R. Bourchier, Archd. Lewis ; J. Evans, Proct. Bang. ; J. Whitefoot, Proct. Norwich ; G. Pooley, Proct. Bath and Wells ; T. Littel, Proct. Norwich."

In May, in the same year, another list of 13, almost the same, (W. Beverege and W. Hayley being substituted for Wichart and Bull,) addressed the Archbishop, by way of protest, on another innovation made by the Lower House. On the 8th, the Prolocutor had refused to read the Archbishop's schedule of prorogation to the Lower House, though urged by some of the members to do so. These members, in consequence, did not consider they could attend on the 16th, which had been fixed for the next Session, without (as far as the form went) obeying the notice of it given by the Prolocutor, instead of the order of the Archbishop, and, in consequence, addressed a letter to the latter to explain their absence.

So much concerning the friends of order in the Lower House, to whom, in 1705, we find added the names, among others, of Gibson, (afterwards Bishop of London, to one of whose tracts I am much indebted in the foregoing account,) Green, Prideaux, Bentley, and Hody. On the other side, besides Spratt, Bishop of Rochester, Trelawney, of Exeter, and Compton, of London, there were Atterbury, Aldrich, Smalridge, Jane, and Hooper.

Here, then, I stop for the present; and, to avoid all mistake, I will just observe that I am far from pretend-tending to have mastered the history of this controversy, though I have attempted to give its outlines correctly, as far as I have gone. I have before me a list of as many as 69 books and pamphlets, written before 1708, on the subject, as affixed to one of them by a publisher.* Wake's work on English Councils, published in 1703, in answer to Atterbury, is itself a thick folio of 850 pages, not to mention the fourth volume of Wilkins' Concilia, a work of a later date. Therefore no one need be sur-prised if he happens to pitch on narratives giving him fuller information than I have collected.

* The reader will find a history of the principal works in the controversy, in the Biographia Britannica; article, Atterbury.

3.

Views of the Lower House in opposing the Upper.

I AM fearful of tiring the reader with the minute details of the quarrel which took place between the two Houses in the Convocations of 1700 and following years; yet it has been my object, as it shall be in what has to come, to confine my account of it to those points which involved some question of right or privilege between them, or between both and the Crown. In continuing the history, I will only remark that such a dissension scarcely can occur again. It arose from a new Upper House being grafted by a new King on an old clergy; whereas, in a settled state of things, there is a regular and close connection between the Bishops and the Lower House, the great majority of the members of the latter being appointed either by the Crown or the episcopal bench. I say it scarcely can recur; because it is not to be supposed that the great body of the clergy will ever again find themselves called upon to shift their allegiance to new Bishops at the command of a foreigner scarcely seated on the throne.

I.

Comparing the two Houses with each other, the dignified and temperate conduct of the Upper House forces itself upon the notice of the reader. However, it should be remembered that nothing is so easy as composure, good humour, and good sense, when we have matters in the main our own way. " Let those laugh who win " is a familiar proverb. The Bishops were at this time on the winning side ; they had the King with them, and their political principles had gained the victory. Besides, a sort of constitutional tranquillity and clearness of head are often the attendants on the cold, unenthusiastical temper which had, at that era, triumphed in Church and State, as may be illustrated in the case of some well-known writers of that and a more recent date. At the same time, there were members of the Upper House as free from the reproach of placidity and insensibility as any of the Lower. On one occasion, Burnet, whose writings had been attacked by the Lower House, was provoked to interpose, in answer to a question from the Prolocutor to the Archbishop, on some immaterial point of dissension. " This is fine indeed," he said, " the Lower House will not allow a committee to inspect their books, and now they demand to see ours ! " and on the Prolocutor replying that he asked nothing but what he was concerned to know, and what of right he might demand, Burnet returned, " This is according to *your usual insolence.*" " Insolence, my lord ! " said the Prolocutor, " do you give me that word ? " " Yes, insolence ! " replied the Bishop ; " you deserve that word and worse. Think what you will of yourself, I know what you are." This Prolocutor was Hooper, soon afterwards Bishop of Bath and Wells, whom Burnet repays in his History, for reporting the above conversation, with a line of description in aggravation of what he then said to his face ; saying, that he was " a man of learning and good conduct hitherto," but " reserved, crafty, and ambitious."

The Convocation of which I have hitherto spoken came to an end by the dissolution of Parliament. A fresh one, summoned in the beginning of 1702, was first interrupted by the death of the Prolocutor of the Lower

House, and then dissolved by the King's death, in spite of Lord Rochester's attempt to give it the same continuance of existence as the Parliament enjoyed, as if it were a constituent part of the civil assembly.

Little need be said of the proceedings of the Convocation for the following nine years. Their dissensions continued unabated, and the situation of the Church and kingdom was such as to supply abundant matter for jealousy and factiousness to act upon. In the opening of the new reign, the Bishops offered, by way of accommodation, to allow the Lower House, during the intervals of Sessions, to appoint committees for preparing matters ; and, further, when business was brought before them, to give them sufficient time, before their prorogation, for debating upon it. The Lower House would not accept these terms, and wished the controversy referred to the Queen's arbitration ; which the Bishops declined, lest they should compromise that right of supremacy over presbyters, inherent in the episcopate. The Lower House then addressed themselves to the Commons, but could only obtain from them a general promise of standing by the just rights of the clergy. Then they addressed the Queen, who referred them to her ministers, and the premier being with them, and the judges (as it was supposed) against them, nothing was done. Lastly, they passed a declaration that episcopacy was of divine and apostolical right ; but the Bishops, apprehensive of incurring a *præmunire* by what would have seemed the enactment of a canon, declined to assent to it.

The sessions of 1705-6 were scarcely begun when a protest was presented to the Bishops against the majority in the Lower House by forty-nine of its members. In this document the following innovations are specified : (1) Their Prolocutor's proroguing the House with the consent and authority of the House itself, not by authority of the Archbishop's schedule (a practice begun in the last Convocation of King William), and the consequent introduction of intermediate Sessions; (2) their claim of a power of putting the Prolocutor into the chair before he was confirmed by the Upper House, and so beginning debates without formal leave from it; (3) their giving leave of absence to members, and of voting by proxy; (4) their electing an actuary, in prejudice of the Archbishop's right, whose officer, the registrar of the whole Convocation, had constantly received fees from the Lower House, in which he acted by deputy; and, (5) their insisting on drawing up an address to the Queen, at the opening of the then Convocation, instead of accepting or amending that sent down to them from the Bishops. It is observable that among these forty-nine protesters, only ten were proctors of the clergy; whereas, in the counter-declaration, subscribed by the majority of the Lower House soon afterwards, there are twenty-nine such, out of seventy-five signatures.

In the Convocation of 1707, the Archbishop was armed by a letter from the Queen (who had already interfered in 1705-6), declaratory of her intention to maintain her supremacy, and the due subordination of presbyters to Bishops in the Church of England. When he sent for the Lower House to communicate it to them, few of them were found assembled, and the Prolocutor was absent; so that the Archbishop found it necessary to communicate it to the clergy generally, in a circular letter, addressed to the Bishops of his province.

2.

However, it is but fair to state the circumstances which led to these strange irregularities on the part of the Lower House. In truth, they found, or thought they found, that their obedience as presbyters to Bishops was to be made use of in order to betray and destroy the Church; they were in a net from which they could not disentangle themselves, and having lately had their Bishops' sanction to the doctrine that, in extreme cases, it was lawful to renounce the Lord's anointed, and his heirs after him, they were tempted to believe that on similar grounds, and much more in a case of conscience, it was religious to engage in a systematic opposition to the successors of the Apostles. In the year 1707, the Act of Union with Scotland was passed, and the body of the clergy saw in it what the event has proved, the depression of the Church Catholic, their own bone and flesh, in that country, and the practical recognition of the kirk by English Protestants. Lords North and Grey had moved the addition of the following proviso to the bill:—"Provided always, that nothing in this ratification shall be construed to extend to an approbation or acknowledgment of the truth of the presbyterian way of worship, or allowing the religion of the Church of Scotland to be what it is styled, 'the true Protestant Religion;'" but it was rejected on the second reading by fifty-five to nineteen, only one Bishop (Hooper, of Bath and Wells,) voting in the minority. The Lower House of Convocation had taken the alarm, and were proceeding to make application to the Commons against the Union, when the Queen (contrary, as the clergy maintained, to the custom of the Church ever since the Reformation,) prorogued the Convocation, while the Parliament sat, for three weeks, that is, till the Act of Union had passed both Houses and received the royal assent. Their indignation at what they considered tyranny added to treachery, occasioned the Queen's letter concerning her own supremacy, and their absence from the Convocation, when the Archbishop communicated it in form, as above related.

Again, their refusal of the Upper House's address to the Queen, in 1705, disrespectful as their conduct was, and irregular, arose from the wish of the Bishops to represent that the Church was in no danger; while the Lower House, fully as they might trust the Queen, did consider that there were parties in the State very hostile and dangerous to its interests.

Nor must it be forgotten, that to the Lower House (aided by the Nonjurors externally) we are indebted that no change was made in our services and discipline in 1689; the innovations contemplated being such as would literally have been fatal to us as a Church, such as cannot be contemplated by any churchman without indignation and affright, and gratitude to a merciful Providence, which ordered things otherwise. What they were shall be given in Mr. Hallam's words:—" The Bill of Comprehension, proposed to Parliament, went *no further* than to leave a few scrupled ceremonies at discretion, and to *admit presbyterian ministers into the Church* without pronouncing on the invalidity of their former Ordination;" as if the recognizing them as ministers were not pronouncing.* Is it then the case that we have a second time risked the Succession? the thought of this, while it is frightful, is consolatory in our present uncertainties. This good act the Lower House of 1689 has done for us; and, while doing it, and attempting other services, its members also gave the alarm that the Government was aiming at the suspension of Convocation, and *the Government party denied it.* We have the event before us.

* [Was not a conditional ordination intended?]

Moreover, with all their faults and mistakes, they certainly had an enlarged view of the duties of an Ecclesiastical Synod ; and grasped the principles, and aimed at wielding the powers, of the Church with a vigour that the court Bishops could not comprehend. The aspect of latitudinarianism and infidelity was very threatening ; and they felt these principles of evil were to be met, not by mere controversy, not by individuals relying on what is called the force of reason, nor again by mere civil authority, but by the moral power of the Church, whether as a body, or in its authorities, by Bishops or Convocations ; by that high influence, in fact, which broke the power of paganism and baffled the schools of philosophy. But so far from exercising this their special gift, the very heads of the Church were in terms of friendship with its enemies. Firmin, the Unitarian, was the friend of Tillotson and Fowler ; and the writers of his party are recommended by Burnet for their "gravity" in the management of controversy, for their temper, and judgment. Sherlock seemed extravagating towards tritheism, Clarke towards Arianism, and Hoadley towards a legion of heresies. Even where orthodoxy was preserved, the depth and fervour of the Laudian era was being supplanted by a cold, dry, and minute theology. A few years after the date under review, the Bishops of the province of Canterbury were all but unanimous in favour of openly recognizing lay baptism ; and were only stopped from declaring themselves on the point synodically, by the Lower House, and, as Bishops, by the opposition of Sharp, Archbishop of York. Such was the less alarming side of things ; but on the worse the prospect was fearful. The rationalism which has appeared in Germany seems in great measure to have originated in England at the period under con-

sideration.   Hickes, in 1707, speaks of pamphleteers of
the day, who wrote

"against making of creeds, and creed-makers who impose upon
men articles of faith.   These men of large minds and free thoughts
will not have them confined and tied up to forms and summaries
of belief. . . .   If they durst, they would write against Scripture-
making, as you may perceive by the table-talk which the reputed
author of the Rights, and some other Grecians, had of them, at a
dinner, the 29th of November last. . . .   They began with Balaam
and his ass, and, with scorn and scurrility enough, asserted the ass
to be the fittest of the two to see an angel, and to have divine in-
spirations and revelations. . . .   Then, for the prophets, they did
God and them the honour to compare them to the Camisars, and
prophecy to deliriums in fevers, and told a story of a physician who
cured a patient of his prophetical deliriums and was refused his
reward.   They also said it was a disease proper, it may be, to
certain places and constitutions, as agues, and . . . observed, that
drunkenness and prophecy was the same thing. . . .   The passing
over the Red Sea, they said, was not miraculous, but natural. . . .
The pillar of fire, they said, was some sort of artificial preparation
in the nature of a phosphorus. . . .   Elijah's sacrifice, they said,
was by artificial fire. . . .   The marriage in Cana was a merry-
making; and He, meaning our Lord, made the water wine with
spirit of wine."

Such being the state of things, the plans of the Lower
House have, at least, the merit of energy and boldness.
They appointed, in 1700, committees for examining
certain attacks upon Christianity; for inquiring into the
causes of the corruption of manners, and the means of
reformation; for making inquiries into seminaries set up
in opposition to the Universities; for the means of pro-
moting religion in the plantations, and among seamen;
for introducing our liturgy to the notice of the French
and other Protestants, and for considering the grievances
of ecclesiastical cognizances.   They desired to restrain
the licentiousness of the press, and the profaneness and

immorality of the stage ; to reform the church discipline, to hinder clandestine marriages, to remove the inconveniences in the mode of recovering church rates, and legal difficulties which lay on the clergy as to the administration of the Lord's Supper. In short, they undertook, as was their duty, all those matters which have ever since either been neglected or taken up by improper parties, whether the Parliament, the public press, or private societies. With some account of their attempts to proceed against irreligious and unsound publications, I shall close this paper and the history of their career.

3.

In 1700, they presented an address to the Upper House, on the subject of Toland's "Christianity not Mysterious," praying for their lordships' judgment on certain extracts they made from it. The Bishops, upon taking advice of counsel, returned answer, agreeably to a former decision in 1689, that since the famous Act of Submission they could not censure judicially any such books without a license from the King, "which they had not yet received." It was conceived that a *judgment on opinions* was of the nature of a *canon*, as indirectly making doctrinal statements, and that thus the Articles of the Church would be liable to continual alteration and variation by successive decisions or precedents ; that, though Coke had decided that the Convocation is a court, nevertheless to judge matters without the King's leave was interfering with his *prerogative*, which the Act of Henry VIII. especially guarded ; and that, in the great Council of Clarendon, 1164, it was resolved, among other things, that no servant or dependent of the King could be excommunicated without his leave ; and that, in case of appeals, the King had the right of final decision. At the same time, it was admitted that each Bishop, in his own court, might proceed against exceptionable publications.

The Lower House was obliged to acquiesce in this determination; but before long they appeared before the Bishops with an attack upon Burnet's Exposition of the Thirty-nine Articles, which, as divers members of the episcopal bench had sanctioned the publication, was, in fact, an attack upon those to whom they were appealing. The Bishops referred their complaint to a committee of themselves, who reported that the Lower House had no power judicially to censure any book ; that they ought not to have entered upon the examination of the work of one of the Bishops without acquainting the Upper House ; that they ought to have been specific in their accusations, which, in the form in which they were presented, were a mere vague defamation ; that the Bishop of Sarum's "*History of the Reformation*" had been approved by Parliament, and, with his other works, had done great service to the English Church, and deserved the thanks of their lordships' House ; and that it did not rest with the Convocation to pass an opinion upon private expositions of the Thirty-nine Articles. Thus matters rested for nine years.

In the summer of 1710 a change of ministry took place, and Parliament was dissolved soon after. This was the consequence of Sacheverell's affair ; and, of course, the accession of the Tories to power was favourable to the wishes of the Lower House of Convocation. The description given, in an address of the new Commons to her Majesty, of the retiring ministry, is curious ; and, though beside my present purpose, I cannot help quoting it. "These ministers framed to themselves wild and unwarrantable schemes of balancing parties, and, under false pretence of temper and moderation, did really encourage faction, by discountenancing and depressing persons zealously affected to your Majesty and to the Church, and by extending their favour and patronage to men of licentious and impious principles, such as shake the very foundation of all government and religion." However, they had now been dismissed from the Queen's councils, and one of the first effects of it was the grant of a license to Convocation to frame canons for the exigencies of the Church. Two bishops, Compton and Hooper, both defenders of the privileges of the Lower House, were delegated, in succession, to supply the place of the Archbishop in his absence, and Atterbury was chosen Prolocutor. The subjects assigned by the Queen for discussion were, the state of religion, with reference to infidelity, heresy, and profaneness; the reform of the proceedings of the courts in the matter of excommunication; the preparing forms for the visitation of prisoners and convicts, and for admitting converts from popery and dissent, and restoring the lapsed; the establishment of rural deans; the providing terriers of glebes, tithes, etc.; and the prevention of clandestine marriages; on all which subjects committees were appointed in this and subsequent years, and delivered in reports. One important measure was actually passed in this Convocation. A correspondence commenced between the Commons and Lower House on the subject of the want of churches in the metropolis, which ended in a vote of the Commons of £350,000 for the erection of fifty additional ones, according to a scheme drawn out by Atterbury and the Lower House. If that House had done no other service to the cause of religion than this, it would deserve to be kindly remembered by posterity, in spite of the temper which it displayed towards the Bishops. On the other hand, it would not be fair to

impute it to the latter that no great measure had hitherto been carried in behalf of the Church.   In their reply
to the Lower House, in 1701, on the subject of censuring
Toland's book, they observe, "that there had been *several
obstructions and stumblingblocks* laid in the way" of their
showing their zeal ; and we can readily understand how
Queen Anne's Tory ministry might be more ready to
co-operate with the heads of the Church than a monarch
of foreign birth and prepossessions.

Passing over these subjects, we are here more especially concerned with the conduct of the Lower House, in
consequence of the first of the recommendations made
by the Queen, viz., to examine into the state of religion.
They first drew up a report, in which they attributed the
growth of irreligion chiefly to the encouragement given
in the former reign to men of latitudinarian principles ;
but, the Upper House objecting to what seemed like
personalities, especially in what had gone by, the matter
dropped.   Next, the Lower House proceeded to censure
Whiston, whose heretical opinions had made great talk
at the time ; and, upon this, the question of the judiciary
power of Convocation revived, which had been stirred
in the case of Toland's publication.

Whiston had been expelled the University of Cambridge for Arianism, in October, 1710 ; and the Lower
House of Convocation addressed the Bishops, praying
for their lordships' opinion how they might best proceed
in relation to him.   They received the request graciously,
and referred it to the Archbishop.   Tenison, in consequence, addressed to them a circular, explanatory of the
state of the case.   He observed that there were three
ways in which a person could be proceeded against
whose writings called for censure :—by means of Convocation ; by Archbishop's court of audience, in which

his suffragans were assessors with him ; or, thirdly, by means of the Bishop's court to whose diocese the accused party belonged, on report of Convocation. He considered the first method to be attended by serious difficulties : first, because the Convocation was a court of final resort, which would interfere with an act of Elizabeth, vesting all ecclesiastical jurisdiction in the Crown ; next, because there had been no such proceeding for the last one hundred years, during which time an Act had passed abolishing the High Commission and *all like* courts hereafter ; thirdly, because, in the statute annulling the writ "de hæretico comburendo," in Charles the Second's time, all established courts, and therefore that of Convocation, were made to give way to episcopal jurisdiction ; lastly, because the Upper House, in 1689, had been advised by counsel to leave such matters to other courts. He ended by recommending an address to her Majesty, praying her to refer the matter to the judges. This was done, and the judges were divided in opinion. Eight were in favour of the jurisdiction of the Convocation in such matters as by the laws of the realm were declared to be heresy, on the ground that an appeal to the Crown from all ecclesiastical courts was implied in the royal supremacy, whether expressly provided for in particular statute or not ; so that the Convocation might exercise its ancient and constitutional powers without incurring a breach of the act of Elizabeth. The other four judges considered that such judgments lay within the ordinary episcopal jurisdiction, and concurred in the apprehensions Tenison had expressed in his letter; however, they allowed that heretical tenets and opinions might be examined and condemned in Convocation, without convening the authors or maintainers of them. Such a public judgment was accordingly passed in Convocation

25

upon Whiston's work, and all Christian people were warned against it; it being thought prudent, in spite of the Queen's encouragement to them to proceed judicially, to abstain from further measures.

In 1714, another lamentable occasion occurred for the Lower House to exert itself in maintenance of the orthodox faith. Dr. Samuel Clarke having published his "Scripture Doctrine of the Trinity," a work especially adapted to harass and confuse sensitive minds, they presented an address to the Bishops, praying them to take the matter into consideration; to which they added, at the Bishops' request, a list of objectionable passages in the work, arranged under distinct heads. The Upper House were unwilling to move in the matter, and professed themselves satisfied with a so-called submission, which Dr. Clarke was prevailed on (chiefly, it is said, by Smalridge,) to offer; in which, without retracting any position he had published, he shut up his sentiments in an ambiguous form of words, and proposed to keep silence for the future. The most natural submission would have been for them to subscribe the Articles before the Convocation; but Bishop Burnet had at that time great influence in the Upper House, and I have been told by a very learned person * (though he did not refer to his authority), that such was Burnet's relative regard for the Church and his Whig friends, that he wrote to dissuade Archdeacon Welchman from answering Clarke, on the ground of the embarrassment which such a procedure would occasion to Protestant politics. This agrees with what we know of the conduct of the Government in the matter, before the publication of the offensive work; when Godolphin and others of the Queen's ministers sent Clarke a message, to the import "that the

* [I think it must have been Dr. Routh.]

affairs of the public were with difficulty then kept in the hands of those who were at all for liberty ; that it was therefore, an unseasonable time for the publication of a book which would make a great noise and disturbance ; and that, therefore, they desire him to forbear till a fitter opportunity should offer itself." Four years after the introduction of his name into the Convocation, he ventured on altering the Doxologies in the Psalm Books used for singing in St. James's parish, which brought upon him the animadversion of the Bishop of London.

In 1714, George the First succeeded to the throne, and the final suspension of the Convocation soon followed. George began his reign with an address to the Archbishops and Bishops on the subject of the "great differences" which had arisen "among some of the clergy of the realm, about their ways of expressing themselves in their sermons and writings concerning the doctrine of the Blessed Trinity," and of the "unusual liberties which had been taken by several of the said clergy in inter-meddling with the affairs of State and government, and the constitution of the realm ; " and, accordingly forbad them preaching either heterodoxy, or politics, except "in defence of the regal supremacy." The next year the Convocation was opened with a license to debate, being the third assembly which had been so favoured. This license was, so far, the result of a more liberal and enlarged policy towards the Church, than Burnet and his friends had advised previous to 1710. The subjects for consideration were (in addition to some of those already specified in former licenses) the preparing a form for consecrating churches and chapels, the better settling the qualifications of candidates for orders, the enforcing discipline on the clergy, the providing more effectually for curates whose incumbents were non-residents, and the improving the catechetical instruction given prior to confirmation. But the career of the Convocation was close on its termination. It soon came into collision with the ruling powers, on the subject of Hoadley's doctrines, and though truth was on the side of the clergy, the interest of the government was against them, and it was easy to see which way the contest would terminate. As early as 1705, the Lower House had ventured to attack a sermon of Hoadley's, as "containing positions contrary to the doctrine of the Church, expressed in the first and second parts of the Homily against disobedience or wilful rebellion;" but the Upper House suffered the matter to drop. In 1715-16, Hoadley was made Bishop of Bangor; and, in the course of the following year, published his "Preservative" and Sermon, which gave rise to the famous Bangorian controversy. These writings were at once brought before the Lower House of Convocation who made a representation of them to the Bishops, on the grounds of their "tendency, first, to subvert all government and discipline in the Church of Christ;" next, "to impugn and impeach the authority of the legislature to enforce obedience in matters of religion by civil sanctions." Before this representation could be taken into consideration by the Upper House, a special order come from the King for the prorogation of the Convocation; and from that time to this, it has only existed as a formal appendage to the first meetings of Parliament.

4.

Its relation to the Ecclesiastical Establishment.

IT may be recollected that I proposed three questions
for consideration on the subject of Convocation :—
what was its real nature and history relatively to the
Church ? what was the principle, and what the actual
extent of the civil governor's jurisdiction over it and
assumption of its powers ? and, thirdly, what was the
place which the Lower House held in its constitution ?
The last of these three has now been discussed, as far as is
necessary to illustrate the history of its suspension in the
beginning of the eighteenth century. And for any other
purpose, one may hope it ever will be unnecessary ; for
it was (to say the least) a heavy calamity that members
of the Lower House should have felt it their duty, from
the circumstances of the times, to stand upon their rights
against the authority of their Bishops. Not to dwell on
the unbecoming appearance of such an opposition, it
must be borne in mind that the privilege actually conceded on all hands to the Lower House, the Veto on the
proceedings of the Upper, is in itself almost too liberal
a grant of power for the episcopal principle ; and is only
defensible (I suppose) on the ground of the size of the
dioceses, and the Crown's prerogative in the choice of
Bishops. "Maximo enim," says Wilkins, "præ aliis
nationibus presbyteri synodi Anglicanæ fruuntur privi-
legio in concilio provinciali, ut dissensus eorum universa
domûs superioris decreta irrita reddere valeat." Having
this Veto upon all proceedings of their superiors, surely

VOL.

the clergy should have been satisfied.   But perhaps those of them who had released themselves from their pledge of canonical obedience to their deprived Bishops, might consider lightly of the obligation which subjected them to those who had come into their place ; perhaps, also, there was reasonable ground of jealousy as regards such as William's government had promoted.   But, though much might have been said in their defence had they refused altogether to recognize the new prelates, one does not see the consistency of taking them for their rulers and then not submitting to them.   But enough on this unpleasant subject.   Now let us pass to the consideration of a second of the questions originally proposed—viz., the nature and history of Convocation relatively to the Church.   And first a few words in statement of the controversy respecting it.

I.

Atterbury, Binckes, and their party, maintained, in the pamphlets mentioned in my first paper, that the Convocation was an essential part of the constitution, established by law, " by the same law as the gentleman receives his rent, or the member enjoys his privilege."   When required to produce the particular law which makes its assembling imperative on the sovereign, instead of its being (as the court party maintained) at his option, they allowed as much as this—viz., that his writ was absolutely necessary for its assembling, but they maintained, at the same time, that it was absolutely necessary that he should grant that writ, and that for two reasons : first, if the meeting of Convocation were a privilege or liberty of the English Church (which no one could deny), the King was by his coronation oath bound in two ways to issue his writ according to custom.   For Magna Charta (they argued), to which the King had sworn, pronounced "quod Ecclesia Anglicana *libera* sit, et *habeat omnia jura et libertates illæsas;*" and again one especial part of the oath administered to him by the Archbishop, contained a promise on his part to "preserve to the Bishops and clergy of this realm, and to the churches committed to their charge, all *such rights and privileges* as by law do or shall appertain to them or any of them;" so that, since the assembly of the clergy in Convocation was, beyond dispute, a privilege recognized by the law, no particular law was necessary to bind the sovereign, who was bound in a more solemn manner by his express oath, which the law imposed.

Secondly, they maintained that their assembling was matter of constitutional right; for the Convocation, they said, was a member or a necessary adjunct of Parliament; so that, independently of law or promise, it could not constitutionally be abolished or suspended. They showed from history that from the earliest Saxon times the clergy had been summoned with the laity to the King's great Council; that, as time went on, the mode of their assembling, from being indeterminate, became definite and regular; then again, from circumstances, was varied; and lastly became fixed in the particular form which had then for centuries been matter of usage; that, on the other hand, during this process and ultimate settlement, the ordinary annual Church Synods gradually came into disuse, so that the Convocation, as then constituted, was the representative both of an important political privilege, and a standing ecclesiastical ordinance of the Church; that at first they met in one body with the Laity, or Parliament (as it is now called), afterwards separated from it, and then again themselves divided into two provincial Synods; that this arrangement was for awhile interrupted by a new writ from the King (the *præmunientes* clause inserted into the Bishops' writ), summoning them to Parliament, which was a fresh evidence of their constitutional right, but that the former custom was again restored and had so continued to that day, the above-mentioned clause being still retained in the Bishops' writ, though not acted on, in token that their right remained where it was ; that under all these changes, under whatever irregularities of time, place, and form of meeting, the great rule obtained that they met in connexion with Parliament, as belonging to it, (closer or more detached, as the case might be,) but still as constitutionally annexed to it ; lastly, that since the Reformation the Convocation had invariably met with the Parliament and been dissolved with it, except in the solitary and extraordinary instance of 1640, when it sat after the Parliament was dissolved, and which no one would urge as a precedent, though after all, even as such, it only affected the question of the termination of Convocation, not of its assembling. They added, that anciently the same general appellation was given to both meetings, the Parliament being called a Wittena Gemote, the Convocation a Church Gemote, and that in various modern documents (besides the *præmunientes* clause above noticed) the Parliament was said to include the clergy, as in a mandate of Bonner's, 1543, which has the words " prelati et clerus Prov. Cant. in parl.," in a petition to the Pope in Henry the Eighth's time, speaking of the " milites et doctores in parl.," and in the phrase in the 5th of November Service, "the nobility, clergy, and commons of this land, then assembled in Parliament ; " this being the reason why a clergyman could not be a member of the House of Commons. They proceeded to argue, that, if the Convocation was thus an adjunct to the Parliament, the King's writ was but the formal instrument, necessary indeed (as a license of marriage may be), but not to be refused without leading to grave political consequences.

The court party, on the other hand, granted that the clergy had this right to be summoned in Convocation, but they drew a distinction between *assembling* and *conferring*. They said that the clergy had nothing beyond a right to be summoned; that a further license was necessary in order to their debating, and that they had no right to demand this; that the utmost extent of their right did not go beyond that of framing petitions to King or Bishops when assembled under the primary writ. This ground of argument, which at first sight looks like an evasion, was maintained, first by the fact that the Convocation had often in matter of fact met without debating; next, by the received opinion of the Church in the century last past; and further by the reason of the thing, the stated meetings of Convocation having been held for the purpose of granting subsidies to the Crown, and the custom naturally coming to an end with its object. Accordingly it was professed that the Convocation had now become only an occasional assembly to provide for especial business, and that old precedents were sufficiently consulted by the King's formally convening them, though without suffering them to debate.

To this it was replied, that the same reasons which made the granting the writ for assembling a right of the clergy, made the license for debate a right also; but if not, then the Convocation did not, in matter of fact, supply the place of ecclesiastical Synod, and thus it became necessary to fall back upon the elementary and essential rights and duties of the Church, and to resume those canonical meetings which had only been suspended from a wish to adjust the principles of the Church to the particular civil polity in which it had been incorporated.

This is an outline of the controversy, which turned upon this :—not whether the meetings of Convocation might be lawfully suspended, this no party maintained, but whether it had a right to debate as well as to assemble, a right to demand a license, as well as the writ. Atterbury, indeed, goes further than this in his view of its rights, denying *in toto* its need of any license for any act short of the positive enactment of a canon ; as if it might frame and pass any measure in the form of a canon, and present it for the royal assent, as a bill in Parliament. On a question of this nature materials of argument lie so widely and plentifully for either side, that it requires a mind practised in weighing evidence, and much careful attention, in order to form an opinion worth putting upon paper. So far I suppose is clear, that at the present day a valid precedent against its right "to be put into a condition to do business," (to use the phrase of Atterbury's party,) exists in the actual suspension of its debates during the last 120 years ; though, to be sure, certain recent changes in the constitution of Parliament, seem to create an opposite precedent of a novel kind, in favour of insisting on inherent rights instead of custom and usage. Now for the history of Convocation.

2.

The Diocesan Council is the simplest form of ecclesiastical assembly, and that which, under the circumstances of the primitive Church, would first come into use. "That the Bishop of each diocese," says Wake, "has, by divine commission, a power of governing the Church of

Christ over which he is placed, and, in order thereunto, to call together the presbyters which minister under him, was the constant sense of all the ancient Councils and fathers of the Church."

In our own Church these diocesan synods were held at first twice a year, but in process of time the direction of the Canon Law was followed, which made them only annual. At this stated assembly all beneficed clergy in the diocese were bound to appear, and the regulars also, except when any were exempted, as time went on, from episcopal jurisdiction. If the diocese were small, and had but one archdeaconry, all the clergy met in one place; otherwise they met by parties, the Bishop moving on from one archdeaconry to another. At these meetings the synodical *inquiries* were one part of the business, of which the ancient form still remains; then the *causes*,— not only clergy, but laity, being at liberty to present complaints before the assembly; then the *Bishop's charge*, in which he communicated to the clergy the decisions, if any, of the Provincial Council, and exhorted them to fulfil the ministry with which they were entrusted; lastly, the *Bishop's diocesan constitutions*, if such there were, were read and agreed to by the Synod, and thenceforth became the law of the diocese, provided they were not contrary to any provincial canons. The mode of celebrating these synods was as follows :—the clergy in solemn procession came to the church where they were to meet, at the day and hour appointed by the Bishop, and took their seats according to the date of their ordination. Then the deacons and laity (even women not excepted) were admitted. The Bishop having entered, prayers were read; and then the Bishop made an address introductory of the Synod. A sermon followed; then the complaints were heard; the diocesan constitutions were promulgated and passed, and the charge, with prayers, ended the meeting, which commonly lasted three or four days. It is easy to see that these Councils are continued to this day in the Bishop's periodical Visitation, which at any moment (were it expedient) might resume the form of a synodal meeting. They were held, as above described, down to the time of Henry the Eighth.

The English Provincial Councils were as carefully conducted, after the pattern of the primitive Church. The Metropolitan summoned them, the business transacted related to the faith and discipline of the Church, and the members were the suffragan Bishops, to whom were sometimes added the heads of the regulars, abbots and the like; parochial presbyters having no place in them, by way of right, but, if summoned, summoned at the Archbishop's pleasure, and for some particular purpose. Here again we have the rudiments, perhaps the substance, of a Provincial Council left to us, (at least as far as political matters of debate are concerned,) in the private meetings of the Bishops in London during the Session of Parliament. So much for ecclesiastical meetings of the clergy; now for civil.

From early Saxon times the prelates of the Church, that is, bishops, abbots, deans, etc., were called to the great Council of the nation to assist in its deliberations, and especially to grant subsidies from the Church property for the use of the State; it being then, as now, the standing principle of the law of England, that no persons could be taxed without their own consent or that of their representatives. In Saxon times the Church lands were taxed for the three objects of castles, bridges, and expeditions. William the Conqueror changed their tenure, and laid the burden of a further service on them. The princes following increased these taxes. However, since they still reached only to a portion of the clergy, and a part only of the revenues of this portion, various methods were adopted to comprehend the general body. First, the Pope laid a tax upon the Church for the use of the King; next, the Bishops, on extraordinary occasions, obliged the clergy to grant a subsidy to the King by way of a benevolence, which was done by means of diocesan Councils, the clergy empowering therein, first their respective Bishops, then their archdeacons, then proctors of their own, to act for them.

Thus matters stood till about the reign of Edward the First, who determined to put them on a securer basis for the interests of the Crown. Accordingly, in 1281, he, of his own authority, bade the two Archbishops call a Council for raising subsidies "coram rege in parliamento." The superior clergy, alarmed at the consequences of a first step in an infringement upon their rights, refused to obey the summons; and the Archbishop of Canterbury, to meet the wishes of both parties, changed the place of meeting so as to disconnect it with the Parliament, while he obtained the grant of the subsidy previously by means of diocesan Councils. This was the first instance of the inferior clergy being summoned to Parliament. Twelve years afterwards, Edward made a new and more systematic attempt. On summoning his Parliament, he inserted a new clause in the writs issued to the Bishops and prelates, which has since been called, from its first word, the *præmunientes* clause, by which he required them to cite such of their inferior clergy to his Parliament as he therein specified, who were to act for the whole body. Here then a general representation of the clergy was introduced into the National Council, and may be called, after Wake in his learned work, (from which, with the assistance of

Wilkins's Concilia, this account is compiled,) the Parliamentary Convention of the Clergy. From that time down to the present day (unless any change has been made since the date of Wake's book [1703]) the clergy have always been summoned to the Parliament, and accounted one of the three estates of the realm. This writ of *præmunientes* has been acted upon, since the Reformation, in the church of York, at the end of Henry the Eighth's reign; in the church of Norwich, in Elizabeth's; in Lichfield, at the end of James the First's; in Lincoln, by the authority of Laud, 1640; and, according to Burnet, by several bishops in 1701.*

Nothing more was done in the reign of our first Edward; but in that of his grandson the clergy resisted. They resolved they would not grant subsidies to the King except in provincial Councils, both as disliking the attendance in Parliament, and as hoping in this way to have more liberty in refusing or lessening the burdens which the King's necessities put upon them. Edward was obliged to give way, and allow these provincial meetings instead of parliamentary; securing, however, their stated meeting, first, by continuing *in terrorem* the *præmunientes* clause in his parliamentary writ to the Bishops; and next, by the periodical issue of a second writ to the Archbishop, formally bidding him to summon them for the purpose of voting subsidies. This is what is now called the Convocation of the Province, the nature of which will easily be gathered from what has been said. It is a kind of provincial Council, assembled (1) on the King's writ, (2) simultaneously in both provinces, (3) for civil, not spiritual purposes, (4) composed, not merely of

---

* Wilkins (p. 11, vol. i.) seems to say that the form of the *præmunientes* was disused after the Restoration. On the other hand vide Wake, passim, e.g. Author. p. 253, and Burnet's History, vol. iii. pp. 389—395.

Bishops and prelates, but of representatives of the body of the clergy ; (5) commonly held with a reference to the time of the meeting of Parliament :—But we must go somewhat more into particulars here, both as to the persons of whom the Convocation consists, and the matters which have come under its cognizance.

As to its *members*, since a money-vote was the object of the meeting, it necessarily consisted of representatives of the whole clergy. This system of representation had been begun in the Legantine Councils, first held, by the Pope's authority, in 1070, with the object of taxing the clergy, in which the regulars were represented by their abbots, etc., and the chapters by their deans, and afterwards by representatives chosen by themselves. The same system obtained in the Convocation. Before the date of its institution, the archdeacon is supposed to have been the original representative of the parochial clergy, in the occasional tax-meetings; but he was present in it in his own right, two proctors being added by election of the clergy of each diocese to support their interests. The members of the Convocation remain the same to this day, (subtracting the abbots and other prelates of the regulars who are extinct,) viz., the bishops, deans, archdeacons, proctors for the chapters, and proctors for the clergy, the Archbishop of the province being president. It should be added, that they gradually formed themselves into several more or less standing committees,—of, for instance, regulars, and of seculars, and of deans and archdeacons, under the Bishops, and then at last into two permanent Houses, which has been the constitutional form of the Convocation from a period earlier than the Reformation ; but on this subject I have already spoken at length.

As to the *subjects* debated in the Convocation, though the King's demand of a subsidy was the direct object of their meeting, yet it was natural that other matters of debate should be brought before it. Money-votes have commonly been used as a fit introduction of grievances ; a statement of these and petitions for redress were accordingly added to the addresses, in which they conveyed to their sovereign intelligence of the grants which they had made him ; and here it was impossible to draw the line between temporal and spiritual matters. Further, a meeting of the clergy was evidently a fit opportunity for discussing and deciding among themselves pure ecclesiastical questions; so that a meeting which had been called as a mere Convocation, was continued in the shape of a provincial Synod, the inferior clergy, of course, falling back into that subordinate rank which would be fitted to the change in the matter of their deliberations, and, by so doing, preparing the way for the formation of a Lower House. Thus, by degrees, ecclesiastical matters were altogether drawn into the Convocation, and the provincial Synod fell into disuse.

This was the condition of the Church, as regards her greater Councils, in which the Reformation found her. At the commencement of it was passed, in Convocation, the famous Act of Submission, to which allusion has been made above, and of which I shall now give the history.

3.

Henry VIII., of unblessed memory, was determined, as Wake says, to "tie up the hands of the clergy, that they might be unable to oppose his designs." With this end he contrived to involve them all in a *præmunire*, which lay against them for appearing in Wolsey's Synods *legantine* unauthorized by the Crown, or for appearing and making suit in Wolsey's courts, as it is variously represented. Wolsey had been in such full possession of Henry's favour, that to have resisted him would have been to provoke the King's anger. He had been made legate with the King's knowledge, and held, besides, the great seal; and, when he put his commands on the clergy to appear before him, it was not for them to ask, or at least they neglected to ask, whether he, the keeper of the great seal, had an express license under that seal for what he commanded. However, by this mistake in a matter of form, they incurred the loss of liberty and estate; and Henry made use of this their difficulty to effect his purposes against the Church. He refused to pardon them unless they paid him £100,000, and recognized him as her supreme Head. After some negotiation they submitted, and passed an Act in Convocation, which was afterwards carried through Parliament, by which the liberties of the Church (as far as they can be lost) were lost for ever. They bound themselves by it, first, not to meet in Convocation, without his authority; and next, lest, when he had called them together (as he was obliged to do, from time to time, in order to obtain their vote of subsidies) they should proceed to act synodically in ecclesiastical matters, they promised henceforth only to act according to his directions,—in other words, not to attempt or make any canons or constitutions provincial without the royal license to make and promulge the same. This latter provision of the Act is the point of debate between Wake and Atterbury; in what follows I have sided with Wake, as having the general judgment of the seventeenth century in his favour.

The negotiations were of the following kind:—First of all, the Commons complained to the King "that they (the clergy) made sanctions and laws of temporal things, not having nor requiring the King's royal assent to the same laws so by them made." The clergy answered, that " they had this power of God, and could not submit it to his authority ; that their authority of making laws was grounded upon the scripture of God, and determination of the Holy Church ; and, as concerning the requiring of the King's assent to the authorizing of such laws as had been made by their predecessors, or should be made by themselves, they doubted not but that the King knew that to depend not upon their will and liberty, who might not submit the execution of their charges and duty, certainly prescribed by God, to his assent." They added, however, some vague promise of being guided by the King's wish in their decisions. This answer (as may be supposed) not satisfying King and Commons, new forms were drawn up, and fresh debates held, how they were to compound the matter with the King, yet give up as little as might be.

First, they gave up the power of *publishing* canons without the King's license, reserving to themselves the power of *making* them. But here they made several important limitations ; first, the canons spoken of must relate to the *laity ;* next, they must not concern *faith* or *good manners*, and the *reformation and correction of sin ;* next, though they went so far as to offer, that they would not enact, promulge, or execute any constitutions in future, unless with his license, still this promise was limited, in the Lower House, to the King's lifetime.

These admissions did not satisfy Henry, and he drew up a form himself for them, in which the clergy were to bind themselves, first, never hereafter to meet in synod without the King's writ ; and next, being assembled by it, never to proceed by virtue of authority of their own, or to make, promulge, and execute canons, without the royal license previously obtained. This promise, after some discussion and alteration, was passed, by Convocation, in the following form :—" We, your most humble subjects, daily orators and beadsmen of your clergy of England, having our special trust and confidence in your most excellent wisdom, your princely goodness, and fervent zeal to the promotion of God's honour and Christian religion, and also in your learning, far exceeding, in our judgment, the learning of all other kings and princes that we have read of, and doubting nothing but that the same shall still continue and daily increase in your majesty, first, do offer and promise, in *verbo sacerdotii*, here unto your highness, submitting ourselves most humbly to the same, that we will never from henceforth enact, put in use, promulge, or execute any new canons, or constitution provincial, or any new ordinance provincial or synodal in our Convocation or synod in time coming, (which Convocation is always, hath been, and must be assembled only by your high commandment or writ,) unless your Highness, by your royal assent, shall license us to assemble our Convocation, and to make, promulge, and execute such constitutions and ordinances as shall be made in the same, and thereto give your royal assent and authority," etc.

It will be observed, that this submission of the clergy, ample as it is, does not go the length of binding the successors of the clergy making it, and it seems to limit itself to the very monarch to whom it was made, by speaking of his personal qualities and endowments ; moreover, it was recalled in Convocation, in Mary's time, and never renewed. However, it became the subject of an Act of Parliament in Henry's, and afterwards in Elizabeth's reign, and with a stronger wording, *by that*

Act (with the penalty of *præmunire* to enforce it) are the clergy at present bound.

Thus stood the relations between Church and State till 1664, the Church being willing to remain in a subjection which the King never abused to her spiritual detriment. On the Restoration, a change was silently made by Sheldon and Clarendon, which was scarcely favourable to her interests. It will be observed, that the sole remaining safeguard which she possessed against the tyranny of the State, was the power of granting subsidies, which gave her a hold of some sort over the earthly masters she had taken to her, "when the Lord was her king." This power gave to Convocation importance, and eventually prevented any attempt at suppressing it. At the era in question, the clergy, impoverished by the recent troubles, felt severely the weight of the subsidies required of them, and perceived (as was really the case) that they paid for their privilege by contributing to the State in a larger proportion than other subjects. An arrangement was agreed upon, in spite of a protest from Heylin against it, between the Bishops and the Commons, by which two subsidies, which the clergy had just voted, were remitted to them, while, on the other hand, they were *sub silentio*, and without formal statute, comprehended in the wording of the money-bills passed in Parliament. The first public Act on this subject was a Tax Act of 1665 (16-17 Car. II. cap. 1), which includes the clergy, discharging them from subsidies, with a saving clause as to their right of taxing themselves, which has never since been exercised. The clergy, on the other hand, soon acknowledged the arrangement by exercising the right of voting in the elections of the Commons, which before was forbidden them, as now it is forbidden peers of Parliament. Burnet speaks of this right, as generally admitted, in a pamphlet, published as early as 1700, and it is assumed in two subsequent Acts of Parliament, 10 Anne, cap. 23, and 18 George II., cap. 18. "Gibson, Bishop of London," observes Speaker Onslow (in a note contained in the last Oxford edition of Burnet's History), "told me that this (the taxing out of Convocation) was the greatest alteration in the constitution ever made without an express law." It is remarkable that (according to Warburton) the clergy had as silently both become and ceased to be an estate in Parliament 300 or 400 years before.

The Church soon began to feel the alarming position in which she had allowed herself to be placed. In 1675, and then in 1677, addresses from the Lords were presented to the throne, praying for the frequent meetings of the Convocation, which (as Mr. Hallam justly observes) probably proceeded from the Bishops, and shows their dissatisfaction with the existing state of things. They were not allowed, however, to feel or express their regrets for any long time. The Revolution which soon followed, "glorious" as it has ever been considered in its political effects, was fatal to the remaining liberties of the Church. William completed what Henry had begun. Nine of her Bishops were sentenced to deposition by a prince who had just ceased to be a Presbyterian, and its Convocation shortly after expired, except as a matter of form, while endeavouring to raise its voice against the doctrines of Hoadley.

5.

Relation of Convocation to the Crown.

THE third and last question I proposed to consider relative to the Convocation was as to the civil governor's *de facto* and *de jure* power over it; a large subject indeed, requiring a depth of thought and an accuracy of historical knowledge which cannot be expected in such papers as I am presenting to the reader. Asking then his indulgence for all defects in my mode of handling it, I will, in return, give him more in one respect than I engaged to do—viz., some account of the State's power over the English Church generally, not merely over the Convocation. To this undertaking I now address myself, and shall so bring my papers to an end.

I.

The King's power over the Church is popularly conveyed in the title "Head of the Church," which has become a familiar phrase. It is a title, however, unknown (as I believe) to the Law at present, having been assumed by Henry, but abandoned by Elizabeth. This would not be worth noticing, except that it is usual, with many persons, to assume it is of authority, and to proceed to deduce conclusions from it; for instance, "the King is head of the Church, and *therefore* he may alter the liturgy;" whereas it is but a generalized term, the sign and symbol of certain defined and specific prerogatives which belong to him, such as the power of appointing bishops. It is not correct to say, "The King appoints the bishops *because* he is head of the Church;" rather, he is head of the Church *because* he appoints the bishops, etc. The simplest answer to such confused statements is to draw attention to the parallel supremacy of the King in civil matters. He is head of the State; yet no one dreams that he may therefore interfere with the constitutional rights of its separate members and functionaries.

With this caution, however, the title of Head will express the relation of the King to the Church, better, perhaps, than any other. The recognized constitutional title, and that which comes nearest to it, is "Supreme Governor;" but this, as we shall directly see, neither includes of necessity his appointment of the bishops, in which he commonly is said to act as the representative of the laity, nor his extensive church patronage, which is held on the same tenure with other patrons, though it is so great as to be virtually a constituent portion of his power. The very vagueness of the term Head is its recommendation.

I confine myself here, however, to the consideration of the *supremacy*, which is a supremacy of *jurisdiction*. The King is supposed to call the Church into being, that is, to develop that member of it existing in his own dominions, which is only *in posse* till he makes it actual ; and, therefore, he claims to have authority over all its movements. In the 26 Henry VIII., the King is said to have "power to visit, repress, reform, order, etc., all such errors, heresies, abuses, etc., which by any manner of spiritual authority or jurisdiction ought to be visited ;" and, in 37 Henry VIII., that ecclesiastical persons, such as archbishops, have "no manner of jurisdiction ecclesi- astical, but by, under, and from him, to whom, by Holy Scripture, all authority and power is wholly given to hear and determine all manner of causes ecclesiastical, and to correct vice and sin whatsoever."

This power is claimed in more accurate language in the instrument under which Cranmer exercised his episcopate in Edward's time, as given in Burnet's History. (Part ii., book 1, Records.) In this document, the King declares that " omnis juris dicendi auctoritas atque etiam jurisdictio omnimodo, tum illa quæ ecclesiastica dicitur, quam sæcularis, â regiâ potestate, velut a supremo capite ac omnium magistratuum infra regnum nostrum fonte et scaturigine, primitus emanaverit."

2.

This being a general account of the Supremacy, let us consider it under the two heads of *executive* and *juridical*.

1. *Executive ;* and here I shall confine myself to the King's *acts* from Henry's time to the accession of the Hanoverians, not, however, professing to do more than approximate to a complete list of them.

(1) Henry's first act of pure Supremacy was in 1536. In all that went before he had had the concurrence of the Convocations ; but, at this time, Cromwell published injunctions about Religion in his name, Cranmer (as it is believed) being the writer of them. These enforced upon all incumbents the reading in church of a declaration against the Pope, and in behalf of the King's Supremacy, confirmed the Articles lately set forth by the Convocation, forbade the superstitious use of relics, etc., and gave sundry directions relative to education, charities, temporalities, etc. Shortly before this, Henry had given orders for the translation of the Bible, but this was at the petition of the Convocation. A more remarkable proceeding of the same year, though still with the sanction of the Con-

vocation, was his interfering in the drawing up and correction of the Articles of Religion, published at that time.

(2) Fresh injunctions were issued out in the King's name in 1538, calling upon the parochial clergy to provide their churches with the English Bible, to instruct their people in the true Gospel, to remove images which had been abused by superstition, to observe holydays and their eves according to the directions set forth, to omit the commemoration of St. Thomas of Canterbury, etc.

(3) In 1539, the King bade the House of Lords appoint a committee of Bishops for framing Articles of Religion. Eight were nominated in consequence, but could not agree. Upon this, six articles were proposed and carried in the House by the Duke of Norfolk, thence passed through the Commons, and lastly received the royal assent, without the Convocation being consulted in the matter, and the Archbishop voting in opposition.

(4) In 1540, a committee of divines was appointed by the King, and confirmed in Parliament, to draw up a declaration of the Christian faith, for the necessary erudition of a Christian man. Some time afterwards, the King prefixed to their Report, which took the shape of a book, a Declaration requiring all his people to read and impress upon their minds the doctrine contained in it. In the same year, another commission of Bishops was appointed to examine the rites and ceremonies of the Church, and to draw up a ritual of worship.

(5) In 1542, the examination of the English version of the Bible, which had begun in Convocation, was taken out of its hands by the King, and committed to the two Universities. And, in 1544, he gave orders for the translation of the prayers for processions and litanies into

English, and sent directions to Cranmer to see to its use all over his province.

(6) Edward the Sixth's reign commenced with a general ecclesiastical visitation, which, during its continuance, suspended all episcopal jurisdiction throughout England. The majority of the commissioners appointed were laymen. Homilies were drawn up and published for general use, and preachers attended the visitors on the same authority.

(7) In the second year of Edward, a committee of select Bishops and divines was appointed for reforming the sacred offices; and the result of their labours was passed through Parliament. And thus the Ordination Service was drawn up by a committee of Bishops and divines, named by the King, at the instance of an Act of Parliament. And several years after, a new Catechism was set forth for the use of schoolmasters by the King's letters patent.

(8) Elizabeth put forth injunctions, in 1559, on the subject of supremacy, superstition, simony, and the like. She also re-enacted the Book of Common Prayer, which, in Mary's reign, had been discarded; doing this without authority of Convocation.

(9) In the reign of James the First, the conference at Hampton Court, the order for the new translation of the Bible, and the proclamation about sports and recreations, were all acts of the King, without the formal sanction of the Church.

(10) Such, moreover, were Charles the First's directions to preachers about the Arminian points. And in the same spirit were that religious King's instructions to Archbishops Abbot and Laud, and Laud's annual report of his province, in consequence.

(11) Charles the Second, in 1661, granted a commission

to a number of Bishops and clergy to review the Book of Common Prayer, which was the occasion of the Savoy Conference. In the next year, he published his directions against seditious, predestinarian, and irregular sermons, and in behalf of the due observance of the Lord's day.

(12) William, in 1689, during Sancroft's suspension, addressed a letter to the Bishop of London, calling upon the Bishops to be careful in their examination of candidates for Orders, and exhorting the clergy to be diligent in their duties, and earnest in enforcing the social virtues. Several years after, he published injunctions concerning ordinations, residence, pluralities, public prayers, the Lord's day, etc., and, soon after, directions concerning preaching on the doctrine of the Trinity.

(13) Lastly, George the First published, like William, directions on the subject last mentioned, and in maintenance of the King's power.

(14) It should be added that the four State Services are imposed on authority of the King, not of the Church.

Now, before summing up the prerogatives contained in this list of precedents, I would observe that some of them have been actually superseded by subsequent precedents of an opposite nature ; for instance, Articles of Religion, which were first imposed by Henry's command, were, in the reign of Elizabeth, regularly passed in Convocation. This was an acknowledgment of the Church's right, and of the informality of Henry's proceedings, while it is a final precedent, and settles the point, for all future times. Again, the liturgy, which, in Elizabeth's time, was imposed by Act of Parliament, was sanctioned in Convocation at the Restoration ; which would not have been done, had not the Church's consent been necessary. In like manner, the Canons of 1603, passed in Convocation, take the place of the irregular State Injunctions of the preceding century. And the High Commission Court, which was the organ of the most exceptionable exercise of the King's power—viz., that of Visitation independent of ecclesiastical functionaries, and even in the case of heresy, etc.—was abolished in Charles the Second's reign. As to the violent act of William, by which nine bishops, including the primate, were marked for deprivation, (a sentence which was executed on all who survived to endure it,) I have not noticed it, because it is evidently a mere *part* of the Revolution itself, which has always been confessedly considered to be an extreme case, and such as ought never to be cited as a precedent for future acts of usurpation.

The prerogatives which remain (even supposing the above acts valid as precedents) are as follows:—1. That of appointing commissions of divines for diverse purposes, for instance, translating scriptures, compiling a liturgy, and framing articles of faith ; 2. Of sending directions to the clergy on the matter of their sermons, whether doctrinal or ecclesiastical ; 3. Of appointing State prayers ; 4. Of addressing the people, through the clergy, on various subjects; as, for instance, the royal Supremacy, education, charities, temporalities, ceremonies, and holydays. To these powers must be added, the most important prerogative, 5. Of appointing the Bishops ; and thus the account of the *executive* power of the King over the Church will be complete.

3.

2. Next, as to his *juridical* power. It is this which is more formally called his Supremacy, consisting chiefly in his presidency in all spiritual courts, and his jurisdiction over Convocation. And here, in order to explain the province and limits of this prerogative, it will be

necessary to give some account of the principle on which the Supremacy over the Church is granted to him.

It is plain that, though our ecclesiastical system is based upon invisible sanctions, it can scarcely be realized in any country without permission from the civil power. The Apostles, indeed, to show their immediate commission from above, asked no earthly aid; and, indeed, because there was no chance of obtaining it, for St. Paul was not backward to avail himself of his existing privilege of Roman citizenship on fit occasions. It is certain all attempts to gain the civil power would have been unavailing, at first; and Christians were obliged, by gaining influence and credit in the world, to show that they were worthy of State protection, before they obtained it. As soon as the chance of recognition on the part of the State appeared, they were not slow to apply for it; and by the middle of the third century they had, on one occasion, employed the Roman power in the defence of their temporalities. This was, in a certain way, acknowledging the State's interference in Church matters; for such a patronage necessarily implied, as its practical correlative, a certain claim of jurisdiction. This, then, is the principle which was publicly avowed and established at the era of the Reformation—the duty of the Church to ask leave of the State (where it could obtain it) to perform its functions, and its protection by the State, and its subjection to the State, thence resulting.

The essential parts of the Church system are few; its elementary functions may be discharged this way or that, according to circumstances. The exact influence of the laity in elections, synods, etc., the form, times, and circumstances of synods, the size of dioceses, the character or the adoption of monastic institutions, chapters, and the like, the celibacy or non-celibacy of the clergy—all these, being but developments of the essential Church element, may well vary according to the country in which that element is found. In other words, the State has practically the power of calling out into existence, this way or that way, the latent energies of the apostolical ministry ; and so far forth as it does so call them out, so far as it recognizes, protects, privileges them by Law, in the same degree does it claim a jurisdiction and superintendence over its own work. Such, for instance, in England are the Spiritual Courts, in which the King presides ; such, in a measure, is Convocation, over which he has kept his hand ; such the temporalities of the Sees, which, converting the episcopate into "the high state of prelacy," may be supposed to give him the right of appointing the Bishops. The essence itself of the Church, the Apostolical element, as it may be called, is not in his power; the ministry of the Word and Sacraments is given to those only whom God especially calls. The developments, again, of this are not necessarily in his power. The Church may not choose to mould itself precisely after the State's design ; while its institutions are unrecognized by Law, they remain apostolical, but as soon as it determines that they shall assume that particular mould to which the State has annexed protection and support, at once they become of a semi-civil nature, or what are commonly called (in the language of the Constitution) *spiritual*. To illustrate what I mean, the King has power over the Convocation, which is a "spiritual" court and assembly ; I conceive he has none over the provincial or diocesan Synod, as being (I suppose) an institution unknown to the Law. Were the Archbishop to hold a metropolitan Council, its decisions indeed would not possess the sanction of civil authority, but at the same time the civil power would have no jurisdiction over it. This, at least, will do to illustrate an important distinction. The King has jurisdiction over the Church only so far as he may be supposed to have called its system into existence and actually sustains it.

And if he has a recognized influence upon it, considered merely as the magistrate well disposed towards it, much more really is he its governor, considered as a Christian prince. In this light he is the father of his subjects, a natural priest ordained of God ; and, as the head of a family is bound to superintend the instruction of his children and servants, so the King has a sort of patriarchal power over the Bishops and clergy. This power is beautifully illustrated in those reports of Laud to King Charles, with the latter's notes upon them, of which I have already spoken ; and it will justify, in some sort, many of those injunctions, directions, and the like, of Henry, Elizabeth, or William,—which most nearly resemble encroachments upon proper Church authority. But, after all, the distinction above drawn between apostolical and mere "spiritual" or "ecclesiastical" functions holds throughout.

4.

Our history sanctions this view of the subject, which I have deduced from the nature of the case ; as I now proceed to show :—

In the first place, I refer to the very instrument above spoken of, in which Edward claims ecclesiastical jurisdiction ; for it explicitly professes, at the same time, to bestow on Cranmer something *additional* to his apostolical power, "per [præter] et ultra ea quæ tibi ex sacris literis divinitus commissa esse dignoscuntur." To the same purpose is the "Declaration made of the function and divine institution of Bishops and Priests" (Burnet's History., part 1, addenda v.), subscribed by Cromwell, Henry's minister in ecclesiastical matters, by Cranmer, the Archbishop of York, eleven other bishops, and others; in which the power of the keys and other Church functions are formally separated from the civil jurisdiction, that is, the apostolical from the spiritual power; and such also the judgment of eight bishops, of whom Cranmer is the first, concerning the King's Supremacy (Record x.), in which it is asserted that the Church's commission is founded, not on princes' power, but on the Word of God, while they confess that that divine commission does not impart civil power over princes, or make the Church independent of them in civil matters, but that she is in the same position towards the State as Christ was on earth, a subject yet with supernatural powers. In further explanation, it may be observed, that Bonner took out the same commission for his bishopric from Henry as Cranmer did from Edward, clearly showing (from the concession of a Romanist) that it was merely a commission for exercising jurisdiction, parallel to the license which the dissenter, at this day, purchases to exercise the privilege of preaching.

Further, the nature of the King's Supremacy is explained in our 37th Article, (which, be it observed, is part of an Act of Parliament,) in a sense quite accordant to that which I have been unfolding, viz.—"that *only* prerogative which we see to have been given *always* to all *godly* princes in holy scripture by God Himself,"— viz., to rule all estates of men, and to use the civil sword. It is plain, from this account of the Supremacy, 1, that it has no reference to the apostolical powers of the Church; for no one pretends, with the instances of Uzziah and Jeroboam before us, that the Jewish kings had right of interfering with the priesthood ; 2, it is only granted to "godly," that is, Christian princes, though Henry, indeed, seemed to make it inherent in the kingly office. There can be no doubt, then, that the oath of Supremacy, in which we swear that the King is " supreme governor, as well in all spiritual or ecclesiastical things or causes as temporal," must be interrupted by this 37th Article, that is, as having no reference to our apostolical rights and powers.

But the history of the beginning of Elizabeth's reign puts this matter in a still clearer light. The Act of Henry VIII., in which the title of "supreme head of the Church " was given to the sovereign, and which had been repealed by Mary, was not revived ; "supreme governor" being substituted for it, in the enactment of that oath which is observed to this day. "This was done," says Burnet (part 2, book iii.), "to mitigate the opposition of the popish party ; but, besides, the Queen herself had a scruple about it." Leslie, who refers to this passage, adds, (Case of the Regale, p. 9,) " the same bishop in his travels, letter 1. from Zurich, quotes a letter of Bishop Jewel's to Bullinger, dated May 22, 1559, wherein he writes 'that the Queen refused to be called Head of the Church,' and adds, 'that that title could not be justly given to any mortal.'"

Moreover, it will be observed, that the 37th Article refers to Elizabeth's Injunctions in explanation of its meaning. These clearly set before us the *drift* of the doctrine of the Supremacy, as it has been held in law ever since Elizabeth's time, whatever extravagant and impious notions Henry may at any time have entertained about it—viz., to secure the kingdom against foreign interference, not to restrain home apostolical authority. "Then followed,"—I quote from Burnet, (part 2, book iii.)— " an explanation of the oath of Supremacy, in which the

27

Queen declared that she did not pretend to any authority for the ministering divine service in the Church, and that *all* that she challenged was, that which had at all times belonged to the imperial Crown of England, that she had the *sovereignity and rule* over all manner of persons under God, *so that no foreign power had any rule over them.*" Indeed, this comment upon the sense of the words is inserted in the latter part of the oath itself.

" Primate Usher," says Leslie, " gave the same explanation of it, in a speech at the council-table at Dublin, upon occasion of some magistrates there, who refused the said oath ; and King James sent him a letter of thanks and approbation of his speech, both which are in print. And none of our succeeding kings or parliaments have given any other explanation of it, or required that it should be taken in any other sense, but all along refer to these." Gibson might be quoted to the same effect. And, lastly, this is, in the main, Burnet's view, who cannot be accused of allowing too much independence to the Church. In a controversial pamphlet on the subject of our Reformation, which he published in Holland, in 1688, he says—" It is a very unreasonable thing to urge some *general expressions,*" (alluding to the preambles introduced into some of the parliamentary Acts of Henry,) *or some stretches of the royal Supremacy,* and not to consider that more strict explanation that was made of it, both in King Henry the Eighth's time and under Queen Elizabeth. . . . In King Henry's time, the extent of the King's Supremacy was defined in the Necessary Erudition of a Christian man, that was set forth as the standard of the doctrine of the time ; and it was *upon this that all people were obliged to take their measures, not upon some expressions, either in Acts of Parliament or Acts of Convocation, nor upon some stretches of the King's juris-*

diction. In this, then, it is plainly said, that with relation to the clergy the King is 'to oversee them, and cause that they execute their pastoral office truly and faithfully, and especially in those points which by Christ and His Apostles were committed to them.'" This is that *patriarchal power* which I have spoken of. "And to this it is added, 'that Bishops and priests are bound to obey all the King's laws, not being contrary to the laws of God.' . . . The *other reserve* is also made of '*all that authority which was committed by Christ and His Apostles to the Bishops and priests.*' And we are not ashamed to own it freely, that we see no other reserves upon our obedience to the King besides these. So that, these being here specified, there was an unexceptionable declaration made of the *extent* of the King's Supremacy. Yet, because the term 'Head of the Church' had something in it that seemed harsh, there was yet a more express declaration made of this matter under Queen Elizabeth. . . . This explanation," [that is, that which is in our Articles,] "must be considered as the *true measure* of the king's Supremacy; and the wide expressions in the former laws must be understood to be restrained by this, since posterior laws derogate from those that were first made. . . . This is all that supremacy which we are bound in conscience to own; and if the letter of the law, or *the stretches of that in the administration of it,* have carried this further, we are not at all concerned in it. But in case any such thing were made out, it could amount to no more than this, *that the civil power had made some encroachments on ecclesiastical authority ; but, the submitting to an oppression, and bearing it till some better times may deliver us from it, is no argument against our church ;* on the contrary, it is a proof of our *temper and patience,*" etc.

5.

To conclude; it would seem, on the whole, that the Royal Supremacy may be viewed under the following aspects :—

1. As the prerogative of governing the Church externally, that is, ruling all the members of it in civil matters, claiming their obedience, to the exclusion of all foreign jurisdiction ; and this is the prerogative of every government, as such, whether heathen or Christian. Vide Canon 1, of 1603.

2. A prerogative of interfering in Church matters, " in ecclesiastical causes," appointing functionaries, directing usages, providing liturgies, etc.,—which is only exercised by the King as Christian, and exercised on two grounds, first, because he allows the Church's jurisdiction in his kingdom, and creates " prelacy," authoritative courts, and the like ; and next, because, by his patriarchal power, he has a claim upon the confidence and devotion of the Church. Vide Canon 2, of 1603 ; agreeably to which is the judgment of the Eight Bishops already referred to, which declares, that " in case the Bishops be negligent, it is the Christian prince's office to see them do their duty."

3. The King has *not* the power (1) of bestowing the ministerial commission, as is plain from Henry and Edward's words, in granting license to Bonner and Cranmer, " ultra ea quæ tibi divinitus," etc. ; (2) of ministering the sacraments, vide Art. 37 ; (3) of excommunicating, vide the Declaration subscribed by Cromwell ; (4) of ministering the Word, (in which, of course, the making Articles, etc., is included,) vide Art. 37.

4. There are a number of details in which the extent of the Supremacy is undetermined—for instance, the King's power of depriving bishops, of creating or destroy-

UNIFORM EDITION OF DR. NEWMAN'S WORKS.

PAROCHIAL AND PLAIN SERMONS.   8 vols.⎫

SERMONS ON SUBJECTS OF THE DAY   .   . ⎬ *Rivington.*

UNIVERSITY SERMONS .   .   .   . ⎭

CATHOLIC SERMONS.   2 vols.   .   .   . ⎫

PRESENT POSITION OF CATHOLICS IN ENGLAND ⎬ *Burns and Oates.*

ESSAY ON ASSENT   .   .   .   . ⎭

TWO ESSAYS ON MIRACLES .   .   .   . ⎫

ESSAYS CRITICAL AND HISTORICAL   2 vols. ⎪

DISCUSSIONS AND ARGUMENTS ON VARIOUS ⎬ *Pickering.*
  SUBJECTS   .   .   .   .   . ⎪

HISTORICAL SKETCHES   .   .   . ⎭

HISTORY OF THE ARIANS   .   .   .   . *Lumley.*

HISTORY OF MY RELIGIOUS OPINIONS (APO- ⎫
  LOGIA)   .   .   .   .   .   . ⎬ *Longman and Co.*

In preparation.

A SECOND AND THIRD VOLUME OF HISTORICAL SKETCHES.

THEOLOGICAL DISSERTATIONS.